TABLE FOR TWO

TABLE
for TWO

One-on-One with Jesus

HEPHZIBAH ISRAEL

ISBN (hardcover): 978-1-965115-00-8
ISBN (paperback): 978-1-965115-01-5
ISBN (ebook): 978-1-965115-02-2

This book is gifted to:

_____

By:

_____

On the occasion of:

_____

Date:

_____

Also by this Author

Just Jesus & Me: A Journal of Praises Prayers Promises and Provisions
ISBN (paperback): 978-1-965115-04-6
ISBN (hardcover): 978-1-965115-03-9

Dedicated for the glory of God.

*To **Jesus Christ** who loved us and washed us from our sins in His own blood and has made us kings and priests to His God and Father, to Him be glory and dominion forever and ever. Amen. Revelation 1:5, 6.*

"In Your presence is fullness of joy"

PSALM 16:11

ACKNOWLEDGEMENTS

I am immensely grateful to my Lord and Savior Jesus Christ for His mercy and grace that have guided this book to its completion.

My deepest gratitude goes to my mother, Mrs. Yohapushpam Livingston, who served as the editor of this book. Her unwavering support, encouragement, and guidance have been instrumental in helping me achieve my goals. This book was made possible only because of her hard work and enthusiasm. Mrs. Livingston, a former Professor of Mathematics at Sarah Tucker College in India, embodies the Scripture, 'Many women do noble things, but you surpass them all' (Proverbs 31:29).

Heartfelt thanks to Mrs. Janet Wilson, a dear friend of my mother and Professor of English Literature at Sarah Tucker College, for her dedication in reading the material and providing a beautiful foreword. May God bless her for her kindness.

I also want to acknowledge my husband, Mr. Israel Thavasikani, for his financial support. He is a humble and steadfast man of God, and I am grateful for his life.

Additionally, I thank my brother, Paul Delightson Livingston, for his assistance with the office staff, and my children, John Thomas Bicket, Rachel Israel Bicket, Sharon Israel, and Joshua Israel, for their constructive feedback and encouragement.

Finally, I am deeply grateful to you, the readers. Without your support and interest, this book would not have been possible. Thank you for making it part of your spiritual journey. May God bless you abundantly.

FROM THE AUTHOR

Dear Reader,

Thank you for purchasing and reading *Table for Two: One-on-One with Jesus*. What started a decade ago as a BlogSpot named "Coffee with Jesus" now feels surreal to see in print. I am truly grateful to God for His boundless mercies that have made this book a reality.

One of the most intimate verses in the Bible, in my opinion, is Revelation 3:20: "Behold, I stand at the door and knock. If anyone hears My voice and opens the door, I will come into him and dine with him, and he with Me." Sharing a meal with our Lord Jesus Christ is a profoundly exceptional and invaluable experience on our Christian journey. It offers an intimate and deeply fulfilling connection.

Table for Two: One-on-One with Jesus is designed to bring you closer to Jesus. Whether it is at daybreak, noon, evening, or bedtime, I encourage you to make a habit of sharing a meal with the Lord Jesus Christ—just you and Him. As you read, imagine yourself sitting with Jesus, being nourished by His Word, and refreshed by His presence. This special time together is a beautiful preview of what heaven will be like.

Throughout writing this book, my prayer has been for the Holy Spirit to guide every word. I hope that this work reflects His wisdom and love, and that as you read, the Holy Spirit will illuminate your heart with fresh revelations. This is my sincere prayer for you.

Once again, thank you for your support. Now, go ahead and enjoy your *Table for Two: One-on-One with Jesus*.

Yours in Christ,
Hephzibah

FROM THE EDITOR

All glory, honor, and praise be to our Lord God, Who has helped us write and publish this book, *Table for Two: One-on-One with Jesus*.

My daughter, Hephzibah Israel, is the author of this book, and it was my privilege to do its editing work. She wrote a blog of daily meditations on Bible verses for 11 years, from September 2010 to November 2021. You can visit her BlogSpot at Coffee with Jesus.

It was her heart's desire to bring out a book based on these blog topics. I have helped her fulfill this desire by collecting, compiling, and editing this book. Instead of publishing the book as daily meditations as in the BlogSpot, the topics are grouped under different headings.

Reading a portion of this book daily will provide great nourishment to your body, mind, and soul. Jesus invites us to dine with Him:

"Behold, I stand at the door and knock. If anyone hears My voice and opens the door, I will come into him and dine with him, and he with Me." – Revelation 3:20

Prophet Jeremiah says, "When your words came, I ate them; they were my joy and my heart's delight." – Jeremiah 15:16

Jesus quoted the verse, "Man does not live on bread alone but on every word that comes from the mouth of the Lord." – Deuteronomy 8:3

This book, *Table for Two: One-on-One with Jesus*, brings the words of our Lord God. Let us eat them and live.

May our Lord God make this book a blessing to every one of you.

— Mrs. Yohapushpam Livingston

FOREWORD BY MRS. JANET WILSON

Table for Two: One-on-One with Jesus by Hephzibah Israel, is a collection of deep, insightful, spiritual observations that prods one on to further thoughts and meditation. Like Mary, sitting happily at the feet of Jesus, eagerly drinking in the living WORD flowing down from the lips of Jesus, treasuring them in her heart and transforming them into workable life principles, Hephzibah's understanding of the WORD as expressed in this book finds clear, practical, spiritual applications from which both young and old could easily gain understanding and inspiration. The book begins with God the Father, God the Son-Jesus, and The Holy Spirit. Meticulously analyzing various topics from the Bible in great detail, the book offers a glance at Christian doctrine with great clarity and serves as extended meditations as well.

For instance, under 'God, the Son-Jesus', within the broad compass of His birth and the Second Coming, other scintillating facets like "Kiss the Son," "I give you My peace," "A lily among thorns," "Lift up your heads, you gates" add profundity and significance to the topics. Other chapters like Prayer, Praise and Worship, Beauty Regimen, Armor of God and so on are the balancing truths for practical application for a holy, spirit-filled life overflowing with joy and blessings.

To conclude, the very title *Table for Two: One-on-One with Jesus* evokes warm images of fellowshipping with Jesus on a day to day, moment by moment basis, and the inspirational thoughts presented in the pages of the book will definitely reverberate and linger in the heart as the precious fragrance of Hephzibah's spikenard poured out on the Lord's feet!

—Janet Wilson

CONTENTS

GOD, THE FATHER

ANCIENT OF DAYS, OUR FATHER AND JUDGE

"As I looked, thrones were set in place, and the Ancient of Days took His seat. His clothing was as white as snow; the hair of His head was white like wool. His throne was flame with fire, and its wheels were all ablaze. A river of fire was flowing, coming out from before Him. Thousands upon thousands attended Him; ten thousand times ten thousand stood before Him. The court was seated, and the books were opened" (Daniel 7:9, 10).

The vision described above, which the Prophet Daniel had of God's judgment, underscores the reverence and fear that we should hold for God above all else. This sentiment is reminiscent of when God appeared to Moses on Mount Sinai. The sight was so awe-inspiring that Moses exclaimed, *"I exceedingly fear and quake" (Hebrews 12:21).* Exodus 24:17 portrays the sight of the Lord's glory as a consuming fire atop the mountain before the children of Israel. Isaiah 29:6 further depicts the Lord's majestic arrival with thunder, earthquake, and devouring fire.

These passages highlight the incomprehensible magnitude of God's presence and the reverence it commands. Throughout the Old Testament, direct encounters with God were rare, emphasizing communication through His Word. It was through Jesus Christ that God chose to reveal Himself fully to humanity, serving as the mediator between us and God. Therefore, we approach God exclusively through Jesus, acknowledging His supreme reverence and sovereignty over all creation.

This reverence is echoed in *Psalm 145:8-9*, describing God as gracious and compassionate **Father**, and in *Jude 1:14-15*, portraying Him as the ultimate **Judge**. Nevertheless, before facing God's judgment, we must first seek His grace, as *Hebrews 4:16* urges us to approach His throne with confidence to receive mercy and find grace in our time of need. Ultimately, our reverence for God should permeate every aspect of our lives, guiding us to approach Him with humility and gratitude for His boundless mercy and grace.

"Let us then approach God's throne of grace with confidence, so that we may receive mercy and find grace to help us in our time of need" (Hebrews 4:16).

THE WHOLE EARTH IS FILLED WITH AWE AT GOD'S WONDERS

You (God) crown the year with your bounty, and your carts overflow with abundance. Psalm 65:11

In Psalm 65, King David eloquently celebrates the wonders and goodness that God continually bestows upon the entire earth, spanning from one end to the other. He expresses gratitude and praise for God's omnipresence and His remarkable deeds.

David begins by acknowledging God's responsiveness to prayers, describing Him as the Savior and hope of all the ends of the earth and the farthest seas. He marvels at God's power in forming the mountains and calming the seas, bringing tranquility even amidst the turmoil of nations.

The psalmist declares that the whole earth is filled with awe at God's wonders, and He brings joy to the morning and evening. David further reflects on God's care for the land, enriching it with abundant provisions through streams and showers, blessing crops and sustaining life.

He acknowledges God's bountiful blessings, crowning the year with abundance and filling His carts with overflowing goodness. David paints a vivid picture of nature rejoicing, with grasslands and hills clothed in gladness, meadows covered with flocks, and valleys mantled with grain, all shouting for joy and singing praises to God.

Throughout the psalm, David emphasizes the depth of God's care and provision, His responsiveness to prayers, and His role as the source of all blessings. He concludes by proclaiming the blessedness of those chosen to dwell in God's courts, filled with the goodness of His house and temple.

You (God) care for the land and water it; you enrich it abundantly. Psalm 65:8

HIS ANGER LASTS ONLY A MOMENT, AND HIS FAVOR A LIFETIME

"His anger lasts only a moment, but his favor lasts a lifetime; weeping may remain for a night, but rejoicing comes in the morning" (Psalm 30:5).

"For a brief moment I abandoned you, but with deep compassion, I will bring you back. In a surge of anger, I hid my face from you for a moment, but with everlasting kindness, I will have compassion on you, says the Lord, your Redeemer" (Isaiah 54:7, 8).

Here, we observe two facets of God's nature: one as a Judge who cannot tolerate sin and is compelled to punish the sinner, and the other as a Father who refuses to see His child punished and would rather bear the punishment Himself. Moses instructed the people that if they were to stray from God and not obey His commandments, they would be chastised by the Lord God, much like a father chastises his son, as mentioned in *Deuteronomy 8:5.*

While our earthly fathers corrected us for a brief period, and we show them respect for it, our Heavenly Father corrects us for our long-term gain and eternal well-being, allowing us to partake in His Holiness *(Hebrews 12:7, 8; Proverbs 3:11, 12)*. This emphasizes the even greater reverence and awe we should have for God.

Though enduring God's discipline may be challenging, it is ultimately for our growth and righteousness *(Hebrews 12:9-11)*. However, it is crucial to remember that God's anger is not everlasting; rather, His mercy endures forever.

'Return, backsliding Israel,' says the Lord; 'I will not cause My anger to fall on you. For I am merciful,' says the Lord; 'I will not remain angry forever" (Jeremiah 3:12).

"My son, despise not the chastening of the Lord; neither be weary of his correction. He corrects as a father even the son in whom He delights" (Proverbs 3:11, 12).

THE ALMIGHTY IS BEYOND OUR
REACH AND EXALTED IN POWER

"The Almighty is beyond our reach and exalted in power" (Job 37:23).

"He says to the snow, 'Fall on the earth,' and to the rain shower, 'Be a mighty downpour.' So that everyone He has made may know His work, He stops all people from their labor. The animals take cover; they remain in their dens. The tempest comes out from its chamber, the cold from the driving winds" (Job 37:6-9).

During Job's numerous trials, three of his friends came to sit and converse with him. Others were also present, listening to these conversations. Among them was Elihu. After the three friends had concluded their arguments, Elihu initiated his discourse, advising Job to recognize that the Almighty God was chastising him due to his perceived wrongdoing.

Elihu emphasized, *"God thunders marvelously with His voice. He does great things with His thunderous voice which we cannot comprehend,"* as stated in Job 37:5.

Elihu emphasized that only God has the power to disrupt human labor with snow, rain, wind, and cold. In essence, he challenged whether a person could generate such an abundance of snow or rain or regulate these natural phenomena. Obviously only God possesses the authority to control them.

Elihu asserted that Job should recognize that the Almighty God does not inflict suffering unjustly and that Job was facing adversity due to some perceived wrongdoing in the eyes of God. However, it is essential to note that Elihu's assessment of Job was inaccurate. God Himself bore witness, stating, *"There is no one on earth like him (Job); he is blameless and upright, a man who fears God and shuns evil" (Job 1:8).*

The Almighty is beyond our understanding and exalted in power, and we cannot give reasons for all His deeds.

6

THE TRAIN OF HIS ROBE FILLS THE TEMPLE

"I saw the Lord seated on a throne, high and exalted, and the train of His robe filled the temple" (Isaiah 6:1).

This verse holds special significance for me because, at the age of thirteen, I had a vision of the Lord's robe filling the tent during a revival meeting. At that time, I was unaware of the Bible verse that mentions the train of His robe filling the Temple. When I shared my vision with my grandmother, she directed me to this verse.

The most remarkable part of this verse is that the train of His robe filled the temple. God's robe envelops everyone, leaving no one out within the Temple. All are embraced by the presence of God. This is why the Psalmist joyfully proclaims, *"I was glad when they said unto me, 'Let us go into the house of the Lord.'" (Psalm 122:1).*

There is divine power in His robe. As told in Matthew 9:20, a woman who had suffered from an issue of blood for twelve years was healed by merely touching the hem of Jesus' robe.

Jesus has given us the promise that He will be in the midst of two or three individuals who gather in His name. When we come together in the name of Jesus, we become the Temple of God. His robe fills our midst, and we experience the power of Jesus forgiving our sins, healing our sickness, and filling us with the joy of the Holy Spirit with His personal individual concern for each one of us.

In Matthew 17:2, when Jesus was transfigured before His disciples, His face radiated like the sun, and His garments became as radiant as pure light. Indeed, our Lord God is described as the *'One who is glorious in His apparel' (Isaiah 63:1).*

When we are touched by His robe, we are enveloped in His beauty, holiness, light, righteousness, power, and all of God's divine qualities. His robe fills the Temple. Keep yourself Holy as the Temple of the living God. Do not neglect the coming together of fellow believers.

NO ONE LIKE OUR GOD, AND NO ONE LIKE HIS PEOPLE

Moses assembled all the Israelites as they reached the end of their expedition through the wilderness. This moment also marked the conclusion of his life's journey. He recounted to the people how God had liberated them from slavery in Egypt and was guiding them on their journey through the wilderness.

Moses proclaimed: *"There is no one like the God of Jeshurun, Who rides the heavens to help you, and in His excellency on the clouds"* (Deuteronomy 33:26).

The term "Jeshurun" pertains to God's people, the Israelites. The God of Israel is our God, and there is truly no god like Him. He rides upon the heavens to assist us and traverses the clouds in His majestic splendor.

We are indeed a blessed people, because we have a God who is unlike any other, setting us apart from all others.

Continuing, Moses declared, *"Blessed are you, Israel! Who is like you, a people saved by the Lord? He is your shield and helper and your glorious sword. Your enemies will cower before you"* (Deuteronomy 33:29).

The prophet Jeremiah confirms the uniqueness of our God: *"No one is like you, Lord; you are great, and your name is mighty in power"* (Jeremiah 10:6).

The Psalmist emphasizes that there are no other people like us, as God has revealed His Word and decrees to us: *"He has revealed His word to Jacob, His laws and decrees to Israel. He has done this for no other nation"* (Psalm 147:19, 20).

Let us strive to be worthy of our God, for there is no one like Him. May we walk in a manner befitting God's people, rejoicing in His Word, laws, and decrees that He has disclosed to us. There is no one like our God, and there is no one like us, His people. Praise the Lord.

El-Shaddai, God Almighty

When Abram was ninety-nine years old, the Lord appeared to him and said,
"I am God Almighty; walk before me and be blameless." (Genesis 17:1)

Isaac blessed his son Jacob, saying, *"May God Almighty bless you and make you fruitful and increase your numbers until you become a community of peoples" (Genesis 28:3).*

God told Jacob, *"I am El-Shaddai - 'God Almighty.' Be fruitful and multiply. You will become a great nation, even many nations. Kings will be among your descendants!" (Genesis 35:11).*

These verses reveal that God introduced Himself as 'God Almighty' to the forefathers Abraham, Isaac, and Jacob. God Himself told Moses, *"I appeared to Abraham, to Isaac, and to Jacob as El-Shaddai - 'God Almighty'" (Exodus 6:3).*

El-Shaddai means 'God Almighty.' God is all-powerful and omnipotent. Therefore, when we pray to our El-Shaddai, our God Almighty, we are, in fact, standing in the presence of an Omnipotent, Supreme, and All-Powerful God. He is the very same God who created the entire earth and everything in it with His Word. He merely said, 'Let there be,' and it came to be. *"He spoke, and it came to be; He commanded, and it stood firm" (Psalm 33:9).*

"With God, all things are possible" (Matthew 19:26). "Is anything too hard for the Lord?" (Genesis 18:14). "For with God, nothing shall be impossible" (Luke 1:37).

Knowing our Lord as God Almighty gives us a fresh perspective when we pray. There is nothing He cannot do, and nothing is impossible for Him. He is Almighty—our El-Shaddai! Amen!

El-Olam, God Eternal

"Abraham planted a tamarisk tree in Beersheba, and there he called on the name of the Lord, the Eternal God" (Genesis 21:33).

Abraham possessed a well of water that had been seized by the servants of the local king, Abimelech. Instead of accepting this injustice, the man of faith rebuked Abimelech for the well. He then entered into a treaty with Abimelech to safeguard his wells from future destruction. Following the successful treaty, Abraham planted a tamarisk tree and invoked the name of the Eternal God, El-Olam. A tamarisk tree is known for its slow growth, and Abraham planted it in faith, believing in God's promise that the land would belong to his descendants forever. Abraham's actions looked ahead to the coming decades and generations.

Eternal or everlasting signifies a state of existence that extends endlessly, forever and ever! *"For this God is our God forever and ever; he will be our guide even to the end" (Psalm 48:14).*

From the book of Isaiah, we are reminded: *"Do you not know? Have you not heard? The Lord is the everlasting God, the Creator of the ends of the earth. He will not grow tired or weary, and His understanding no one can fathom" (Isaiah 40:28).*

In the Epistle to the Hebrews, we find the affirmation: *"Jesus Christ is the same yesterday and today and forever" (Hebrews 13:8).*

In the book of Revelation, God is described as *the 'One who lives forever and ever' (Revelation 4:9, 5:14, 10:7, 15:7).*

"The Lord reigns forever and ever" (Exodus 15:18), and "From everlasting to everlasting you are God" (Psalm 90:2).

Indeed, our Lord and Savior Jesus Christ is El-Olam! All glory, honor, and power belong to Him forever and ever. Amen!

El-Elyon, God Most High

"Blessed be God Most High, who has delivered your enemies into your hand" (Genesis 14:20).

"How awesome is the Lord Most High, the great King over all the earth!" (Psalm 47:2).

"Sacrifice thank offerings to God, fulfill your vows to the Most High" (Psalm 50:14).

"I cry out to God Most High, to God who fulfills His purpose for me" (Psalm 57:2).

In the original Hebrew Scriptures, "El-Elyon" is consistently translated as "God Most High" in English versions.

The term "God Most High" implies that there is no one, in the past, present, or future, who surpasses God. There is no one superior to Him. He is the ultimate authority to whom we can turn with our requests.

Our God is El-Elyon, the Most High God. He esteems a humble and contrite heart and makes it His temple. It is a blessing to be esteemed by Him.

"This is what the Lord says: "Heaven is My throne, and the earth is My footstool. Where is the house you will build for Me? Where will My resting place be? Has not My hand made all these things, and so they came into being?" declares the Lord. "This is the one I esteem: he who is humble and contrite in spirit, and trembles at My Word"" (Isaiah 66:1, 2).

'But will God really dwell on the earth? The heavens, even the highest heaven, cannot contain Him" (1 Kings 8:27).

What a remarkable blessing it is that God Most High values a humble and contrite heart and transforms it into His Temple.

EL-ROI, GOD WHO SEES

She gave this name to the Lord who spoke to her: "You are the God who sees me," for she said, I have now seen the One who sees" (Genesis 16:13).

El Roi, the 'God who sees,' prompted Hagar to exclaim, "I have seen God who sees me," in her moment of excitement during her encounter with God in the wilderness. She was alone and on the run from her mistress Sarai, who had mistreated her. At the time, she was pregnant with Abram's child. God recognized her dire circumstances, called out to her, and instructed her to return to Sarai, assuring her that her son would become the patriarch of a great nation. God saw her in her time of need and encouraged her to persevere.

King David passionately sought the presence of the Lord, desiring to encounter Him in his lifetime. In Psalm 27:8-9, he declared, "When You said, 'Seek My face,' My heart responded, 'Your face, Lord, I will seek.' Do not hide Your face from me; Do not turn Your servant away in anger; You have been my help; Do not leave me nor forsake me, O God of my salvation." Similarly, in Psalm 17:15, David expressed his longing: "As for me, I will see Your face in righteousness; I shall be satisfied when I awake in Your likeness."

Job also expressed his hope in seeing his Redeemer on the final day of history, firmly declaring, "For I know that my redeemer lives and that He shall stand at the latter day upon the earth. And though after my skin worms destroy this body, yet in my flesh shall I see God. Whom I shall see for myself, and mine eyes shall behold, and not another, though my reins be consumed within me" (Job 19:25-27).

Do we seek the Lord's presence like David? Do we hold hope of encountering Him at life's end? Are we in desperate situations, like Hagar, crying out for help? God sees our hearts, desires, and despair. He is El-Roi, 'the God who sees.' One day, we will all meet Him face to face. Are you ready to meet El-Roi?

The Lord is our Healer

"If you will give earnest heed to the voice of the Lord your God, and do what is right in His sight, and give ear to His commandments, and keep all His statutes, I will put none of the diseases on you which I have put on the Egyptians; for I, the Lord, am your healer." Exodus 15:26

Often, we find ourselves anxious and concerned about news of illness affecting our friends, family, church members, colleagues, and our community. Our hearts are filled with fear when we must await test results at the doctor's office. However, these anxieties are unnecessary. If we worry in the same manner as those who lack faith, what distinction does our faith make in our lives? Instead of fretting over matters beyond our control, let us offer praise to God for the blessings we have—the joy of salvation, the promise of eternal life. Let us thank Him for the gift of each breath and the ability to move. Let us express gratitude for everything that functions well in our lives. Even when we receive a diagnosis of a serious illness, regardless of how life-threatening it may seem, worrying does not provide relief. I apologize if this comes across as insensitive, but it is the guidance we find in Scripture.

In Luke 12:25-26, Jesus wisely stated, *"Who of you by worrying can add a single hour to his life? Since you cannot do this very little thing, why do you worry about the rest?"*

While we have breath in our nostrils, we can praise the Lord; let us make the most of our lives by continually praising Him. As *Psalm 115:17-18* reminds us, *"The dead do not praise the Lord, nor do any who go down into silence; but as for us, we will bless the Lord from this time forth and forever. Praise the Lord!"*

The Lord is indeed our Healer! Whether He chooses to heal us and grant us life, or whether He calls us home, there is no denying that He is our ultimate Healer. He paid the price for our sickness on the cross, just as He did for our sins. Let us cast out all fear, doubt, worry, and any sickness affecting our loved ones and seek refuge under His protective wings. As Romans 14:8 reminds us, *"If we live, we live to the Lord; and if we die, we die to the Lord. So, whether we live or die, we belong to the Lord."*

HE SPOKE, AND IT CAME TO BE

"For He spoke, and it came to be; He commanded, and it stood firm."
Psalm 33:9

This verse holds a special place in my heart, and I incorporate it into almost all my prayers, whether they are for myself or someone else. The power of His words is truly remarkable.

Consider the incident when a centurion approached Jesus seeking healing for his servant. He humbly said, 'Lord, I do not deserve to have you come under my roof. But just say the word, and my servant will be healed' (Matthew 8:8). Jesus responded by telling the centurion, 'Go! Let it be done just as you believed it would,' and his servant was healed instantly (Matthew 8:13).

In Genesis 1:3, we read, 'And God said, 'Let there be light,' and there was light.' The rest of creation also came into existence through His spoken words.

In the beginning was the Word, and the Word was with God, and the Word was God (John 1:1).

Jesus rebuked Satan, saying, 'Man does not live on bread alone, but on every word that comes from the mouth of God' (Luke 4:4).

Mark 4:39 recounts how Jesus calmed the storm: 'Then He arose and rebuked the wind and said to the sea, 'Peace, be still!' And the wind ceased, and there was a great calm.'

Romans 8:34 informs us that Jesus Christ sits at the right hand of God, making intercession for us. What He prays for us shall undoubtedly come to pass, for 'He spoke, and it came to be.'

Let us cling to these verses and pray to the Lord in this manner: 'You spoke, and it came to be, Lord; You commanded, and it stood firm, Lord. Please speak to me, Lord. Please speak for me, Lord! For I believe that if you speak and command, it will be so. And I thank you for speaking for me, Lord. Amen!'

GOD THE SON, JESUS CHRIST

OUT OF BETHLEHEM WOULD COME THE RULER

"But you, Bethlehem Ephrathah, though you are small among the clans of Judah, out of you will come for me one who will be ruler over Israel, whose origins are from of old, from ancient times." - Micah 5:2

The Prophet Micah lived during the same era as the Prophet Isaiah, approximately 700 years before the birth of Christ. Micah accurately prophesied the birthplace of the ruler over Israel, Jesus Christ, as Bethlehem.

There are those who argue that because Jesus did not establish His earthly kingdom during His first coming, He cannot be the ruler foretold in this prophecy. However, they overlook the dual role of the Messiah. The first role is that of a suffering servant who bears the sins of His people, which Jesus fulfilled during His first coming. The second role is that of a triumphant ruler who will exercise authority over the nations, which will be fulfilled by Jesus at His second coming.

Regarding the statement that His origins are from old and from ancient times, it signifies that there is no beginning for Jesus Christ that we can comprehend with our human understanding. He is eternally pre-existent, having been with God from ancient times. As John writes, *"In the beginning was the Word, and the Word was with God, and the Word was God. He was with God in the beginning. Through Him all things were made; without Him, nothing was made that has been made"* (John 1:1-3). Even before the creation of the earth, Jesus was with God.

Proverbs 8:29-30 further illustrates the eternal nature of Jesus Christ: *"When He assigned to the sea its limit so that the waters would not transgress His command and when He marked out the foundations of the earth, then I was beside Him as a master craftsman; and I was daily His delight, rejoicing always before Him."*

Jesus Christ is the Alpha and the Omega, the beginning and the end, and He lives forever and ever. He is the Eternal Son of God the Father and is God Himself incarnate in the flesh.

It was the night before Christmas

It was the night before Christmas. All was calm and all was well. But was it truly so? Not quite! On that night, many cities in Israel were bustling with travelers and pedestrians. The streets were teeming with people and their animals, while the sidewalks were crowded with small shops and eateries. Businesses were thriving, and everyone seemed to be on a spending spree. All the hotels, motels, and every lodging option in between were completely booked. The scene was almost festive.

Joseph and his pregnant wife, Mary, who had travelled about 70 miles from Nazareth, had just reached Bethlehem. They made several stops in search of accommodation, but every place had a sign that read, 'House Full!' or 'No Room!' Not one room was available. However, one kind man offered them his cow shed, saying, 'Perhaps you could use this?' Joseph inspected the place with Mary and realized it wasn't ideal. The walls, floors, and roof were far from perfect, but it would have to suffice for now. Time was running out, and Mary was eager to end the uncomfortable donkey ride. They had travelled a great distance, and rest was much needed.

Joseph helps Mary off the donkey and settles her into the cowshed. He places her on some hay and quickly begins to clean the place. The animals had just been moved out, so the place was quite unpleasant. There wasn't much he could do, and they would have to make do for the night. Perhaps tomorrow, he would set off early to knock on a few more doors in search of a better place. But for tonight, this would have to suffice.

Mary is not in the mood to inspect her lodging. She is just relieved the journey is over. She tells herself it will be a short night, and soon it will be day. She is not much worried about the baby either. If all that the angel had told her about this child is true – that He is the Savior of the world – then there's no way she's giving birth tonight, not in this dirty, cramped cowshed. The Savior must be born in more comfortable sur-roundings, with maids to attend to her, warm water, and clean clothes at her disposal. So, she's least concerned about the rest of the night.

Elsewhere in Bethlehem, the shepherds had finished their work for the day. They had gathered their flocks from the mountainsides, plains, and valleys, counted them, and were satisfied with the numbers. One of them had started a fire, and they were now resting, chatting, and tending to the sheep.

Suddenly, an angel appeared before them, lighting up the night sky and delivering the good news: "There is born to you this day in the city of David a Savior, who is Christ the Lord" (Luke 2:11). And with the angel, a multitude of heavenly hosts appeared, praising God and proclaiming, "Glory to God in the highest, and on earth peace, good-will toward men" (Luke 2:13-14). They vanished, leaving the shepherds in awe and wonder.

Mary had been mistaken; the Savior was indeed born that very night, in the humble cowshed. She had to make do with whatever rags she could find. As she looked at the child – the Godchild, God Himself in human form – she was moved to tears, blaming herself for not being better prepared to receive Him. Joseph was speechless, overwhelmed by the realization that the child he was holding was God Himself in human form. He couldn't believe his eyes.

If only He had been born at their home, maids would have been there to clean the child, assist Mary, and ensure the needs of the mother and Child were met. Now they were all alone with the newborn. Joseph was filled with concern. How should he care for the baby? Could he quickly go out to buy something for Mary? Would she manage while he was away? Were the rags warm enough for the child? Was the hay too prickly for His back? Is Mary okay? Countless thoughts raced through his mind, and he wasn't sure where to begin.

If only he had some help… Suddenly, a few shepherds arrived at the stall to pay their respects to the King Child. They brought milk and other foodstuffs with them and began to assist with the situation. They knew how to keep the Baby warm for the night and were eager to help. The child was lovely – their Savior. Indeed, He was!

Years later, this very Child's body would be wounded, His hands and feet nailed, His words ridiculed, and He would endure scorn, derision, and abandonment, to His very death. He endured it all. For you and me… as our Savior.

The Word became flesh and made His dwelling among us

The Word became flesh and made His dwelling among us. John 1:14

In the beginning was the Word, and the Word was with God, and the Word was God. In Him was life; and the life was the light of men. John 1:1, 4

True! The Word became flesh! But making a dwelling among us is not something He forces on us. The Bible often uses the metaphor of Jesus standing at the door and knocking (Revelation 3:20) as an invitation for individuals to open their hearts and lives to Him. Allowing Jesus to dwell within us is a personal choice and an act of faith.

We share meals with the people we love and are friends with, not with strangers. When Jesus wishes to dine with us, it signifies His desire to be our friend, His love for us, and His wish to communicate with us. He initiates this, asking us to allow Him into our lives. What a profound love! Dining together creates an intimate experience where we let down our guard, reveal our true selves, engage in open conversations without concern for our backgrounds or social differences, and come together to form deeper connections.

What a privilege it is to have our Lord Jesus Christ dwell in us, dining with us! It is truly wonderful to experience His presence so closely, within arm's reach, sharing a meal with us, participating in our everyday conversations, understanding our thoughts, and reassuring us that He will always be with us. Jesus is eager to enter our lives, and all we must do is open our hearts, inviting Him to make a home within us.

However, we must remember that the Holy God will not remain with us if we persist in living in unholiness. It is our responsibility to maintain our cleanliness and holiness so that Jesus can continue to dwell within us and among us. The Holy Spirit is ready to sanctify us and prepare us as a worthy dwelling place for Jesus.

A SIGN FROM THE LORD

The Lord spoke again to Ahaz, the king of Judah, through the prophet Isaiah, saying, "Ask a sign for yourself from the Lord your God; ask it either in the depth or in the height above." But Ahaz said, "I will not ask, nor will I test the Lord!" The Lord said that He Himself will give you a sign: Behold, the virgin shall conceive and bear a Son, and shall call His name Immanuel. Isaiah 7:10-12, 14

God had promised a miraculous sign that no one could have imagined – a virgin giving birth to a Son. This promise was a prophecy about the birth of Jesus Christ. About 600 years later, this remarkable promise came to fruition in the life of a virgin named Mary. She willingly submitted herself as a servant of God, allowing His promise to be fulfilled through her.

Mary and Joseph were betrothed to each other, preparing for their marriage. However, Mary became pregnant through the power of God even before their marriage was formalized. When Joseph learned of Mary's pregnancy, he contemplated how to disassociate himself from marrying her while safeguarding her reputation. As he pondered these concerns, an angel of the Lord appeared to him in a dream and reassured him, saying, "Joseph, son of David, do not be afraid to take Mary as your wife, for the Child she carries is conceived by the Holy Spirit. She will give birth to a Son, and you are to name Him Jesus because He will save His people from their sins" (Matthew 1:20-24). When Joseph woke up, he did as the angel of the Lord had commanded him and embraced Mary as his wife.

This Son, Jesus, was the Immanuel foretold by Isaiah. The name Immanuel means 'God is with us.' God Himself was born through the virgin Mary.

God promised a unique sign, one that could not be found anywhere else, and He fulfilled this promise through the birth of His Son, Jesus, from the womb of a virgin girl. Indeed, all things are possible with God.

The words of Jesus from the cross

We should rejoice in Jesus' death on the Cross because without it, we would be eternally doomed. Thanks to His sacrifice, we are now redeemed! Praise the Lord! Therefore, the day of Christ's crucifixion is indeed a day of celebration for us, not necessarily a day of mourning. While hanging on the Cross, despite the intense pain, Jesus made seven significant statements. Let us reflect briefly on these words:

Father, forgive them: for they do not know what they are doing.
Luke 23:34

Even as He endured suffering on the cross, His concern was for the people who would undoubtedly face the consequences of their actions against His beloved Son. He offered a prayer to the Father, asking Him not to punish them. This prayer continues to hold true today. Whether knowingly or unknowingly, we subject Jesus to crucifixion again and again through our sins. Thanks to Jesus' prayer, God has shown us mercy, forgiving our sins repeatedly.

Today you will be with me in Paradise. Luke 23:43

Two thieves were crucified alongside Jesus, one on each side. One of the thieves recognized that Jesus was unjustly being crucified, and he understood that after His death, Jesus would enter His kingdom. He prayed to Jesus, asking Him to remember him when He entered His kingdom. Jesus assured the thief that he would be with Him in Paradise that very day. This is a crucial prayer that we should all offer to Jesus before our own deaths. We shouldn't be hard-hearted, thinking that we can postpone this prayer until our death is imminent, just as the thief did. This would be a disservice to ourselves because we cannot predict the timing of our death or our mental state at that moment. Instead, we should pray to Jesus today, asking Him to remember us when He enters His kingdom, as mentioned in Luke 23:42.

Woman, behold your son!.., Behold your mother! John 19:26, 27

Jesus demonstrated His respect and love for His mother by arranging for His beloved disciple, John, to take care of her after His death. He entrusted them to each other for mutual consolation and support. This serves as a valuable lesson for us, emphasizing the importance of honoring, loving, and caring for our parents and relatives.

My God, my God, Why have you forsaken me? Matthew 27:46

When Jesus was on the cross, darkness covered the land for three hours. In His anguish, Jesus cried out, "My God, my God, why have you forsaken me?" This cry of anguish was due to Jesus bearing the sins of the world and feeling a temporary separation from God the Father, who had hidden Himself. In our own lives, we may encounter situations where it seems like God has forsaken us and our prayers go unanswered. However, we must hold onto God's promise that He will never forsake us. Even in moments when it appears that God is hidden from us, it is only a temporary state. God's power is such that even if we face death, He is mighty enough to resurrect us.

I Thirst. John 19:28

While hanging on the cross, Jesus experienced thirst and desired a refreshing drink. However, a soldier offered Him a sponge soaked in bitter vinegar, which He could not drink. It is a poignant contrast to a few days earlier when Jesus had invited all those who were thirsty to come to Him and partake of the living water He offered. Now, on the cross, He was thirsty with no one to satisfy His thirst. Jesus was enduring the agony of the cross solely because of His thirst for the salvation of people. This leads us to reflect on our own actions – are we providing Him with a bitter drink or bringing souls to Him to satisfy His thirst?

It is finished. John 19:30

The work of salvation, the complete task that Jesus had to accomplish for the redemption of humanity, was completed through His death on the cross. His final words, "It is finished," are a triumphant proclamation that He has fulfilled His mission on the cross. Through His sacrifice, Jesus achieved victory, defeating Satan. As we contemplate the end of our earthly journey, can we likewise declare victoriously that we have fulfilled God's purpose for our lives?

Father, into Your hands I commit My spirit. Luke 23:46

Jesus surrendered His spirit to the Father. No matter what suffering we endure in our lives, it is essential to entrust our spirit to God when facing death. May our final prayer in this world be: "Father, into Your hands, I commit my spirit."

Water and blood came mingling down

One of the soldiers pierced His side with a spear, and immediately blood and water came out. John 19:34

Many of us are devastated, remembering the sufferings our Lord bore on our behalf. Rest assured, He is alive and well! Indeed, He overcame the sting of death!

The day on which Jesus was crucified was the day before the Sabbath, and dead bodies should not remain upon the cross on the Sabbath day. The Jews asked Pilate to break the legs of those on the cross to expedite their death so that the bodies could be taken down from the cross. The Roman soldiers broke the legs of the two thieves who were crucified with Jesus. When they came to Jesus, they saw that He was already dead, so they did not break His legs. However, one of the soldiers pierced His side with a spear, and blood and water came out (John 19:31-34).

The following two prophecies about Jesus were fulfilled in this incident:

He keeps all his bones: not one of them is broken. Psalm 34:20

And they shall look upon me whom they have pierced. Zechariah 12:10

Medical terms explain the gushing out of blood and water from the pierced side of Jesus to be due to a ruptured pericardium membrane that surrounds the heart. Clearly, Jesus had suffered deeply from the beating, the nails on the hands and feet, and the crown of thorns. His body was literally torn. It is all for me, for you, for us, for humanity, to atone for our sins!

Let us pray that not a single drop of His blood goes to waste but saves mankind for which it was shed. He is our Rock and Living Water flows from Him. Let us pray that not a single drop of this flowing water goes wasted but refreshes the weary souls of mankind. Let us remember His sufferings not just today, but every single day! Let us not hurt Him anymore by our disobedience to His teachings.

HE WAS PIERCED FOR OUR TRANSGRESSIONS

He was pierced for our transgressions, he was crushed for our iniquities;
the punishment that brought us peace was upon him, and by his wounds,
we are healed. Isaiah 53:5

We sometimes tend to forget the essence of the Gospel in our lives. We become less sensitive to the ultimate sacrifice our Lord and Savior Jesus Christ offered for us.

We can personalize the above Scripture as below:

- My Lord Jesus Christ was pierced for my transgressions.
- My Lord Jesus Christ was crushed for my iniquities.
- My Lord Jesus Christ bore my punishments upon Himself.
- My Lord Jesus Christ brought me peace.
- My Lord Jesus Christ was wounded for me.
- My Lord Jesus Christ healed me.

The Gospel is very personal, folks! It is not as generic as we tend to think at times. True, He died for the entire human race. But more importantly, He died for me! For you! On a personal level. One-on-one! It is like dying many times all over again for the entire humanity.

Let us not be light-hearted about the sufferings of Jesus for each one of us. Let us not let His blood go wasted. Let us be cleansed all over again, engulfed by His supreme love. Let us be mindful of the fact that He took our place on the cross! Amen!

Jesus, by the grace of God, tasted death for every man, to deliver all from the fear of death. Through His death, He destroyed the devil who had the power of death.

Why do you seek the Living One among the dead?

Why do you seek the living One among the dead? He is not here, but He has risen. Luke 24:5, 6

Easter is the day when we remember and celebrate the Resurrection of the Lord Jesus Christ from the dead. After Jesus died on the Cross, His body was taken down, wrapped in fine linen, and placed in a tomb hewn out of rock, where no one had ever laid before (Luke 23:53). This occurred on a Friday evening, and He remained in the tomb on the Sabbath, which was Saturday.

On the following day, the first day of the week, very early in the morning, a few women came to the sepulcher, bringing spices they had prepared to embalm Jesus' body. The Jewish custom at that time was not to bury the dead body but to keep it inside a chamber in a cave. A large stone was placed at the entrance of the grave, and the women were concerned about who would roll away this stone for them. As they approached the sepulcher, they found the stone already rolled away. Upon entering, they discovered that the body of the Lord Jesus was not there. Instead, they saw two men in shining garments who said to the women, "Why seek the living among the dead? He is not here, but has risen" (Luke 24:5, 6). The women then returned from the sepulcher and shared these events with the eleven disciples and others (Luke 24:9).

After the Resurrection, Jesus presented Himself alive by many infallible proofs, being seen by them for forty days and speaking of the things pertaining to the kingdom of God. (Acts 1:3)

The main message of the disciples was witnessing the fact that Jesus died on the cross and was raised up from the dead on the third day.

"If you declare with your mouth, 'Jesus is Lord,' and believe in your heart that God raised him from the dead, you will be saved." (Romans 10:9)

Jesus declares, "I am He who lives, and was dead, and behold, I am alive forevermore. Amen." (Revelation 1:18)

KISS THE SON

Kiss the Son, lest he be angry and you be destroyed in your way, for his wrath can flare up in a moment. Blessed are all who take refuge in him.
Psalm 2:12

Kissing is a token of love and affection. We reserve kisses for those we truly love—our close family and friends. Kissing the Son means loving the Son of God and accepting the love and relationship He offers.

How do we develop a personal relationship with Jesus, enabling us to express our love through a kiss? Whoever confesses that Jesus is the Son of God, God abides in him, and he in God (1 John 4:15). If you confess with your mouth the Lord Jesus and believe in your heart that God has raised Him from the dead, you will be saved (Romans 10:9). When we believe that Jesus is the Son of God and that He died for us, we initiate a personal relationship with Him.

He is our deliverer and Savior. He has made us God's children, and thereby, He is our brother. Fondly, He calls His disciples friends, making Him our friend. He is our teacher and leader, our gardener, our Shepherd, our lover, and our bridegroom. He is our King, our Lord, and our God. Having redeemed us with His own blood, He is our owner.

With the bouquet of these relationships and more, He stands and knocks at our hearts, offering us this bouquet. We cannot help but accept this great love and, thereby, kiss Him. Refusing such love saddens Him because a day is coming when His wrath will flare up and destroy those who have not kissed Him.

WHO DO YOU SAY HE IS?

"Jesus and His disciples went out to the towns of Caesarea Philippi; and on the road, He asked His disciples, 'Who do men say that I am?' They answered, 'John the Baptist; but some say, Elijah; and others, one of the prophets.' He said to them, 'But who do you say that I am?'" (Mark 8:27-29)

Simon Peter answered, 'You are the Christ, the Son of the living God.' Jesus answered and said to him, 'Blessed are you, Simon Bar-Jonah, for flesh and blood has not revealed this to you, but My Father who is in heaven. And I also say to you that you are Peter, and on this rock, I will build My church, and the gates of Hades shall not prevail against it.'" (Matthew 16:16-18)

Who is Jesus to you? Amidst the varied opinions surrounding us — some proclaiming Him as a deity, a distinguished teacher, a catalyst for social change, or even a miraculous worker — the question remains deeply personal. Despite others' assertions, what is your conviction? Can you confidently declare Him as Christ, the Son of the living God, sent to redeem you? Can you acknowledge Him as the anointed Savior, appointed by God to offer Himself as a sacrifice for your sins? As Jesus himself indicated, this revelation of His identity as the Son of the living God is granted by God the Father alone.

Jesus said that His Church will be built on the truth that Jesus is the Son of God, which means Jesus is God revealed in man. When Peter witnessed that Jesus was Christ, Jesus promised him, 'I will give you the keys of the kingdom of heaven, and whatever you bind on earth will be bound in heaven, and whatever you loose on earth will be loosed in heaven.'" (Matthew 16:19)

Whoever witnesses to this truth that Jesus is the Son of the living God will receive the keys of the kingdom of heaven. They will be given the authority to lead people into the kingdom of God, the authority to heal the sick, deliver them from the devil, and lead people from darkness to light.

The Son of Man came to seek and save the lost

The Son of Man came to seek and to save the lost. Luke 19:10

Jesus was passing through Jericho. Zacchaeus, a very wealthy chief tax collector lived there. He wanted to see Jesus. But he could not see Him over the crowd because he was small in stature. So, he ran ahead to the road that Jesus would pass through and climbed a sycamore tree to see Jesus.

Jesus knew that Zacchaeus was waiting to see Him. He also knew who he was and how he had accumulated his wealth by corruption in tax collecting. He knew the desire of his heart to see Him. When He came under the tree on which Zacchaeus was, He stood and looked up and said, "Zacchaeus, hurry down, for I must stay at your house today."

Tax collectors were looked down upon and were mentioned along with sinners by society. The religious leaders did not wish to be associated with them. But Jesus Who had come to save sinners, was entering the house of a sinner as his guest. Zacchaeus hurried down to welcome Jesus. All who saw this began to grumble saying, "He has gone to be the guest of a sinful man." Zacchaeus was afraid that Jesus might leave him because of what the people were saying. He wanted Jesus to come to his house at any cost. Hastily he said to Jesus *"Lord, half of my possessions I give to the poor, and if I have cheated anyone I will repay it fourfold." Jesus said to him, 'Today salvation has come to this house, because this man, too, is a son of Abraham'. Luke 19:9*

The saving grace and power of Jesus Christ will work towards the salvation of any sinner who believes in Jesus Christ and repents his sins. Abraham believed in God, and it was considered as righteousness to him. When a sinner believes in Jesus Christ, God makes him righteous and accepts him as His child. God accepts everyone who desires to see Him. Jesus has promised: *Whoever comes to me I will never drive away. John 6:37 This is a faithful saying, and worthy of all acceptances, that Christ Jesus came into the world to save sinners. 1Timothy 1:15*

I GIVE YOU MY PEACE

Peace I leave with you; my Peace I give you. I do not give to you as the world gives. Do not let your hearts be troubled and do not be afraid. John 14:27

And the Peace of God, which transcends all understanding, will guard your hearts and your minds in Christ Jesus. Philippians 4:7

'Shalom' which means 'peace,' and 'nothing missing, nothing broken,' is a regular greeting among the Jews. This salutation is generally a matter of custom and polite ceremony, given without much thought to it. However, here the Prince of Peace is not saying mere empty words but brings attention to the word PEACE as in consolation. When He says, 'my peace', He means the kind of peace only He can impart. This promised peace is quite different from the empty promises given by the world.

When we are at peace it gives us a tranquil spirit. We are not in a rush to find a solution for any situation. We learn to unwind at the feet of Jesus and be still. We completely surrender to His will. Have you sensed this peace? If not, join me in this prayer:

Jesus, our dear Savior, we thank You for the heavenly peace You have promised us. Often times we are so overwhelmed by many things that we tend to forget the peace You have promised us. Today, we surrender all matters at Your feet, Lord. Forgive us for running away from Your presence trying to find our own solutions to our problems. Thank You that You are in control, and You will take care of all our struggles. The battle is Yours, Lord.

Let the peace of God, which transcends all understanding, guard our hearts and our minds, dear Lord. We thank You and praise You for the peace You are giving us at this very moment. We give all glory, honor, and praise to Your Holy Name Lord. In the Name of Jesus, our Prince of Peace, we pray. Amen.

HERE I AM, I STAND AT THE DOOR AND KNOCK

Jesus says: 'Here I am! I stand at the door and knock. If anyone hears my voice and opens the door, I will come in and eat with him, and he with me.' Revelation 3:20

The King of Kings, Lord of Lords is standing outside our hearts asking us to open our hearts to Him. We recognize the voice of Jesus and are excited that Jesus is talking to us. But have we opened our hearts to Him? Or do we want to live as we please satisfying our worldly desires without subjecting ourselves to the rule of Jesus? You may not be given another knock. Your heart may become too hardened to hear His voice.

Today, if only you would hear his voice, do not harden your hearts. Psalm 95:7, 8

In Song of Solomon, we read that the maiden was sleeping but she could hear her beloved asking her, *'Open to me, my sister, my love, my dove and my undefiled.'* In spite of the endearing words of her lover, she began to give excuses saying she could not get up to open the door for him. When her beloved put his hand through the hole of the door, her innermost being was moved for him. She rose up to open the door for him, but her beloved was gone. She sought him, but she could not find him; she called him, but he gave her no answer. Finally, after much searching and struggle, she was able to find him. *Song of Solomon 5:2-6*

Jesus Christ is the lover, and His Church is the maiden. Jesus knocks at our hearts asking us to wake up from our sleep and to get ourselves ready to meet Him. We hear His voice, but we do not wake up immediately. When Jesus reminds us about His love which was manifested in the Cross, our heart is filled with love for Him, and we get up to open the door. But He may not be there.

The Spirit of God shall not always strive with man. Genesis 6:3

Jesus may not be always knocking at our door. When you hear His voice, be ready to invite Him into your lives.

My lover is mine and I am His

My lover is mine and I am His; He browses among the lilies. Song of Solomon 2:16, 6:3

I belong to my lover, and his desire is for me. Song of Solomon 7:10

The relationship between each one of us with Jesus is that of a couple betrothed to each other to get married in due time. In the book of Hosea, God's love for His people is described as the love of a person for his wife who had gone after other lovers. Though the wife had cheated on him, God asked the prophet to take her back. This is symbolic of the love of God for His people, who were not faithful to God.

Though the wife had chosen other lovers, Hosea calls her back with the endearing words, *'And I will betroth you unto me forever; yea, I will betroth you unto me in righteousness, and in judgment, and in loving-kindness, and in mercies and in faithfulness.' Hosea 2:19, 20*

This is similar to the covenant made by God with His people, we read about in *Jeremiah 31:33:* "I will put My law within them and on their heart I will write it, and I will be their God, and they shall be My people."

Our relationship with Jesus is like that between a husband and wife, which is stated as follows: *A man shall leave his father and his mother and shall cleave unto his wife: and they shall be one flesh. Genesis 2:24*

This love is a deeply personal one that cannot be expressed in words. They live for each other and surrender themselves to each other completely. We speak here about the Church and Christ.

Christ loved the church and gave Himself for it that He might sanctify and cleanse it with the washing of water by the word, that He might present it to Himself a glorious church, not having spot, or wrinkle, or any such thing; but that it should be holy and without blemish. Ephesians 5:25-27.

A LILY AMONG THORNS

Beloved: *"I am a rose of Sharon, a lily of the valleys."* Lover: *"Like a lily among thorns is my darling among the maidens."* Song of Solomon 2:1, 2

Where is Sharon? What is so special about the rose of Sharon? Sharon is a fruitful pastureland in Judea, a place where David's cattle also were fed (*1 Chronicles 27:29*).

In *Isaiah 35:2*, we read about *the excellence of Carmel and Sharon.* Sharon is a plain from Joppa to Caesarea, between the hill - country and the sea, and travelers have remarked on the abundance of flowers with which this plain is still carpeted in spring.

A rose of Sharon is a common scene, but it is not extraordinary. Same way lily of the valleys is quite common. It is like the bride saying, "I am just a commoner; not quite fit to marry you." But the Lover reassures her that she is very special among the maidens, 'like a lily among the thorns'.

Of all the 'flowers' in the pasture, our Christ has found us to be special, worthy of His love! Isn't that awesome? We are commoners, ordinary folks. But our Lord has chosen us to be His bride, His flawless bride.

It is not Sharon that is special nor the rose from Sharon; it is the love of the Lord that makes us special. Let us cherish His love.

The rose is surrounded by thorns and the lily blooms in the low places of the valleys. Our circumstances may be full of thorns and lowly. Whatever maybe our situations, let us remember that God loves us. Let us bloom for Jesus and spread His fragrance.

LIKE AN APPLE TREE

Like an apple tree among the trees of the forest is my beloved among the young men. I delight to sit in his shade, and his fruit is sweet to my taste. Song of Solomon 2:3

There are many trees in the forest, and they all have their uses and are being used in various ways. But when one is hungry, faint, and thirsty, the forest trees yield no succor, and we must look elsewhere to quench our thirst and hunger. The trees of the forest yield shelter, but no refreshing nutriment.

If, however, in the midst of the wood, one discovers an apple tree, he there finds the refreshment which he needs; his thirst is alleviated, and his hunger removed.

The above verse means to say that there are many things in the world that yield us a kind of satisfaction — people, truths, institutions, earthly comforts, arts, games, and the like. There are many manmade and God-made splendors, and many talents that attract and please us. But there are none which yield us the full solace which our soul requires; none which can give the spiritual food for which it hungers. Jesus Christ alone supplies the needs of the souls of men.

Jesus told the Samaritan woman, *'Everyone who drinks this water* (which momentarily quenches man's thirst) *will be thirsty again, but whoever drinks the water I give him will never thirst. Indeed, the water I give him will become in him a spring of water welling up to eternal life.' John 4:14*

Jesus alone caters to our needs for Eternal life. *Jesus said to them, "I am the bread of life; he who comes to Me shall not hunger, and he who believes in Me shall never thirst." John 6:35*

"Truly, truly, I say to you, unless you eat the flesh of the Son of man and drink His blood, you have no life in you; he who eats My flesh and drinks My blood has eternal life, and I will raise him up at the last day." John 6:53, 54

Only Jesus has the food and drink that nourishes and leads us to eternal life.

HIS BANNER OVER ME IS LOVE

He has taken me to the banquet hall, and his banner over me is love. Song of Solomon 2:4

Let us visualize a banquet hall. A feast has been prepared to celebrate the bride by her groom. All nobles who were invited were seated. There is merriment between the young and the old. All are rejoicing over the wedding that has just taken place or soon will be taking place. It is a joyous occasion for sure.

Now the groom presents a banner to the bride. I sometimes imagine it like a sash with the words "MY LOVE" written across it. Or it could be a flag-like banner of fine red with the golden words "MY BELOVED" embroidered on it in big bold letters. It is, indeed, a beautiful sight.

Jesus is our Bridegroom and He is preparing us to be His bride. He has redeemed us from a miry pit and elevated us to the honorable state of being His own bride. His love for His bride is unfathomable. He has prepared a banquet for His bride and honors her in the banquet hall with His love. *You prepare a table before me in the presence of my enemies. You anoint my head with oil; my cup runs over. Psalm 23:5*

To become the bride of Jesus we will have to undergo a sanctification and purification process. In the book of Esther, we read how the maidens contesting to be the wife of the king had to go through a lengthy beautification process for one year. Each young woman went into King Ahasuerus after she had completed twelve months' preparation, according to the regulations for the women: six months with oil of myrrh, and six months with perfumes and preparations for beautifying women. *Esther 2:12*

No doubt Jesus loves us and reveals His love for us. Still, we cannot take this love for granted. We must work to earn His love. Our thoughts and deeds should be entered on how to please our Lord. We cannot meet our Bridegroom without the sanctification and the purifying process.

RETURN, RETURN, O SHULAMITE!

Return, return, O Shulamite; return, return, that we may look upon you.
Song of Solomon 6:13

The Song of Solomon was written by King Solomon to show his special love for Shulamite, a village girl whom he loved. God in His wisdom has made this love song to describe the love of Jesus for His Church.

The name Solomon means, 'a man of peace'. Jesus is the Prince of Peace.

The name Shulamite is the feminine form of Solomon. Thus, Shulamite means a woman of peace. Jesus has left His peace with His church:

Peace I leave with you, my peace I give unto you. John 14:27

King Solomon and the Shulamite exalt each other. The maiden sings, *'My beloved is white and red, and He is the chiefest among ten thousand and He is altogether lovely.' Song of Solomon 5:10, 16.*

The king says that the Shulamite is the fairest among women and she is his beloved. He declares that there are three queens and fourscore concubines and virgins without number. But His beloved is undefiled and is the only one (*Song of Solomon 6:1, 8, 9*).

Our Bridegroom Jesus Christ is white and red since He is Holy and He shed His blood for us. He is the chiefest of ten thousand and more. To Jesus, each one of us is the fairest among all women and He loves us as though we are the only ones for Him. When the lover was describing her beauty, Shulamite's heart quickened like a speedy chariot, and it began to fly into high places. Her friends called her back to go to them and describe her lover more.

When we describe the love and greatness of Jesus, our friends would like to hear more and more about Him. There is no jealousy or competition for the love of Jesus. His love for each one of us is unique.

The Lamb of God, a Good Shepherd

Jesus Christ declares of Himself: *"I am the good shepherd. The good shepherd gives His life for the sheep. John 10:11*

The Apostle Peter testifies that Jesus Christ, *'Himself bore our sins in His own body on the tree, that we, having died to sins, might live for righteousness—by whose stripes you were healed. For you were like sheep going astray but have now returned to the Shepherd and Overseer of your souls.' 1 Peter 2:24, 25*

The writer to the Hebrews says *May the God of peace who brought up our Lord Jesus from the dead, that great Shepherd of the sheep, through the blood of the everlasting covenant make you complete in every good work. Hebrews 13:20, 21*

Jesus Christ who is our great and good shepherd is also the Lamb of God who sacrificed Himself to redeem us with His blood.

The Apostle John saw Jesus coming toward him, and said, *"Behold! The Lamb of God who takes away the sin of the world!" John 1:29*

In the Book of Revelation, John saw a vision of God sitting on His throne and the Lamb of God in the midst of the throne: *'For the Lamb who is in the midst of the throne will shepherd them and lead them to living fountains of waters. And God will wipe away every tear from their eyes.' Revelation 7:17*. This verse clearly says that the Lamb and the Shepherd are the same person, and we know that it is Jesus Christ.

Surely Jesus Christ is the sacrificial lamb that was killed for our sins so that we do not have to die. When we accept Jesus as our sacrificial Lamb we are gathered into His flock. And He becomes our good and great Shepherd. He protects us from the claws of the devil and leads us along good pastures and still waters.

The Comfort of Christ's coming

For the Lord Himself will come down from heaven, with a loud command, with the voice of the archangel and with the trumpet call of God, and the dead in Christ will rise first. After that, we who are still alive and are left will be caught up together with them in the clouds to meet the Lord in the air. And so, we will be with the Lord forever. Therefore encourage one another with these words. 1 Thessalonians 4:16-18

The Apostle Paul asks us to comfort one another with these words regarding the second coming of Jesus. When He comes back He will bring with Him those of His people who have already died.

But I do not want you to be ignorant, brethren, concerning those who have fallen asleep, lest you sorrow as others who have no hope. For if we believe that Jesus died and rose again, even so, God will bring with Him those who sleep in Jesus. 1 Thessalonians 4:13, 14

Christ's coming comforts us in two ways:

- When He comes He will bring with Him all who have died in Him. We can see all our beloved who had gone earlier.
- Christ's coming also brings us the comfort of entering God's rest, which is rest from our toils on this earth.

Therefore, since the promise of entering His rest still stands, let us be careful that none of you be found to have fallen short of it. There remains, then, a Sabbath rest for the people of God; for anyone who enters God's rest also rests from their works, just as God did from his. Let us, therefore, make every effort to enter that rest, so that no one will perish by following their example of disobedience. Hebrews 4:1, 9-11

Even though comfort and rest when Christ comes are promised, we must make every effort for the fulfilment of these promises by obeying the Word of God.

LIFT UP YOUR HEADS, YOU GATES

Lift up your heads, O you gates! And be lifted up you everlasting doors! And the King of glory shall come in. Who is this King of Glory? The Lord is strong and mighty, The Lord mighty in battle. Psalm 24:7, 8

This passage is one of exuberance, excitement, and great commotion. It is not just the typical mundane incident of life. But something HUGE is happening that should attract our attention and make us all "lift up our heads"! So, what is happening? The King of Glory shall be entering. We are preparing for the "King of Glory" to come in! Who is this King of Glory? He is our Lord God who is strong and mighty, mighty in battle. God Almighty is coming in!

Many times, the presence of God is undervalued. Did you know that God Almighty comes every time we meet for life group in His name? Did you know that God Almighty shows up for every church service? Did you know that God Almighty is amongst us when simply two or three believers gather in His name?

However, there are occasions when it appears that we attend church or life group merely as if it were "just another gathering." Perhaps we find ourselves overly preoccupied with who will be present, who will be speaking, or who will be leading worship. We may even prioritize whether the meeting aligns with our schedule and other considerations. Well, the truth is this. It is not just another meeting. It is not just another church service. It is not just another quiet time.

It is a big deal! Because somebody is coming, THE KING OF GLORY, THE LORD STRONG AND MIGHTY. He is going to be there. So "lift up your heads, that the King of Glory may come in".

As we pray today, let us remember. We have Almighty God in our midst. Let the gates of our hearts be lifted up and wide open for our King of glory to enter our midst. Along with Him comes the power to win our battles. He is strong and mighty, mighty in battle.

THE LAST TRUMPET CALL

And He will send His angels with a loud trumpet call, and they will gather His elect from the four winds, from one end of the heavens to the other. Matthew 24:31

In a flash, in the twinkling of an eye, at the last trumpet. For the trumpet will sound, the dead will be raised imperishable, and we will be changed. 1 Corinthians 15:52

For the Lord himself will come down from heaven, with a loud command, with the voice of the archangel and with the trumpet call of God, and the dead in Christ will rise first. After that, we who are still alive and are left will be caught up together with them in the clouds to meet the Lord in the air. And so, we will be with the Lord forever. 1 Thessalonians 4:16, 17

The most important event we as Christians ought to look forward to on a daily basis is the Last Trumpet Call!

What is meant by the last trumpet call? The last trumpet call is the imminent return of our King and Savior Jesus Christ at the least conceivable time to gather His Church in mid-air. The dead in Christ will rise and the faithful living will be transformed to be caught up with Him. This is also widely referred to by the term 'pre-tribulation rapture'.

When will the last trumpet call be? No one knows the exact date/time/hour of the last trumpet call - which makes it all the more difficult to be ready for it.

What does it take to be ready? Knowing Jesus Christ as our personal Savior and having our name written in the Book of Life is all it takes to be rapture ready. When Apostle Paul was in prison, a jailer asked him, "What must I do to be saved?" Paul's answer was: *"Believe in the Lord Jesus, and you will be saved—you and your household." Acts 16:31*

If we believe in the Lord Jesus Christ, then we are ready for the trumpet call.

GOD, THE HOLY SPIRIT

DID YOU RECEIVE THE HOLY SPIRIT
WHEN YOU BELIEVED?

When Apostle Paul came to Ephesus during his missionary journeys, he found some disciples there. Apollo had already preached the gospel of Jesus Christ in Ephesus and because of his ministry; there were some believers when Paul came there. Paul met with them and could see that they lacked the Holy Spirit in their lives. The believers in Ephesus had not heard the name of the Holy Spirit when they took baptism. This is not what Jesus had commanded in *Matthew 28:1,* to *"go and make disciples of all nations, baptizing them in the name of the Father and of the Son and of the Holy Spirit"*. When Paul explained this, they took baptism in the name of the Father and of the Son, and of the Holy Spirit. When Paul placed his hands on them the Holy Spirit came on them, and they spoke in tongues and prophesied (Acts 19: 1-7).

From the above passage, we make the following conclusions: * There is an outward manifestation of the Holy Spirit if we have received Him.

- There is a connection between the word 'Holy Spirit' and the baptism we take.
- We need to pray with others so that we receive the Holy Spirit.
- When we receive the Holy Spirit, there is an outward manifestation of speaking in tongues and utterance of prophecies.
- It is not enough that we have believed the gospel and become disciples of Jesus.
- We need to pray for and receive the Holy Spirit.

Did you receive the Holy Spirit when you became a believer? If you are not sure, pray to God to fill you with the Holy Spirit, so that you too can receive Him.

THE DAY OF PENTECOST

When the Day of Pentecost had fully come, they were all with one accord in one place. And suddenly there came a sound from heaven, as of a rushing mighty wind, and it filled the whole house where they were sitting. Then there appeared to them divided tongues, as of fire, and one sat upon each of them. And they were all filled with the Holy Spirit and began to speak with other tongues, as the Spirit gave them utterance. Acts 2:1-4

Pentecost is the fourth festival following Passover. Passover, Unleavened Bread, and First Fruits are the three festivals celebrated before Pentecost. The first three are celebrated in the same week however Pentecost is celebrated 50 days later, following the festival of First Fruits.

What is the significance of the day of Pentecost?

It is not a coincidence that Jesus was killed as our Passover Lamb, broken as our unleavened bread, and rose again on the third day as the First Fruit! Forty days later our Lord Jesus Christ ascended into heaven promising that He would soon send a Comforter. Ten days later, that is fifty days after His resurrection, the Holy Spirit - the promised Comforter descended on His disciples on the day of Pentecost!

How does Pentecost apply to us?

The same Comforter is available for us to experience the same infilling of the Holy Spirit, even today! Some people argue that the Holy Spirit dwells in us from when we got saved or were born again. It is true that the Holy Spirit convicts us of our sins and helps us to believe in Jesus and to get saved. However, we need the Pentecostal experience of the Holy Spirit descending on each one of us making us speak of God's wonders in different tongues. After being born-again and baptized in water, we should receive the baptism of the Holy Spirit. It was not an experience for only first-century Christians. It is for all of us too. The Holy Spirit descended on the disciples when they were praying in one accord and gathered together. Let us also come together in prayer and fellowship to be filled with the Holy Spirit.

WATER ON THIRSTY LAND; HIS SPIRIT ON OUR OFFSPRING

*For I will pour water on the thirsty land, and streams on the dry ground;
I will pour out my Spirit on your offspring, and my blessing on your
descendants. Isaiah 44:3*

Jesus has promised, *"If anyone thirsts, let him come to Me and drink.
He who believes in Me, as the Scripture has said, out of his heart will
flow rivers of living water." John 7:37, 38*

God invites, *"Everyone who thirsts, Come to the waters." Isaiah 55:1*

When we thirst for the filling/refilling of the Holy Spirit in us, God
will pour His Spirit abundantly on us, and also on our children and
children's children. What a great loving God!

The Holy Spirit is a must-have in our Faith journey without Whom
we cannot successfully complete our Christian walk. Let us thirst to
receive the Holy Spirit.

Let us cry out with King David, *"O God, you are my God, earnestly I
seek you; my soul thirsts for you, my body longs for you, in a dry and weary
land where there is no water." Psalm 63:1*

Another Psalmist cries out, *"As the deer pants for streams of water,
so my soul pants for you, O God. My soul thirsts for God, for the living
God." Psalm 42:1*

Do we have such a longing and thirst for the Holy Spirit?

Then surely God will fulfil His promise, *"I will pour water on the
thirsty land, and streams on the dry ground; I will pour out my Spirit on
your offspring, and my blessing on your descendants."*

THE SPIRIT TEACHES YOU WHAT IS TRUE

But the anointing which you have received from Him abides in you, and you do not need that anyone teach you; but as the same anointing teaches you concerning all things, and is true, and is not a lie, and just as it has taught you, you will abide in Him. 1 John 2:27

Above Scripture tells us that when we receive the Holy Spirit and He lives within us, He will teach us what is true.

Who is the Holy Spirit?

God is one God in three persons, God the Father, God the Son, and God the Holy Spirit. They exist and act together. May be a little beyond our understanding. But God cannot be bound by our understanding. A simple example may be a man as a triune person with his mind, soul, and body, existing together.

In *Isaiah 11:2,* we have the following names given to the Holy Spirit. He is the Spirit of the Lord; the Spirit of wisdom and understanding; the Spirit of counsel and might; and the Spirit of knowledge and of the fear of the Lord.

When we believe in the name of God, the Son, and accept Him, we become the children of God, the Father. When we ask God to give us the Holy Spirit, He baptizes us with God the Holy Spirit. The promise of Jesus, "Anyone who loves me will obey my teaching. My Father will love them, and we will come to them and make our home with them" is fulfilled in us.

When Jesus was preparing His disciples for His ascension to heaven leaving them behind, He promised them that even if He would not be with them physically, another counselor would come to stay with them. *"But the Counselor, the Holy Spirit, whom the Father will send in my name, will teach you all things and will remind you of everything I have said to you." John 14:26.* If we have the Holy Spirit living within us, He will teach us the truth and help us live a holy life just as He is holy.

The Holy Spirit up close

Who is the Holy Spirit?

The Holy Spirit is God Almighty! He is God Himself living in us and guiding our every path. With the help of the Holy Spirit, we acknowledge that Jesus Christ is the Son of God.

How can we receive the gift of the Holy Spirit?

Repent and be baptized, every one of you, in the name of Jesus Christ for the forgiveness of your sins. And you will receive the gift of the Holy Spirit. Acts 2:38

What is the evidence of the Holy Spirit living in us?

The Holy Spirit acknowledges that Jesus is Lord. All of us who believe and acknowledge that Jesus is Lord and revere His name already have the Holy Spirit living in us!

What are the functions of the Holy Spirit in our lives?

- The Holy Spirit prays for us in accordance with God's will. *The Spirit helps us in our weakness. We do not know what we ought to pray for, but the Spirit himself intercedes for us with groans that words cannot express. And he who searches our hearts knows the mind of the Spirit because the Spirit intercedes for the saints in accordance with God's will. Romans 8:26, 27*
- The Holy Spirit seals us to be God's sons and daughters! Amen! *For you did not receive a spirit that makes you a slave again to fear, but you received the Spirit of sonship. And by Him, we cry, 'Abba, Father' Romans 8:15*
- The Holy Spirit guides us in the path of truth. *But when he, the Spirit of truth, comes, he will guide you into all the truth and he will tell you what is yet to come. John 16:13*
- The Holy Spirit empowers us to be witnesses to Jesus. *You will*

receive power when the Holy Spirit comes on you, and you will be my witnesses in Jerusalem, and in all Judea and Samaria, and to the ends of the earth. Acts 1:8

And do not grieve the Holy Spirit of God, with whom you were sealed for the day of redemption. Ephesians 4:30

Manifestation of the Holy Spirit – tongues

All of them were filled with the Holy Spirit and began to speak in other tongues as the Spirit enabled them. Acts 2:4

Frequent disagreements arise among believers regarding the phenomenon of "speaking in tongues," primarily involving those who have experienced this gift and those who haven't. At the most intense end of this debate, some contend that one cannot attain salvation without speaking in tongues, while others counter by suggesting that those who do speak in tongues are influenced by malevolent forces.

We must exercise caution in making such assertions since both arguments contradict the teachings of the Bible – the Word of God. Jesus says, *'Whoever blasphemes against the Holy Spirit will never be forgiven; he is guilty of an eternal sin.' Mark 3:29*

There are many instances recorded in the Acts of the Apostles where, whenever people were filled with the Holy Spirit, there was an outward manifestation of speaking in tongues.

The Apostle Paul says, *"He that speaks in an unknown tongue speaks not unto men, but unto God." (1 Corinthians 14:2).* Paul wishes for all the believers to speak in tongues. However, he asks those who speak in tongues to pray for and receive the gift of interpretation which will benefit the hearers. *1 Corinthians 14:2, 5, 13*

Speaking in tongues is a true experience of the Holy Spirit. I have personally experienced speaking in tongues. It is the Holy Spirit dwelling within me, praying on my behalf in an unknown language to God. We ourselves do not know what He is praying for us. It is an unknown language even to the one who speaks in tongues. It is a mystery. But it is God's mystery, and it is a blessed experience of being connected to God and loving Him better. Ask God to fill you with the Holy Spirit. Ask and you will receive. When the Holy Spirit comes and fills you, He will teach and lead you in all truth. Amen.

MANIFESTATION OF THE HOLY SPIRIT – LOVE

And hope does not disappoint us, because God has poured out his love into our hearts by the Holy Spirit, whom he has given us. Romans 5:5

Because you are sons, God sent the Spirit of his Son into our hearts, the Spirit who calls out, 'Abba, Father'. Galatians 4:6

The primary and most profound gift of the Holy Spirit is the love He lavishly pours into our hearts. This love overflows abundantly, directed towards God, our Lord Jesus Christ, our neighbors, all humanity, and even towards sinners. Alongside this abundant love, another gift of the Holy Spirit is the intimate sense of closeness to God, allowing us to address Him as "Abba, Father," fostering a profound connection and intimacy with our Creator.

Clarke's Commentary on the Bible states: "This love is the spring of all our actions; it is the motive of our obedience; the principle through which we love God, we love Him because He first loved us, and we love Him with a love worthy of Himself. Speaking in tongues and prophesying are other signs that accompany the infilling of the Holy Spirit. But if we lack the fundamental love then these external signs are of no use."

This is exactly what Paul writes:

Though I speak with the tongues of men and of angels, but have not love, I have become sounding brass or a clanging cymbal. And though I have the gift of prophecy, and understand all mysteries and all knowledge, and though I have all faith, so that I could remove mountains, but have not love, I am nothing. And though I bestow all my goods to feed the poor, and though I give my body to be burned, but have not love, it profits me nothing. 1 Corinthians 13:1-3

When God fills us with the Holy Spirit, He pours out His love in us. We should walk in this love. As much as we give importance to speaking in tongues and prophesying, we should give more importance to manifesting this love.

HE WHO HAS AN EAR, LET HIM HEAR WHAT THE SPIRIT SAYS

In the Book of Revelation, the Apostle John wrote what Jesus revealed to him. Jesus had told John, *"I am the Alpha and the Omega, the First and the Last,' and, 'What you see, write in a book and send it to the seven churches which are in Asia: to Ephesus, to Smyrna, to Pergamos, to Thyatira, to Sardis, to Philadelphia, and to Laodicea."(Revelation 1:11)*

> *Write the things which you have seen, and the things which are, and the things which will take place after this. Revelation 1: 19*

Jesus gave specific messages to the above seven churches and asked John to send these messages to those churches. He asked him to finish His message to each church with the words, *"He who has an ear, let him hear what the Spirit says to the churches." 2:7, 11, 17, 29, 3:6, 13, 22.*

In each of these churches, the conditions varied. Some were commended for their deeds, while others were admonished. Jesus addressed their shortcomings and urged them to repent from their spiritual decline, guiding them towards actions that would be pleasing to Him. He understood their spiritual struggles, trials, and the persecutions they endured for His sake. Moreover, He promised rewards for those who remained steadfast and overcame their challenges.

Jesus affirmed that the messages addressed to each individual church represent the words inspired by the Holy Spirit. While specific churches were mentioned, the teachings hold relevance for all churches and people, spanning across time—past, present, and future—who have ears to hear and hearts to understand.

Every message in Scripture is inspired by the Holy Spirit and meant for us all. We shouldn't disregard any verse, thinking it is only for certain individuals, churches, or times. Instead, we should realize these messages are for all who will listen and comprehend. Let us heed what the Holy Spirit communicates through Scripture, given to us by Jesus Christ to draw us closer to God the Father.

WHERE THE SPIRIT OF THE LORD
IS, THERE IS FREEDOM

Now the Lord is the Spirit; and where the Spirit of the Lord is, there is liberty. 2 Corinthians 3:17

Pentecost is an ancient festival observed by the Israelites fifty days after the commencement of the barley harvest. However, in the New Testament, Pentecost holds a spiritual significance. It was on the day of Pentecost when the Holy Spirit descended upon the disciples, marking a pivotal moment in the early Christian church. The resurrection of Jesus had infused them with renewed spirit and hope, yet they remained uncertain about what lay ahead.

On the day of Pentecost, they assembled in unity, and it was there that they encountered the infilling of the Holy Spirit, as chronicled by Luke in the Book of Acts, Chapter 2. Since that momentous occasion, countless individuals have undergone a similar experience of being filled with the Holy Spirit. Regardless of our denominational affiliations or labels—whether Baptist, Methodist, Evangelical, Pentecostal, non-denominational, or any variation thereof—the Holy Spirit continues to work actively among us. Praise the Lord!

The Holy Spirit plays a crucial role in convicting people of their sins, an essential step in becoming Christians. Our connection to the Holy Spirit is indispensable; it is He who guides us towards salvation, whether we consciously acknowledge or recognize His presence. Once we accept salvation, the Holy Spirit takes up residence within us.

The baptism of the Holy Spirit, however, represents a distinct experience. It is a gift from God available to those who desire and ask for it. Through this gift, the Holy Spirit empowers us to continually sanctify ourselves—a lifelong process. It is the Holy Spirit who works within us, gradually transforming us to become more like Jesus with each passing day.

And we all, who with unveiled faces contemplate the Lord's glory, are being transformed into his image with ever-increasing glory, which comes from the Lord, who is the Spirit. 2 Corinthians 3:18

May we seek and receive a fresh outpouring of the Holy Spirit, renewing and replenishing us, leading to our transformation into the likeness of Jesus Christ, our Lord, and Savior. May this transformation prepare us to behold His glorious face in eternity. Amen.

The Holy Spirit living in us

This is how you can recognize the Spirit of God: Every spirit that acknowledges that Jesus Christ has come in the flesh is from God. 1 John 4:2

What is the evidence of the Holy Spirit living in us?

The answer is plain and simple from today's Scripture. Holy Spirit acknowledges that Jesus is Lord, which means that as believers who confess Jesus as Lord, we already have the Holy Spirit dwelling within us!

How can we receive the gift of the Holy Spirit?

Repent and be baptized, every one of you, in the name of Jesus Christ for the forgiveness of your sins. And you will receive the gift of the Holy Spirit. Acts 2:38

What more can we expect from the Holy Spirit?

In the same way, the Spirit helps us in our weakness. We do not know what we ought to pray for, but the Spirit himself intercedes for us through wordless groans. And he who searches our hearts knows the mind of the Spirit, because the Spirit intercedes for God's people in accordance with the will of God. Romans 8:26, 27

The Holy Spirit brings us a step closer to God. We are no longer ordinary mankind but God's sons and daughters! Amen! *The Spirit you received does not make you slaves, so that you live in fear again; rather, the Spirit you received brought about your adoption to sonship. And by him we cry, "Abba, Father." Romans 8:15*

Why do we need more of the Holy Spirit?

But you will receive power when the Holy Spirit comes on you, and you will be my witnesses in Jerusalem, and in all Judea and Samaria, and to the ends of the earth." Acts 1:8.

We should seek the power of the Holy Spirit or an abundant over-flow of His anointing, enabling us to be effective witnesses wherever we go. The more we are filled with the anointing of the Holy Spirit, the more our lives reflect holiness. Our thoughts, actions, hobbies, and prayers will align with God's will, progressively shaping us into His image.

PRAISE AND WORSHIP

Praise the Lord, my soul

Praise the Lord, my soul; all my inmost being, praise His holy name. Praise the Lord, my soul, and forget not all His benefits; Psalm 103:1, 2

In Psalms 103, King David expresses profound praise to God and encourages his soul to remember and exalt the Lord for His countless blessings. David lists several ways in which God has demonstrated His goodness to him and to all who fear Him:

God's grace extends to every aspect of our lives: He forgives all our iniquities and heals all our diseases. Our redemption from destruction is coupled with His loving kindness and tender mercies. He satisfies us with good things, renewing our strength like the eagle's. In executing righteousness and judgment, He defends the oppressed. The Lord's mercy is boundless, slow to anger and abounding in compassion. He doesn't hold onto anger forever or deal with us according to our sins. His mercy reaches as high as the heavens above the earth, removing our transgressions infinitely far from us. Like a compassionate father, He understands our weaknesses and remembers our frailty. The everlasting mercy and righteousness of the Lord encompasses both us and our children.

Let us also lift our voices in wholehearted praise to the Lord, offering Him our deepest adoration and gratitude. Praise the Lord. Amen.

A call to praise the Lord

Praise the Lord! Praise the Lord from the heavens; Praise Him in the heights! Psalm 148:1

Praise the Lord from the earth, You great sea creatures and all the depths. Psalm 148: 7

In Psalm 148, King David summons the heavens, the earth, and all that dwells within to join in praising the Lord. This call to worship stems from the recognition that God's name is supreme, and His glory surpasses even the heavens and the earth. The Psalm commences and concludes with the word "Hallelujah," which translates to "Praise the Lord," signifying a continuous exhortation to praise and worship God. The Psalmist extends an invitation to the angels and the celestial beings, the heavenly hosts, to offer praise to God. He then calls upon the sun, moon, and stars—all the luminous celestial bodies—as well as the highest heavens and the waters above the skies, urging them to glorify the name of the Lord. The reason for this exhortation lies in the fact that all these creations were brought into existence by God's command and are sustained by His ongoing providence.

Verses 7-9 summon the earth, sea creatures, depths, fire, hail, snow, vapors, winds, mountains, hills, trees, and all such entities to praise the Lord. Similarly, verses 10-12 call upon beasts, cattle, creeping things, flying fowls, kings, princes, judges, and all people—regardless of age or status—to offer praise to the Lord. The Psalmist's inclusive list encompasses both celestial and earthly beings, including even inanimate objects, emphasizing that all creation should give praise to the Lord. The universal summons to worship stems from the reality that the Lord God is the Creator of the heavens, the earth, and all that dwell therein. His unmatched splendor exceeds even the loftiest domains, rendering Him worthy of adoration.

The paramount reason for us to praise the name of the Lord is highlighted in Psalm 148:14, which declares: *"He has raised up for His people a horn"*. This "horn" raised for us is none other than His Son, Jesus Christ. Therefore, we should offer praise to the Lord for this invaluable gift bestowed upon us—His Son, who embodies salvation, redemption, and eternal life.

Exalting our Lord with songs of praises

When the Israelites were liberated from slavery in Egypt and crossed the Red Sea, they witnessed the drowning of the pursuing Egyptian army. In response to this miraculous deliverance, Moses, Miriam, and all the Israelites sang a song of praise to the Lord:

I will sing to the Lord, for He is highly exalted. Both horse and driver He has hurled into the sea. Exodus 15:1

Each of us has undoubtedly experienced numerous miracles in our lives. Have we taken the time to express gratitude to the Lord God Almighty for our deliverance, provision, and protection by lifting our voices in songs of praise?

Even when the foundations of the earth were fastened and its cornerstone was laid, the morning stars sang together, and all the sons of God shouted for joy (*Job 38:6, 7*). God has lifted us from the pit of our sins, established us on the rock of Christ, and has given us new songs in our mouths to praise Him (*Psalm 40:2, 3*).

The Book of Psalms contains 150 songs composed and sung by various individuals in diverse circumstances. Following significant victories over their adversaries, the Israelites expressed praise to God through songs of deliverance and triumph. Upon the establishment of the Temple in Jerusalem, King Solomon and later Nehemiah meticulously organized arrangements for singing and worship.

When Jesus was born, a heavenly chorus was sung by a multitude of angels, praising God and singing, '*Glory to God in the highest, And on earth peace, goodwill toward men!' Luke 2:13, 14*

Indeed, Our God lives among the praises of His saints (*Psalm 22:3*). Therefore, we must exalt Him with praises and songs.

I will praise God's name in song and glorify him with thanksgiving. Psalm 69:30.

Come, let us bow down and worship the Lord

Come, let us bow down in worship; let us kneel before the Lord our Maker.
Psalm 95:6

The primary purpose of God concerning humanity is that humans should worship God, their Creator, and not any of God's creations or idols crafted by humans. All the commandments, statutes, and ordinances given by God to humanity revolve around loving and worshiping God alone. Indeed, God called Abraham and set him apart to become the patriarch of a nation dedicated to worshiping Him alone. When the Israelites were enslaved in Egypt, God sent Moses to confront the Pharaoh, commanding him to release His people so they could worship Him freely.

During their journey from Egypt to Canaan, God instructed Moses to construct the Tabernacle, a portable sanctuary where the Israelites could offer sacrifices and worship God according to His specifications. After settling in Canaan, King Solomon built the Temple in Jerusalem, a permanent place of worship for the Israelites to honor and adore God.

It is indeed a tremendous privilege that God has called us to worship Him. He has instructed us on how to approach Him in worship: through sanctification by the blood of the sacrificial Lamb (*1 Peter 1:18-19*). Christ offered Himself on the cross, shedding His precious blood to cleanse us from sin. Additionally, the Holy Spirit purifies us like fire and water, preparing us for worship. Through sanctification by the blood of Jesus and the work of the Holy Spirit, we become worthy to worship God. Worshiping God is the primary expectation He has of us.

The Psalmist asks us to bow and kneel down in the presence of God to worship Him. We should humble ourselves before God. There is no place for our pride when we stand before God.

Give to the Lord the glory due His name; bring an offering and come before
Him. Oh, worship the Lord in the beauty of holiness! 1 Chronicle 16:29

A NEW SONG IN MY MOUTH

He put a new song in my mouth, a hymn of praise to our God. Many will see and fear and put their trust in the Lord. Psalm 40:3

King David here expresses his distress and cries out to God for deliverance from the "miry clay" of his sins. God hears his plea, lifts him out of the pit, and sets his feet upon a firm foundation. In response to God's deliverance, David receives a new song of praise to extol God's faithfulness and deliverance. David anticipates that many will witness his transformation and be inspired to fear and trust the Lord.

This sentiment resonates deeply with the biblical concept of praising God with new songs, celebrating His ever-present mercies and grace in our lives. As each day dawns, God's mercies are renewed, and His loving-kindness manifests in countless ways. Therefore, it is fitting for us to offer new songs of praise and thanksgiving, rejoicing in God, our Savior. This becomes especially poignant when we have waited patiently for answers to our prayers. When God graciously delivers us in ways that exceed our expectations or imagination, He indeed places a new song of praise in our mouths. This hymn of praise not only glorifies God but also serves as a testimony to others, encouraging them to place their trust in the Lord.

The need for a new song arises when the old songs fail to adequately express our gratitude for God's deliverance from the pit of our sin. Each fresh deliverance we experience demands new words and melodies to praise God. It is God Himself who inspires these new songs within us, overwhelming us with the joy of His deliverance when our hearts are bursting with gratitude, but words seem insufficient. When we sing these new songs of praise, our overflowing hearts bear witness to God's goodness, prompting others to revere Him and place their trust in Him. Through our new songs, we share our testimony of deliverance, inviting others to experience God's saving grace alongside us What an awesome way to share our testimony!

GOD IS SPIRIT. WORSHIP HIM IN SPIRIT AND TRUTH

"God is Spirit, and those who worship Him must worship in spirit and truth." John 4:24

The Lord is near to all who call on Him, to all who call out to Him in truth. Psalm 145:18

God is Spirit. He does not have a physical form. n Exodus 20:4-5, one of the Ten Commandments given to Moses includes the prohibition against making any graven images or idols to represent God. The commandment states: *"You shall not make for yourself an image in the form of anything in heaven above or on the earth beneath or in the waters below. You shall not bow down to them or worship them"* *Exodus 20:4, 5.*

Worshiping God in truth involves meditating on His greatness, His mighty deeds, His promises, His Word, and His commandments. We engage our minds and intellect in this form of worship. On the other hand, worshiping God in spirit involves becoming deeply united with God. In this state, we transcend our surroundings, and our spirits become immersed in the indescribable joy of God's presence. To worship God in spirit, we require the filling of His Spirit. Jesus assured us that the heavenly Father will indeed give the Holy Spirit to those who ask for Him. Therefore, we should earnestly seek God's Spirit to enable us to worship Him in spirit and in truth.

Now the Lord is the Spirit; and where the Spirit of the Lord is, there is liberty. 2 Corinthians 3:17

God grants us the freedom to worship Him without hindrance. The Spirit assists us in our weaknesses, interceding for us when we are unsure of what to pray for, as stated in Romans 8:26. In our worship, the Spirit praises God on our behalf and enables us to join in worshiping God along with Him. Therefore, we are called to worship God both in spirit and in truth, fully engaging our hearts and minds in communion with Him.

Is our worship made up only of rules taught by men?

The Lord says: "These people come near to me with their mouth and honor me with their lips, but their hearts are far from me. Their worship of me is based on merely human rules they have been taught. Isaiah 29:13

Each Sunday, believers gather to honor our Lord in worship, guided by various principles and regulations, both divine and human.

According to 1 Chronicles 16:29, we are urged to render to the Lord the reverence He deserves, presenting offerings and approaching Him with sanctified hearts. Psalm 96:9 instructs us to worship God with awe, acknowledging His holiness and grandeur. Similarly, Psalm 100:2, 4 encourages us to worship the Lord joyfully, expressing gratitude through song and praise as we enter His presence with thanksgiving and praise. These verses emphasize a fundamental principle for worship: to approach God with holiness, gratitude, and joyful praise.

The Apostle Paul also emphasizes the importance of orderly worship, ensuring that even unbelievers who attend our gatherings can witness the presence of God among us. In 1 Corinthians 14:40, he advises, "But everything should be done in a fitting and orderly way."

This prompts us to reflect on the authenticity of our worship. Are we merely paying lip service to God, or do we genuinely love Him with all our hearts? Are we more focused on outward appearances, or do we prioritize the purity and integrity of our inner beings before God?

If we find ourselves entangled in man-made rules or rituals that detract from true worship, let us earnestly seek correction and alignment with God's intended form of worship. Today is an opportunity to realign our hearts and intentions with the essence of worship that God desires from us. Let us pursue worship that is sincere, genuine, and centered on loving God with our whole being.

WORSHIP THE LORD IN THE
SPLENDOR OF HIS HOLINESS

Worship the Lord in the splendor of His holiness. Psalm 96:9

A s we prepare to worship the Lord, let us always remember to approach Him with reverence and awe, honoring His holiness and majesty. In another translation, we are instructed to "Worship the Lord in holy attire," which brings to mind the parable of the wedding banquet in Matthew 22:11-13. In this parable, a guest who did not have the proper wedding clothes on was thrown out into the darkness. This serves as a reminder of the importance of coming before God with hearts purified and adorned in righteousness, ready to honor Him with our worship.

Indeed, attire or clothing can symbolize our salvation and righteousness. As Isaiah 61:10 beautifully expresses, "I delight greatly in the Lord; my soul rejoices in my God. For he has clothed me with garments of salvation and arrayed me in a robe of righteousness." This imagery highlights how God clothes us with the garments of salvation and adorns us with the robe of righteousness.

As we prepare for the ultimate banquet in the presence of our King in heaven, let us ensure that we are adorned with these spiritual garments of salvation and righteousness. May our hearts rejoice in the Lord, and may our lives reflect the beauty of His salvation and righteousness as we worship Him with reverence and joy.

In Revelation 3:4-5, Jesus speaks to the church in Sardis, acknowledging that there are some individuals who have not defiled their garments, and they will walk with Him in white because they are worthy. Those who overcome will be clothed in white garments. Additionally, in Revelation, John sees the Bride of the Lamb adorned in fine linen, clean and bright. This fine linen represents the righteous acts of the saints. He also observes the elders worshiping around the throne of God, clothed in white garments, as well as the armies in heaven, clothed in fine linen, white and clean (Revelation 4:4, 19:8, 14).

In Revelation 7:9, a multitude of people clothed in white robes stands before the Throne, praising God. It is revealed that these individuals have come out of the great tribulation and have washed their robes, making them white in the blood of the Lamb (Revelation 7:14).

We too must cleanse our robes in the blood of the Lamb to make them white and pure. This spiritual cleansing is accomplished through the redemptive work of Jesus Christ. We must pray and ask God to apply the blood of Jesus to every aspect of our being—our body, mind, and soul—so that we may be purified and made holy. It is through this ongoing process of spiritual cleansing and renewal that we are empowered to live lives that glorify God and reflect His righteousness.

Worship the Lord with gladness

Worship the Lord with gladness; come before him with joyful songs. Psalm 100:2

Rejoice before the Lord your God, you, your sons and daughters. Deuteronomy 12:12

In *Isaiah 35:10* we read, *"...the ransomed of the Lord will return. They will enter Zion with singing; everlasting joy will crown their heads. Gladness and joy will overtake them, and sorrow and sighing will flee away."*

As those redeemed by the Lord, we will rejoice in His presence, singing joyful songs and worshiping Him wholeheartedly. Through our worship, the joy of our salvation is continually renewed within us, a joy that cannot be taken away by anyone. God has appointed the Sabbath and numerous festivals for His people to gather together and rejoice before Him with gladness. He deeply cares about our rejoicing and happiness, ensuring that the fullness of joy is found in His presence. As Psalm 16:11 declares, *"You make known to me the path of life; in your presence there is fullness of joy; at your right hand are pleasures forevermore."*

Moses emphasized the significance of worshiping the Lord with gladness to the Israelites. He conveyed that if they did not serve the Lord their God with joy and gladness of heart, acknowledging His abundance in all things, they would be subjected to serving their enemies (Deuteronomy 28:47-48). In *Isaiah 58:13, 14,* we read how to worship the Lord with gladness.

- Consider the worship day delightful, holy, and honorable.
- Stay away from doing your own work.
- Do not find your own pleasures.
- Do not speak your own words.

When we worship God with gladness, He will lift us up with His blessings.

GIVE THANKS TO THE LORD; MAKE KNOWN WHAT HE HAS DONE

Give thanks to the Lord, call on His name; make known among the nations what He has done. 1 Chronicle 16:8

G iving thanks or expressing gratitude is understandable, but how does it relate to the task of spreading this message among different nations? Words possess the power to sway someone in favor of or against a particular issue. Marketing experts often attest to the effectiveness of "word of mouth" as a highly impactful marketing strategy. The Epistle of James, in chapter 3, delves into the influence of the tongue, likening it to a rudder guiding a large ship and a fire capable of consuming an entire forest.

In the Gospel of Luke, we encounter the account of Jesus journeying to Jerusalem in a procession, riding on a colt, with a multitude of people following Him. As He approached the descent of the Mount of Olives, the entire assembly of disciples began to rejoice and praise God loudly for the mighty works they had witnessed, declaring, "Blessed is the King who comes in the name of the Lord! Peace in heaven and glory in the highest!" However, some Pharisees in the crowd urged Jesus to silence His disciples. In response, Jesus declared, "I tell you that if these should keep silent, the stones would immediately cry out" (Luke 19:37-40).

This underscores the importance of proclaiming God's wonders and works. If we fail to do so, even the stones would testify to His glory, leaving us ashamed for our silence. Indeed, "making known among the nations" involves more than simply offering a brief expression of gratitude. It entails boldly proclaiming our acknowledgment, support, and affiliation with the brand called Jesus!

We are called to go beyond mere thanksgiving and instead announce, proclaim, and broadcast to the nations all that Jesus has accomplished for us. Just as the disciples rejoiced and praised God loudly for the mighty works they had witnessed, let us follow in their footsteps, rejoicing and praising God with resounding voices for all the incredible things He has done in our lives!

GIVE THANKS TO GOD

Give thanks to the Lord, for He is good! For His mercy endures forever.
Who remembered us in our lowly state, For His mercy endures forever.
Psalm 136:1, 23

U ndoubtedly, each of us has encountered challenging periods in our lives at one time or another. Whether it was a health setback, feelings of unhappiness, unemployment, or another struggle, these experiences are relatable to many. During those difficult days, assistance seemed distant, leaving us unsure of where to turn or how to cope. Our faith was put to the test, and we found ourselves grappling with uncertainty and loneliness. It was a time when supportive friends were scarce, and we felt as though we had hit rock bottom.

However, even in those trying moments, God did not forsake us. He remembered our struggles, and out of His boundless mercy, He stepped in. Through His intervention, our faith was fortified, and our hearts were filled with renewed hope. We found solace in the restoration of our joy, knowing that God's love and care endure through every trial.

Let us take a moment to reflect on how God remembered us in our times of need, casting our minds back to those challenging moments. As we recall His faithfulness and provision during those low points, let us express gratitude to Him for His unfailing love and care.

It is important to share our stories and testimonies of God's faithfulness with others, including our friends, family, and especially our children. By doing so, we can encourage and uplift those around us, reminding them of God's faithfulness even in the darkest of times.

Furthermore, let us extend kindness and assistance to those who may be experiencing hardships similar to what we once faced. Just as God remembered us in our low estate, let us show compassion and support to others in need, offering help in whatever way we can.

Reflecting on our own lives, we can see abundant evidence of God's grace and provision, demonstrating that His grace has indeed been sufficient for us in the past. Therefore, let us remember to give thanks to the Lord who remembered us in our low estate, offering praise and adoration for His continued faithfulness and love.

He raises the poor from the dust and lifts the beggar from the ash heap, To set them among princes And make them inherit the throne of glory. 1 Samuel 2:8

He raises the poor out of the dust and lifts the needy out of the ash heap, that He may seat him with princes—with the princes of His people. Psalm 113:7, 8

Give thanks to the Lord, for He is good! For His mercy endures forever. Psalm 136:1

WORSHIP THE LORD YOUR GOD, AND SERVE HIM ONLY

Worship the Lord your God and serve Him only. Matthew 4:10

Worship the Lord with gladness; come before Him with joyful songs. Psalm 100:2

Worship the Lord in the splendor of His holiness. Psalm 96:9

Worship the Lord your God, and His blessing will be on your food and water. Exodus 23:25

Let us analyze our worship. Do we worship the Lord only because it is one of the rules formed by men for a Christian way of life? or Is our worship streaming from the sincere desire of our heart to worship God? Do we only go to Him with our outward love and honor Him with our lips, or do we truly love Him in our hearts of hearts? Are we giving more importance to our appearance, or are we concerned with keeping our inner beings holy and presentable to God?

If, whether knowingly or unknowingly, we find ourselves ensnared in teachings or practices dictated by human rules rather than the true essence of worship, let us endeavor to liberate ourselves from such constraints today. It is imperative that we exercise caution and discernment, refusing to blindly adhere to any form of worship or doctrine that deviates from the teachings of God's Word.

Instead, let us approach our worship of the Lord with genuine sincerity of heart. We must remember that He alone is deserving of all praise, honor, power, and majesty, and He alone is truly worthy of our worship.

God is spirit and those who worship Him must worship in spirit and truth. John 4:24

Ascribe to the Lord the glory due his name; bring an offering and come before Him. Worship the Lord in the splendor of His holiness. 1 Chronicles 16:29

Prayer

GIVE US THIS DAY OUR DAILY BREAD

Give us today our daily bread. Matthew 6:11

"..give me neither poverty nor riches but give me only my daily bread."
Proverbs 30:8

Our physical sustenance is vital for survival, but similarly, our spiritual well-being depends on nourishment. The prayer, "Give us this day our daily bread," reflects not only our reliance on God's provision for our physical needs but also our dependence on His Word for spiritual sustenance. Regrettably, many of us overlook regular engagement with the Word of God. Just as our physical strength declines with prolonged hunger, our spiritual vitality wanes when we neglect spiritual nourishment.

Nourishing our soul holds greater significance than nourishing our body. So, what constitutes the sustenance for our spiritual growth?

- **The Word of God.** Both Moses and Jesus have said, *"Man does not live by bread alone, but by the Word that proceeds from the mouth of God" (Deuteronomy 8:3, Luke 4:4).*
- **Hunger and thirst for righteousness.** *"Blessed are they who hunger and thirst after righteousness, they shall be filled." Matthew 5:6*
- **Jesus is the living bread.** *"I am the living bread that came down from heaven. If anyone eats of this bread, he will live forever." John 6:51*

Encourage daily devotion to reading and meditating on the Word of God. Foster a deep longing for righteousness and actively pursue it every day. Remember and believe in the sacrificial death of Jesus on the cross for our redemption on a daily basis. Through these practices, we engage in the spiritual nourishment graciously provided by our Heavenly Father. Just as we pray, "Our Father in Heaven, give us this day our daily bread," let us wholeheartedly receive and embrace the sustenance He graciously provides for us each day. Amen.

GOD IS NEAR US WHENEVER WE PRAY TO HIM

What other nation is so great as to have their gods near them the way the Lord our God is near us whenever we pray to Him? Deuteronomy 4:7

Consider these reflective questions: Do we engage in prayer with sincerity? Do we possess the unwavering conviction that God hears our prayers? Can we perceive the nearness of God's presence when we pray to Him? Do we genuinely believe that the Word of God is the ultimate truth?

If our answer is affirmative, it naturally leads us to the understanding that prayer is essential. We should approach prayer with steadfast assurance, knowing that God hears our supplications and comes close to us. This certainty finds its foundation in the Word of God itself.

For those who require further reinforcement of this truth, consider these additional scriptures:

"The Lord is near to all who call on Him, to all who call out to Him in truth." (Psalm 145:18)

"The Lord is near to the brokenhearted; He saves the contrite in spirit." (Psalm 34:18)

"Seek the Lord while He may be found; call on Him while He is near." (Isaiah 55:6)

With these assurances from Scripture, we can confidently affirm that God is indeed close to us when we pray. Let us embrace this reality and approach prayer with faith and assurance, knowing that our Heavenly Father hears and responds to our heartfelt supplications.

Blessed be the Lord, because He has heard the voice of my supplications! Psalm 28:6

Cleanse me from hidden faults

Who can understand his errors? Cleanse me from secret faults. Psalm 19:12

For the ways of man are before the eyes of the Lord and He ponders all his paths. Proverbs 5:21

Nothing escapes the Lord's gaze. Every thought, desire, and prayer, no matter how hidden, is fully known to Him. While it is comforting to acknowledge this truth, we must also recognize that the Lord is aware of our hidden sins, impure thoughts, and malicious intentions. Despite our hesitations to expose these aspects to God's scrutiny, the reality remains unchanged.

As *Hebrews 4:13* states, *"Nothing in all creation is hidden from God's sight. Everything is uncovered and laid bare before the eyes of Him to Whom we must give account."* Similarly, *Ecclesiastes 12:14* emphasizes that *"God will bring every deed into judgment, including every hidden thing, whether it is good or evil."* Additionally, *Matthew 6:18* reminds us that *"Your Father who sees in secret will reward you openly."*

Truly, nothing is concealed from God's view. We stand naked and exposed before the Lord. Therefore, let us reflect on our lives and make a commitment to prayerfully address any hidden faults or offensive ways within us. Like King David, let us earnestly pray, *"Cleanse me from secret faults"* (Psalm 19:12) and *"See if there is any offensive way in me and lead me in the way everlasting" (Psalm 139:24).* Amen!

Prayer of Daniel

Now when Daniel knew that the writing was signed, he went home. And in his upper room, with his windows open toward Jerusalem, he knelt down on his knees three times that day and prayed and gave thanks before his God, as was his custom since early days. Daniel 6:10

Daniel found himself in exile in Babylon. Despite this, King Darius bestowed upon him the highest office in the kingdom, much to the envy of other officials. Seeking to discredit Daniel, these officials scrutinized his actions, hoping to find fault. When their efforts failed, they resorted to cunning tactics. They persuaded the king to issue a decree stating that anyone who prayed to any god or man other than the king for the next thirty days would face punishment by being thrown into a den of lions. Aware of Daniel's unwavering devotion to the God of Israel, they knew this decree would ensnare him. Daniel, however, remained steadfast in his daily prayers, even though he knew of the decree.

In this context, we recall the prayer offered by King Solomon during the dedication of the Temple of God in Jerusalem. He petitioned that if any of God's people were taken captive and prayed facing the direction of Jerusalem and the Temple, their prayers would be heard and answered (*1 Kings 8:48*). It is reasonable to assume that Daniel would have been aware of Solomon's prayer, especially given his deep knowledge of scripture and his faithful devotion to God.

Daniel's enemies maliciously plotted against him, leading to the king reluctantly throwing him into the den of lions. Early the next morning, filled with worry, the king rushed to the den and called out to Daniel, hoping for a miracle. To his relief, Daniel responded, affirming that God had sent an angel to protect him, ensuring the lions did not harm him. Daniel emphasized his innocence before God and the king. Witnessing this miraculous deliverance, the king issued a decree urging all in his kingdom to revere Daniel's God, recognizing Him as the living God who delivers His faithful servants. This event further solidified Daniel's reputation and the reverence for his God among the people. (Daniel 6:19-26)

OUR WORDS AND OUR MEDITATION
BE PLEASING IN GOD'S SIGHT

Let the words of my mouth, and the meditation of my heart, be acceptable in your sight, O Lord, my strength and my Redeemer. Psalm 19:14

Psalm 19 opens by vividly illustrating how the skies declare the glory of God, portraying each day and night as teachers imparting wisdom and knowledge. The majestic journey of the sun, rising and setting with purpose, serves as a reminder of the joyous fulfillment found in following our ordained paths and illuminating the world with God's light. Just as the natural world reflects God's glory, so too should we, as believers, cast aside any hindrances and run with endurance the race set before us (Hebrews 12:1). Our delight in God's law and continual meditation upon it lead to true blessedness, as stated in Psalm 1:1-2. Thus, we are called to emulate the faithful example set by creation, embracing God's law and wisdom in our lives to shine brightly in a world in need of His light.

King David meditated on the law, statutes, commandments, and judgments of God and His meditation filled His heart with praises to God. His meditations made him feel his unworthiness and realize his secret faults and sins. He was warned by the law. He concludes with the following prayers:

Cleanse me from my secret faults. Keep your servant also from willful sins; may they not rule over me. Let the words of my mouth, and the meditation of my heart, be acceptable in your sight. Psalm 19:12-14

Few more Scriptures along those lines, to prompt us to be vigilant regarding both our speech and the thoughts of our hearts, aiming to please God:

Be not rash with the words of your mouth. Do not be hasty to say anything before God. Let your words be few. Ecclesiastes 5:2

Let your speech be always with grace, seasoned with salt. Colossians 4:6

Prayer of King Hezekiah

*But Hezekiah prayed for them, saying, 'May the Lord, who is good, pardon
everyone who sets their heart on seeking God the Lord, the God of their
ancestors, even if they are not clean according to the rules of the sanctuary.'
And the Lord heard Hezekiah and healed the people.* 2 Chronicles 30:18-20

King Hezekiah followed the ways of the Lord faithfully, unlike his
father King Ahaz, who condoned idol worship and desecrated
the Temple. Hezekiah took action to purify the Temple, demolishing
idolatrous sites, cleansing the sanctuary, reinstating priests and Levites,
establishing a choir for praising God, and reviving the tradition of celebrating the Passover in Jerusalem, which had been neglected for years.

Hezekiah dispatched messengers throughout Israel and Judah,
urging them to join in celebrating the Passover in Jerusalem. A vast
multitude from all the tribes gathered in Jerusalem for the occasion.
While many sanctified themselves for the Passover, some who had
journeyed from distant lands had not undergone purification rituals.
Despite this, Hezekiah prayed for forgiveness on their behalf, acknowledging their sincere desire to seek the Lord. In response to his prayer,
the Lord granted forgiveness to all who had assembled, even those who
were not ritually clean according to sanctuary regulations.

Let us model our prayers for friends, family, and others whose
approach to seeking the Lord may differ from ours after Hezekiah's
prayer. Instead of resorting to criticism or condemnation, let our
prayers be filled with intercession for their acceptance by God, provided they have sincerely come seeking His favor. Rather than judging,
may we petition for their understanding and forgiveness, trusting
that God will guide them onto the right path in due time through
our prayers.

God is willing to welcome all who approach His presence, whether
they adhere to certain outward rituals or not. So, why should we condemn those whose worship practices differ from our own?

PRAYER OF KING ASA

And Asa cried unto the Lord his God, and said, Lord, it is nothing with thee to help, whether with many, or with them that have no power: help us, O Lord our God; for we rest on thee, and in thy name we go against this multitude. O Lord, thou art our God; let not man prevail against thee. 2 Chronicles 14:11

King Asa, the great-grandson of King Solomon, ruled over the Kingdom of Judah. Despite the division of the kingdom after King Solomon's death, Asa remained steadfast in his commitment to God. He undertook righteous actions, pleasing to the Lord, by removing altars dedicated to foreign gods, demolishing idols, and cutting down the groves where idol worship took place. Moreover, Asa urged the people of Judah to seek the Lord, the God of their ancestors, and to adhere to His Law and Commandments. (2 Chronicles 14:2)

When the Ethiopian army, consisting of a million soldiers and three hundred chariots, marched against Judah, King Asa found himself vastly outnumbered, with only five hundred thousand men and eighty thousand warriors. Recognizing the dire situation, Asa turned to the Lord for assistance, pleading that God would not let mere mortals triumph over Him. (2 Chronicles 14:11) In response to Asa's earnest prayer, the Lord intervened, defeating the Ethiopian forces, causing them to flee before Asa and Judah. Despite the brevity of the prayer, its potency was evident as Asa secured the victory he sought by placing his trust in God's name.

Likewise, when we lead lives of righteousness and goodness in the eyes of God, our prayers become vehicles for achieving victory. Despite our own limitations, God's strength is magnified and perfected in our moments of weakness.

Some trust in chariots and some in horses; but we will remember the name of the Lord our God. Psalm 20:7

ASK, KNOCK, AND SEEK

Ask, and it will be given to you; seek, and you will find; knock, and the door will be opened to you. For everyone who asks receives; he who seeks finds; and to him who knocks, the door will be opened. Matthew 7:7, 8

- **Ask:** Asking God is praying to God. Jesus repeatedly taught His disciples to pray to God. He taught them to believe and pray.

Whatever you ask for in prayer, believe that you have received it, and it will be yours. Mark 11:24

If you remain in me and my words remain in you, ask whatever you wish, and it will be done for you. John 15:7

- **Seek:** In Luke 15, Jesus tells the parables of the lost sheep and the lost coin, illustrating the value of seeking what is lost. A shepherd searches diligently for his lost sheep, rejoicing when it is found, just as a woman meticulously seeks her lost coin and celebrates its recovery. Similarly, in Luke 18, Jesus shares the parable of the persistent widow who repeatedly seeks justice from an unjust judge. Though initially indifferent, the judge grants her request to avoid further inconvenience. These parables emphasize the importance of persistence and determination in seeking God's help and justice.
- **Knock:** Knock at the doors of heaven till God hears our prayer and opens the doors for us. Our sin has shut and barred the doors of health, wealth, and happiness in front of us. Knock till our sins are forgiven and the doors are open.

Jesus has promised, *"Ask, and it will be given to you; seek, and you will find; knock, and it will be opened to you. For everyone who asks receives, and he who seeks finds, and to him who knocks it will be opened. Matthew 7:7, 8*

Vindicate me, Lord

Vindicate me, O Lord, for I have led a blameless life; I have trusted in the Lord without wavering. Psalm 26:1

In Psalm 26, David appeals to the Lord for vindication, seeking to demonstrate the righteousness of his actions despite accusations of wrongdoing. He presents his case before God, asserting that he has walked in integrity, trusted in the Lord without wavering, and adhered to God's truth.

David claims to have avoided association with vain persons and hypocrites, expressing hatred for evildoers and a refusal to sit with the wicked. He declares his innocence by washing his hands and approaching God's altar with thanksgiving, praising God's wondrous works. Additionally, David expresses his love for God's Temple, where His honor dwells.

David, having listed out his rightful deeds, asks God to test him, try him, and examine his heart and mind. He implores God not to gather his soul with sinners and his life with murderers, who deal in mischief and bribes. David repents and seeks forgiveness, trusting in God's mercy and ultimate vindication. He pleads with God to redeem him and show him mercy (Psalm 26:9-11).

When we err, praying for vindication is not appropriate. Yet, despite David's shortcomings, his repentance and forgiveness serve as testament. By striving for blamelessness in God's sight, we can trust in His eventual vindication.

If any of you lacks wisdom, ask God

If any of you lacks wisdom, let him ask of God, who gives to all liberally and without reproach, and it will be given to him. James 1:5

King Solomon beseeched God: "Give your servant an understanding heart to judge your people and to discern between good and evil" (1 Kings 3:9). God granted his request, and Solomon became renowned as the wisest of all people. King David also acknowledges the wisdom he received from God, affirming, "Surely You desire truth in the inmost being You teach me wisdom in the inmost place" (Psalm 51:6). The Prophet Daniel confirms that wisdom comes from the Lord, stating, "He gives wisdom to the wise and knowledge to the discerning" (Daniel 2:21). Similarly, the Apostle Paul teaches that God has made Christ Jesus our wisdom, righteousness, sanctification, and redemption (1 Corinthians 1:31).

How to obtain wisdom:

- If we do not have Jesus in lives, we lack wisdom. Therefore, let us accept Jesus as our Lord and God. As Proverbs 9:10 states, *"The fear of the Lord is the beginning of wisdom."* Fearing God entails obeying His commandments. Therefore, to receive wisdom, let us obey God's commandments diligently.
- According to Isaiah 11:2, the Spirit of the Lord encompasses wisdom, understanding, counsel, knowledge, and the fear of the Lord. Therefore, let us earnestly pray to God to fill us with His Spirit. When we are filled with the Spirit, we will be imbued with wisdom and all these virtues.
- If any of us lack wisdom, let us ask God, who generously bestows wisdom upon us without reproach. As it is written, "Ask and it will be given to you." *Matthew 7:7*
- The Word of God teaches us wisdom. Study the Word of God and be instructed.

Finally, *Do not be wise in your own eyes; fear the Lord and shun evil. Proverbs 3:7*

INCREASE OUR FAITH

The apostles said to the Lord, 'Increase our faith!' He replied, 'If you have faith as small as a mustard seed, you can say to this mulberry tree, 'Be uprooted and planted in the sea,' and it will obey you. Luke 17:5, 6

Truly I tell you, if you have faith as small as a mustard seed, you can say to this mountain, 'Move from here to there,' and it will move. Nothing will be impossible for you.', Matthew 17:20.

In essence, Jesus teaches us that when we pray, we should have faith and believe without doubt in our hearts. He assures us that whatever we ask for in prayer, if we truly believe, we will receive it. *Whatever things we desire, when we pray, believe that we have received them and then we shall have them. Mark 11:23, 24*

The disciples sought greater faith through prayer. Jesus assured them that even with a tiny amount of faith, they could achieve incredible feats, even moving obstacles as massive as mountains. Recognizing their limited faith, they understood their dependence on Jesus to bolster their faith.

Likewise, we possess a measure of faith. We trust that God responds to our prayers for healing the sick, driving out demons, and performing miracles in His name. Jesus teaches us that even with this small amount of faith, we are capable of achieving remarkable wonders.

Jesus is the author and the finisher of our faith. Just as a sower plants the seed of faith within us, we must cultivate our hearts to nurture this seed, allowing it to flourish and produce a bountiful harvest. We strive for a yield of thirty, sixty, or even a hundredfold. To safeguard this seed of faith, we must not permit the distractions and concerns of the world to choke it. Instead, we diligently water it with the Word of God, the guidance of the Holy Spirit, and fervent prayer.

How long Lord?

King David initiates Psalm 13 with a series of inquiries, each beginning with the phrase "how long".

How long, Lord? Will you forget me forever? How long will you hide your face from me? How long shall I take counsel in my soul, having sorrow in my heart daily? How long shall mine enemy be exalted over me? Psalm 13:1, 2

King Saul relentlessly pursued David, driving him into a life on the run, seeking refuge in caves, forests, and deserts to evade Saul's wrath. Accompanied by his family and around six hundred followers, David bore the responsibility of protecting and providing for them amid their fugitive status, enduring approximately ten years of hardship and scarcity. Under the weight of his circumstances, David cried out in anguish, repeatedly asking, "How long, Lord, how long?"

Even amidst his troubles, a glimmer of hope emerges for David, reigniting his trust in God. David remained confident that God would eventually deliver him from the clutches of his enemies and fulfill His promise of David becoming the King of Israel. With this restored trust and hope, David offers his prayer: "Consider and hear me, O Lord my God: open my eyes to see your plans so that I do not sleep the sleep of death. Do not allow my enemies to say, I have prevailed against him. Do not make those that trouble me rejoice when I am moved." (Psalm 13:3, 4) David concludes the Psalm on a note of victory: "But I trust in your unfailing love; my heart rejoices in your salvation. I will sing the Lord's praise, for he has been good to me." (Psalm 13:5, 6)

Despite facing adversity and questioning when God's promises will be fulfilled in our lives, let us continue to trust in His faithfulness and offer our prayers to Him. We may cry out, "How long will we have to endure these sufferings?" Yet, we must remember that God is merciful and faithful to fulfill His promises to us. Therefore, let us rejoice in His mercies and remain steadfast in our trust in Him.

Praying and Fasting

But this kind does not go out except by prayer and fasting. Matthew 17:21

A man brought his demon-possessed son to the disciples of Jesus for deliverance, but they were unable to cure him. When Jesus arrived, he rebuked the demon, and the son was delivered. The disciples later asked Jesus why they had been unsuccessful. Jesus explained that certain demons required prayer and fasting to be cast out, highlighting the importance of both practices in spiritual warfare.

Fasting entails more than just refraining from food and water; it involves dedicating our time, energy, and resources to prayer and supplication before the Lord. It requires abstaining from worldly distractions like TV shows, shopping, food addiction, and other indulgences. The persistent desire to engage in these futile activities can only be overcome through prayer and fasting.

Fasting serves as a means to draw closer to God, fostering a deeper connection with Him as individuals keep themselves in His presence (James 4:8). Throughout Scripture, figures like King David and Ezra utilized fasting as a way to humble themselves before God, acknowledging His sovereignty and seeking His guidance and mercy (Psalm 35:13, 21; Ezra 8:21). The people of Nineveh's collective fasting spared their city from destruction, showcasing the efficacy of fasting coupled with repentance in eliciting God's compassion and forgiveness (Jonah 3:5). Additionally, the story of Esther highlights the protective power of fasting and prayer, as Esther's intercession on behalf of her people led to their deliverance from impending danger (Esther 4:16, 5:2). Isaiah 58:6-7 outlines the type of fasting that God desires, emphasizing acts of compassion and justice toward others, such as breaking the bonds of wickedness, alleviating burdens, liberating the oppressed, and caring for the needy and marginalized.

Let us also engage in fasting and praying as prescribed in Scripture, thus empowering us to overcome our adversary, the devil.

Prayer of Agur

Two things I request of You (Deprive me not before I die): Remove false-hood and lies far from me; Give me neither poverty nor riches—Feed me with the food allotted to me; lest I be full and deny You, And say, "Who is the Lord?" Or lest I be poor and steal and profane the name of my God.
Proverbs 30:7-9

The prayer above originates from Agur, a man who humbly identified himself as lacking in wisdom and knowledge of the Holy, as stated in Proverbs 30:3. However, as one delves into the entirety of Proverbs 30, Agur's profound wisdom shines through. Despite his initial claim, he demonstrates a deep understanding of the ways of God and His divine Son (*Proverbs 30:4*), filling the chapter with insights that reflect his reverence for the Holy.

Agur's prayer to God was twofold: Firstly, he petitioned to be distanced from the allure of vanity and deceit, recognizing the inherent truthfulness of God. His earnest desire was for personal integrity, steering clear of falsehood and lies. Secondly, he implored for a balanced provision, neither desiring poverty nor excessive riches. Agur sought contentment in God's allotted portion for him, expressing a profound trust in divine provision for his sustenance.

Agur's prayer reflects a timeless wisdom akin to the prayer later taught by Jesus to His disciples, as recorded in the Gospel of Matthew: *Give us this day our daily bread (Matthew 6:11);* and *"do not lead us into temptation but deliver us from the evil one (Matthew 6:13).*

Agur wisely prayed for a state, that he might be kept at a distance from temptations. He asked for the daily bread needed by him. He was afraid that if he had poverty then he may steal and defile the name of the Lord, and if he had riches he may deny God. And so, he prayed for a middle state with neither poverty nor riches, but whatever is needed for daily living.

Shall we make this our prayer too?

Do we ask with the wrong motives?

Ask and it will be given to you; seek and you will find; knock and the door will be opened to you. For everyone who asks receives; he who seeks finds; and to him who knocks, the door will be opened. Luke 11:9, 10

Despite Jesus' assurance that "everyone that asks receives," there are instances where prayers seemingly go unanswered. The apostle James provides insight into this phenomenon, suggesting that prayers remain unanswered when motivated by selfish desires.

When you ask, you do not receive, because you ask with wrong motives, that you may spend what you get on your pleasures. James 4:3

James explains that requests are denied because they stem from improper motives, intended for personal gratification rather than alignment with God's will. Thus, James highlights the importance of praying with pure intentions, seeking God's guidance and purposes rather than indulging in self-serving desires. James and John, chosen by Jesus as disciples, once asked Him for positions of honor in His glory. Jesus responded, questioning if they were prepared for the challenges He faced. They affirmed their readiness, and Jesus acknowledged that they would indeed share in His trials. However, He explained that granting specific positions of honor was not His decision but reserved for those designated by God. (Mark 10:37-40)

What is it we are asking God for? What is the motive behind our plea? Do we intend on spending whatever we are asking for on our pleasure or for His glory? Let us examine our hearts and intentions as we pray. May our prayers be marked by humility, sincerity, and a genuine desire to align our desires with God's purposes. Let us seek His guidance and wisdom, trusting that He will fulfill our needs according to His perfect will and for His glory.

OPEN OUR HEARTS

*Now a certain woman named Lydia heard us. She was a seller of purple
from the city of Thyatira, who worshiped God. The Lord opened her heart
to heed the things spoken by Paul. Acts 16:14*

In Philippi, the Apostle Paul and his companions gathered by a riverside for prayer and engaged with the women present, including Lydia. By God's grace, Lydia's heart was opened to receive Paul's message, leading her to offer her home for his ministry. Through her hospitality, a doorway for spreading the gospel was unlocked in the city. Let us pray that, as we listen to God's Word proclaimed by His servants, our hearts too may be opened by Him, and that we may generously offer our resources for His work.

Jesus says, *"I stand at the door and knock. If anyone hears my voice and opens the door, I will come in and eat with him, and he with me."* *Revelation 3:20*

Indeed, while Jesus calls upon us to open our hearts, it is God who provides the assistance we need to heed His voice and embrace His presence. Let us pray to our loving heavenly Father in heaven asking Him to open our hearts in various ways: to hear the gentle knocking of the Lord Jesus, inviting Him into our lives; to cultivate our hearts into fertile soil, allowing His Word to bear abundant fruit; to recognize the miracles unfolding in our lives, trusting in His ultimate goodness; to follow and obey His teachings and commands faithfully; and to be filled with His Spirit, overflowing with love, joy, and peace for all.

Prayer: Our Heavenly Father: We pray that You open our hearts to understand Your Word more and to know You more. We pray in the name of Jesus. Amen.

CLEANSE ME WITH HYSSOP

Cleanse me with hyssop, and I will be clean; wash me, and I will be whiter than snow. Psalm 51:7

Psalm 51 expresses a heartfelt plea for cleansing and restoration, uttered by King David in a prayer of repentance. These words convey more than mere guilt; they reflect the sincerity of a contrite heart and a spirit humbled by wrongdoing.

King David's response to his wrongdoing stands in stark contrast to Adam's attempt to evade God's presence after sinning. Instead of hiding, David approached God with humility, begging for forgiveness and crying out in repentance. In verse 4, he says, *"Against you, you only, have I sinned and done what is evil in your sight."*; acknowledging his sin against God alone, expressing deep remorse and complete acceptance of his wrongdoing. His words convey profound agony, total surrender, and a sincere acknowledgment of the gravity of his actions.

As he was praying, he asked to be cleaned by hyssop. What is hyssop? Hyssop is an herb that holds significant symbolic meaning in the Israelite tradition, particularly in rituals of cleansing and purification. It was commonly used in ceremonies where blood or water was sprinkled for purification purposes, symbolizing spiritual cleansing from sin and impurity. David's request to be cleansed with hyssop in his prayer reflects his deep understanding of the need for thorough purification of the heart. Just as the blood of the Passover lamb was applied to protect the Israelites, David sought a similar cleansing to safeguard his spiritual well-being..

When we sin, let us not run from God like Adam did. Instead, we should come humbly before Him, asking for cleansing through the blood of Jesus Christ and the Holy Spirit is purifying work. God will accept us when we approach Him with a repentant heart.

The blood of Jesus Christ cleanses us from all sin. 1 John 1:7

ASK THE LORD FOR RAIN IN THE SPRINGTIME

"Ask the Lord for rain in the springtime; it is the Lord who makes the storm clouds. He gives showers of rain to men, and plants of the field to everyone." Zechariah 10:1

The message is clear: ask the Lord for showers of blessings. Today, let us bring all our pressing needs to Him. Whether it is a need for a job, a vacation, financial or spiritual freedom, or healing, let us unite in prayer and ask God to send His showers of blessings in our lives. Let us pray:

Dear Heavenly Father,

We praise Your holy name and thank You for the abundant provisions You have blessed us with thus far in our lives. We trust that Your provision will continue to sustain us throughout our journey. According to Your Word, we come before You, asking for the rain You have promised us. Please send Your refreshing rain upon us this very moment, this very day, Lord.

Thank You, Jesus, for Your faithfulness. Please send the rain according to the unique needs we've brought before You in this moment. We trust in Your mighty power to save, and we hold firm to Your promises that are always fulfilled. As You have said, if we ask anything in Your name, You will do it. So now, Lord, we ask for Your showers of blessing. May our faith be rewarded, and may we not be disappointed. Hear our prayers, Lord, and send the much-needed rain upon us. In the name of Your beloved Son, our Savior Jesus Christ, we pray. Amen.

Now that we have sought the Lord for rain and showers of blessings in our lives, let us rejoice in His promise.

"He gives showers of rain to men, and plants of the field to everyone." Zechariah 10:1

SUSTAIN ME ACCORDING TO YOUR PROMISE

Sustain me according to your promise, and I will live; do not let my hopes be dashed. Psalm 119:116

When faced with delayed blessings, it is natural to feel weary. Drawing from examples in Scripture, we see how godly men coped with this stress.

King David, for instance, turned to prayer and supplication. Throughout the Psalms, we find numerous instances of him crying out to God. In Psalm 54:4, he expresses his certainty that help will come from the Lord, affirming, *"Surely God is my help; the Lord is the one who sustains me."*

Prophet Jeremiah exemplified the art of waiting upon the Lord. Despite the trials he faced, he found solace in God's enduring mercies, which prevented his utter destruction. In Lamentations 3:22, 24-26, Jeremiah's soul declares, *"Through the Lord's mercies, we are not consumed, because His compassions fail not. "The Lord is my portion," says my soul, "Therefore I hope in Him!" The Lord is good to those who wait for Him, to the soul who seeks Him. It is good that one should hope and wait quietly for the salvation of the Lord."* He recognizes God's goodness to those who patiently wait and seek Him. Thus, Jeremiah encourages us to maintain hope and wait quietly for the salvation of the Lord.

When our blessings seem delayed, we may feel weary and hopeless, much like the people of Israel in Ezekiel 37:11. However, God reassures us through His promises. In Ezekiel 37:13-14, He declares that He will restore His people, breathing life into their dry bones and settling them in their land.

Likewise, we can trust that God will fulfill His promises in His perfect timing. Let us hold onto His assurances and remain steadfast in faith, knowing that He will bless us according to His plan.

A KING'S PRAYER FOR RAIN

"When the heavens are shut up and there is no rain because they have sinned against You, when they pray toward this place and confess Your name, and turn from their sin because You afflict them, then hear in heaven, and forgive the sin of Your servants, Your people Israel, that You may teach them the good way in which they should walk; and send rain on Your land which You have given to Your people as an inheritance. 1 Kings 8:35, 36

This scripture is from King Solomon's prayer of dedication for the newly built Temple in Jerusalem. Standing before the entire congregation of Israelites with hands raised towards heaven and voice clear, Solomon presented a range of requests. Among them was a plea for rain in times of drought due to the people's sins. He prayed that if the people repented and sought forgiveness by confessing the Name of the Lord and turning from their sin, God would hear their prayer, forgive them, and send rain upon the land.

Indeed, this prayer is a powerful example of humility, repentance, and intercession on behalf of the people of Israel. King Solomon's heartfelt plea for forgiveness and compassion reflects a deep understanding of God's mercy and faithfulness. As history unfolds, we witness how God remembered Solomon's prayer, responding with grace and intervention whenever the people repented and sought Him. This demonstrates the enduring impact of genuine prayer and the faithfulness of God to His promises throughout the history of Israel.

Just as King Solomon prayed for the well-being and forgiveness of the people of Israel, we can intercede for our descendants, asking God to guide, protect, and bless them. Our prayers have the power to shape the trajectory of their lives and to establish a legacy of faithfulness for generations to come. Let us commit to lifting up our future generations in prayer, trusting in God's faithfulness to answer and fulfill His promises for them.

Conditions for our Prayers to be answered

*If my people, who are called by my name, will humble themselves and pray
and seek my face and turn from their wicked ways, then will I hear from
heaven and will forgive their sin and will heal their land. 2 Chronicles 7:14*

God appeared to King Solomon, offering a clear directive: if the
children of God humble themselves, pray, seek God's face, and
turn from their wicked ways, their prayers will be answered, their sins
forgiven, and their land healed.

How to humble ourselves?

Being humble means having a modest estimate of one's own importance. The Apostle Paul writes in *Romans 12:3*: *"Do not think of yourself
more highly than you ought."* James too echoes this sentiment: *"God
resists the proud But gives grace to the humble." (James 4:6)*

Whenever pride attempts to steal credit for an achievement, let us
consciously redirect all glory to God Almighty, who enabled us in the
first place. Let us continually remind ourselves that it is God's grace
that sustains our well-being, happiness, and contentment, enabling us
to acquire what we need and fostering strong family bonds filled with
peace, love, and joy. It is His grace that saves us, prevents our downfall,
and lifts us up each time we stumble. As Prophet Jeremiah affirms,
*"Through the Lord's mercies, we are not consumed, Because His compassions
fail not" (Lamentations 3:22)*. Recognizing that our existence is solely
by God's grace humbles our hearts, leading to answered prayers and
divine elevation.

How to pray

Our prayers may go unanswered if we haven't prayed in the manner
taught by Jesus. Jesus provided the Lord's Prayer as a model, highlighting the importance of forgiveness as a condition for our prayers to be
heard. He warned against praying like hypocrites who seek to be seen
by others, urging instead to pray in private to our Father who sees in

secret and rewards openly (Matthew 6:5-6). Jesus also cautioned against babbling like pagans, emphasizing that God already knows our needs before we ask (Matthew 6:7-8).

How to seek the face of God

As Psalm 123:2 beautifully expresses, just as the eyes of a servant look to their master or maid to their mistress, so our eyes should be fixed on the Lord our God until He shows us His mercy. Until we receive the answer to our prayers, we are encouraged to continue seeking the face of the Lord, adopting a posture of humility akin to that of a servant or maid.

How to turn away from our wicked ways

Depart from evil and do good; Seek peace and pursue it. Psalm 34:14

Though we discern what is good and evil, we may still struggle, finding it difficult to act rightly. The Apostle Paul candidly acknowledges this internal battle in Romans 7:20, 24, attributing it to the sin dwelling within us. Yet, he finds hope in Jesus Christ, who transforms us into new beings, as stated in 2 Corinthians 5:17, *If anyone is in Christ, he is a new creation; the old sinful nature has gone and the new has come!*

By accepting Jesus as our Savior, we become new creations, shedding our old sinful nature and embracing righteousness. This transformation offers the ultimate solution to turning away from wickedness and living in alignment with God's will.

Lord, set a guard over our mouths and lips

Set a guard over my mouth, Lord; keep watch over the door of my lips.
Psalm 141:3

We are reminded in Proverbs 10:19 that *"Too much talk leads to sin. Be sensible and keep your mouth shut."* Additionally, Proverbs 13:3 advises that *"those who guard their lips preserve their lives, but those who speak rashly will come to ruin."*

It is crucial to recognize the power of our words, as Proverbs 18:21 states, *"Death and life are in the power of the tongue, and those who love it will eat its fruit."*

Indeed, the tongue holds immense power—it can speak life or death, joy or depression, victory or defeat, cheer or gloom. It's influence extends to shaping the dynamics of relationships, whether fostering a happy marriage or contributing to a broken family life.

In the beginning, God created the heavens and the earth and all therein through His spoken word. He simply said, "Let there be," and it came to be. As beings created in His image, we too possess a similar power in our words. With our spoken words, we can build or destroy, encourage or discourage, boast or praise, love or hate. Our words carry tremendous influence, reflecting the profound impact of our Creator's spoken word upon creation.

Indeed, we must exercise great caution in our use of words, as they hold the power to either glorify God or bring disgrace upon ourselves. It requires conscious effort to use our words for His glory rather than misusing them for our disgrace. Let us diligently watch our words and be willing to correct our course if they veer in the wrong direction. We rely on the power and grace of God to restrain our mouths from speaking words of destruction and instead open them to speak words of grace and praise. Let us earnestly pray for God's guidance in guarding our mouths and lips.

Lord, open our mouths and lips

O Lord, open my lips, and my mouth will declare your praise. Psalm 51:15

May my lips overflow with praise, for you. Psalm 119:71

Apostle Paul humbly requests the prayers of the believers in Ephesus, writing, *"Pray also for me, that whenever I open my mouth, words may be given me so that I will fearlessly make known the mystery of the gospel" (Ephesians 6:19).*

King Lemuel's mother imparts wisdom, teaching him, *"Open your mouth for the speechless, in the cause of all who are appointed to die. Open your mouth, judge righteously, and plead the cause of the poor and needy" (Proverbs 31:8-9).*

It is a liberating experience when our lips overflow with praise. In *Psalm 81:10*, we are encouraged: *"Open wide your mouth and I will fill it, says the Lord."* When the Lord fills our mouths, our lips overflow with praises, glorifying Him with utterances given by God.

The prophet Hosea urges us to turn to God using our words. In *Hosea 14:2*, he says, *"Take with you words, and turn to the Lord: say unto him, Take away all iniquity, and receive us graciously: so, will we render the calves of our lips."* Here, "the calves of our lips" refer to the thanksgiving sacrifices we offer to God through our words.

Praying from the depths of our hearts is crucial, but it is equally important to articulate our prayers with our mouths. If you are unsure about it, give it a try—you will feel the difference. As promised, the Lord will fill our mouths—with praise, Scripture, the Holy Spirit, tongues, His prophetic words, and more praise.

Therefore, by Him (Jesus Christ) let us continually offer the sacrifice of praise to God, that is, the fruit of our lips, giving thanks to His name. Hebrews 13:15

REMEMBER ME WITH FAVOR, O MY GOD

Remember me, O my God, concerning this, and do not wipe out my good deeds that I have done for the house of my God, and for its services! Nehemiah 13:14

Remember me, my God, for good, according to all that I have done for these people. Nehemiah 5:19

And I commanded the Levites that they should cleanse themselves and that they should go and guard the gates, to sanctify the Sabbath day. Remember me, O my God, concerning this also, and spare me according to the greatness of Your mercy! Nehemiah 13:22

Nehemiah, a captive in Babylon serving as the cupbearer to the King, sought and obtained permission to rebuild the walls of Jerusalem. Gathering volunteers and securing resources, including skilled craftsmen and quality wood, he led the monumental project. Generations later, Jerusalem stood restored, with people returning to worship in the temple. Levites and priests resumed their duties, and a proficient choir was established. Nehemiah's leadership culminated in a resounding success for him and his people.

It is intriguing to note Nehemiah's recurring prayer throughout his book: *"Remember me with favor, O my God!"* This suggests that Nehemiah may not have received the recognition he deserved for the successful execution of his work.

There may be occasions when we embark on significant endeavors for the Lord, exceeding even our own expectations and those of others. Yet, appreciation may elude us. However, the one who will remember our diligence and sincerity, and bless us, accordingly, is the Lord. Therefore, instead of being disheartened, let us join Nehemiah in making it our prayer: "Remember me with favor, O my God." Amen.

Prayer of Jesus at Gethsemane

After celebrating the Passover Feast, Jesus, and His disciples came to a place called Gethsemane. Jesus told His disciples, *"Sit here while I pray."* He took with Him Peter, James, and John, to go and pray at a place a little farther away. He began to be deeply troubled and distressed. Then He said to them, *"My soul is consumed with sorrow to the point of death. Stay here and keep watch."* Going a little farther, He fell to the ground and prayed that, *if it were possible, the hour would pass from Him. "Abba, Father,"* He said, *"all things are possible for You. Take this cup from Me. Yet not what I will, but what You will."*

Then Jesus returned and found them sleeping. *"Simon, are you asleep?"* He asked. *"Were you not able to keep watch for one hour? Watch and pray so that you will not enter into temptation. For the spirit is willing, but the body is weak."* Again, He went away and prayed, saying the same verse. And again, Jesus returned and found them sleeping—for their eyes were heavy. And they did not know what to answer Him. When Jesus returned the third time, He said, *"Are you still sleeping and resting? That is enough! The hour has come. Look, the Son of Man is betrayed into the hands of sinners. Rise, let us go. See, My betrayer, is approaching!" Mark 14:32-42*

In the above passage, Jesus has set an example for us to follow, especially in times of despair. There may be instances where those we trust to pray for and with us fail to do so, leaving us to struggle alone in prayer with God. Even Jesus experienced this solitude in prayer. In such moments, we should not rely solely on family members, friends, church leaders, or fellow believers to intercede for us. Sometimes, it is just us and God. Yet, we should not be disheartened, for God hears our prayers and may send an angel to comfort us in our despair.

Ultimately, regardless of whether we pray alone or with others, it is God's will that will prevail.

Father in Heaven gives good gifts to those who ask Him

If you then, being evil, know how to give good gifts to your children, how much more will your heavenly Father give the Holy Spirit to those who ask Him!" Luke 11:13

Isn't it true that when it comes to buying gifts for our children, we always want the best, even if it means stretching our budget a bit? We go above and beyond to fulfill their wishes and make them happy, right?

Now, consider this: as sinful human beings, we prioritize the best for our children. If we, imperfect as we are, care so deeply for our kids, how much more would our loving Father in heaven care for us? He is holy, sinless, abounding in grace and mercy, and loves us unconditionally. Would it be beyond His ability to grant us the best when we ask for it? Definitely not!

God has graciously sent His Holy Spirit into the world to fulfill numerous roles in our lives. The Holy Spirit leads us into all truth, comforts us in times of need, reminds us of the teachings of Jesus Christ, intercedes for us in prayer, fills us with love for God and others, speaks on our behalf, empowers us with spiritual gifts, and enables us to live for Christ. The work of the Holy Spirit in our lives is truly magnificent, preparing us to meet Jesus when He returns.

The urgency of being filled with the Holy Spirit cannot be overstated.

Jesus Christ assures us that if we earnestly pray to our heavenly Father to fill us with the Holy Spirit, He will surely answer our prayers.

Receiving the Holy Spirit is indispensable in our lives. Let us boldly ask God and receive Him.

TEACH US TO NUMBER OUR DAYS

Teach us to number our days, that we may gain a heart of wisdom. Psalm 90:12

In Psalm 90, Moses prays to God to teach us to number our days, so that we may gain a heart of wisdom. Although we are aware that our days are passing swiftly and our time on earth is finite, we often fail to dwell on this reality. Instead, we live as if our lives will never end. Moses encourages us to join him in praying for wisdom to recognize the brevity of life. These additional scriptures serve as poignant reminders of the transient nature of our days on earth:

Show me, Lord, my life's end and the number of my days; let me know how fleeting my life is. (Psalm 39:4); My days are swifter than a runner; they fly away without a glimpse of joy. (Job 9:25); My days are swifter than a weaver's shuttle, and they come to an end without hope. (Job 7:6); and My days are like the evening shadow; I wither away like grass. (Psalm 102:11).

Moses reflects on the brevity and trouble-filled nature of life, particularly due to our iniquities. Yet, he prays for God's unfailing love to satisfy us each morning, bringing joy and gladness throughout our days. He asks for God's favor to rest upon us and for His deeds to be shown to us and our children. Moses concludes his prayer by asking God to establish the work of our hands.

Let us therefore join with Moses in his plea for God's favor to be upon us. Despite our iniquities, we trust in God's mercy to forgive us and grant us the grace to journey through life with hope, looking forward to seeing Him in glory.

WHAT IS MAN THAT GOD IS MINDFUL OF HIM?

THE STATUTES AND ORDINANCES
THAT GOD HAD TAUGHT US

*Now, O Israel, listen to the statutes and the judgments which I teach you
to observe, that you may live, and go in and possess the land which the
Lord God of your fathers is giving you. Deuteronomy 4:1*

As the Israelites prepared to enter Canaan, the promised land, Moses,
nearing the end of his life, gathered them to impart his final words.
Knowing he would not lead them further; he emphasized the importance of God's commandments. In Deuteronomy 4:1-10,

Moses reiterated God's instructions, underscoring their significance
for the Israelites' journey ahead. Moses instructed the Israelites to
carefully heed the statutes and ordinances that God had given them,
emphasizing their importance for living a long and prosperous life. He
urged them not to alter or tamper with these divine commandments,
underscoring that they originated directly from God and not from
any human source.

By faithfully observing these laws, they would demonstrate wisdom
and understanding before others, showcasing their status as a blessed
and favored nation. Moses reminded them to remain vigilant, never
forgetting that these laws were delivered to them by God speaking
from fire. He emphasized the need for continual adherence to these
commandments, ensuring that they would be passed down through
the generations by teaching them diligently to their children and
grandchildren.

No other nation has a God as near to them as the Lord our God,
always ready to answer when we call. Who else has such righteous
statutes and ordinances as God's law? His commandments are given
for our benefit.

Let us obey them carefully, reading and learning from Scripture,
and diligently following them. In doing so, we remain a blessed people.

I HAVE PLACED BEFORE YOU AN OPEN DOOR

To the angel of the church in Philadelphia write: These are the words of him who is holy and true, who holds the key of David. What he opens no one can shut, and what he shuts no one can open. I know your deeds. See, I have placed before you an open door that no one can shut. I know that you have little strength, yet you have kept my word and have not denied my name. Revelation 3:7, 8

The city of Philadelphia was originally founded to promote Greek culture globally, but Jesus repurposed its doors to spread the gospel and the Word of God worldwide through the church established there. To the church in Philadelphia, Jesus reveals Himself as the One who has the key of David, the king of Israel. signifying his authority over the kingdom of Israel and beyond. As the descendant of David, he holds dominion over the entire world. With this authority, he can unlock doors of blessing, freedom, and the spread of the gospel. Whatever he opens cannot be closed by any other power.

Amidst the trials and tribulations faced by the first-century churches due to the Roman government and its authorities, believers persevered despite their limited strength. Their unwavering faith led them to hold onto their convictions and refuse to renounce the name of Jesus. In recognition of their steadfastness, Jesus placed before them an open door that no one could shut.

Whatever doors are shut before you, Jesus is going to open them. God will not only open doors for the spread of the gospel but also close doors of opposition. The doors He opens cannot be shut and the doors He shuts cannot be opened. He knows you have only a little faith, yet you have kept His Word and have not denied His name. God sees your efforts and your faithfulness.

I AM WITH YOU AND WILL WATCH
OVER YOU WHEREVER YOU GO

*Behold, I am with you and will keep you wherever you go and will bring
you back to this land; for I will not leave you until I have done what I
have spoken to you. Genesis 28:15*

Jacob, fleeing from his brother Esau's wrath, sought refuge for the
night. Resting his head on a stone, he fell into a profound sleep and
had a remarkable dream. In this vision, he witnessed a ladder extending
from earth to heaven, with angels ascending and descending upon it,
revealing a divine connection between heaven and earth.

*And behold, the Lord stood above it and said: 'I am the Lord God of Abra-
ham your father and the God of Isaac; the land on which you lie I will give
to you and your descendants.' Then Jacob awoke from his sleep and said,
'Surely the Lord is in this place, and I did not know it.' And he was afraid
and said, 'How awesome is this place! This is none other than the house
of God, and this is the gate of heaven!' Then Jacob made a vow, saying, 'If
God will be with me, and keep me in this way that I am going, and give
me bread to eat and clothing to put on so that I come back to my father's
house in peace, then the Lord shall be my God.' Genesis 28:13, 16, 17, 20, 21*

The God who was previously known as the God of Jacob's forefathers, Abraham and Isaac, now extends His covenant to Jacob himself.
This same God is also ours; His promises are for us as well. We, too,
can claim the assurances of God's presence and provision in our lives.

Jesus has promised us, *'I am with you always, even to the end of the
age.' Matthew 28:20*

Amen. God will indeed watch over us wherever we go, guiding us
safely to our ultimate destination, our Father's house in heaven.

VICTORY BELONGS TO THE LORD

The horse is prepared for the day of battle, but the victory belongs to the Lord Proverbs 21:31

Some trust in chariots and some in horses, but we trust in the name of the Lord our God. Psalm 20:7

The lot is cast into the lap, but it's every decision is from the Lord. Proverbs 16:33

These verses emphasize a common theme: our victory ultimately comes from the Lord, not from earthly resources like chariots, horses, or lots. We trust in the name of the Lord our God and the victory belongs to the Lord.

The story of Gideon (*Judges 6,7*) further illustrates this principle. Despite having only a small army, Gideon trusted in the strength given by the Lord. With just 300 men, he achieved a mighty victory over the Midianites, proclaiming the power of the Lord as they fought. This narrative serves as a powerful reminder that our reliance on God's strength and guidance is paramount, leading to triumph even in the face of overwhelming odds.

David's victory over Goliath serves as a powerful testament to this principle that true triumph comes from the Lord. Armed only with a sling and a stone, David faced the giant Philistine warrior Goliath. Despite the vast difference in size and weaponry, David's faith in the name of the Lord enabled him to defeat his formidable opponent. As recounted in *1 Samuel 17:50*, David's single stone struck Goliath, resulting in his demise and securing victory for the Israelites. This remarkable feat underscores the potency of trusting in God's strength and guidance, demonstrating that even the most daunting challenges can be overcome with unwavering faith.

Let us fight with our limited strength, trusting the Lord for victory. Cast aside fears and doubts, carrying only our faith in God. He fights our battles, securing triumph for us. The Lord of Hosts leads the way, ensuring victory belongs to Him.

BLESSED BE THE LORD, WHO
TRAINS MY HANDS FOR WAR

*Blessed be the Lord my Rock, Who trains my hands for war and my fingers
for battle. Psalm 144:1*

*He trains my hands for battle; my arms can bend a bow of bronze. Psalm
18:34*

We all know the story of how young David defeated the giant
Goliath. Armed with only a stone and a sling, David struck
Goliath on the forehead, causing him to fall face down on the ground
(1 Samuel 17:49). Despite his lack of formal training for battle, David
had been prepared by God while tending his flock. He had previously
killed lions and bears that threatened his flock, honing his skills with a
sling and stones. This training enabled him to overcome Goliath with
confidence and precision.

Moses received elite education and martial arts training during his
first forty years in the palace of the Egyptian king. However, his character was further developed during the subsequent forty years spent
tending flocks in the wilderness. This dual training equipped Moses
to become a formidable leader for God's people.

The Apostle Paul received top-tier education under the renowned
scholar Gamaliel, enabling him to effectively preach the gospel to
influential leaders and kings. Likewise, Peter, John, and James were
personally trained by Jesus Himself for the ministry of preaching the
gospel.

God equips us with abilities and trains us to utilize them according
to His divine purpose. While some may boast about their own strength
or resources, attributing success to their own efforts, we choose to boast
in the name of our Lord God, recognizing that He is the one who has
trained and empowered us.

You will be the head, not the tail

The Lord will make you the head, not the tail. If you pay attention to the commands of the Lord your God that I give you this day and carefully follow them, you will always be at the top, never at the bottom. Deuteronomy 28:13

In the scripture cited above, we are assured that by keeping all of the Lord's commands and diligently following them, we will rise to prominence, never relegated to a position of inferiority. This encompasses not only the Ten Commandments but all of God's commandments found throughout Scripture. Keeping these commandments is not a singular event but a continual journey throughout life. Remarkably, even as we navigate this ongoing process, the promise of being elevated to a position of prominence is fulfilled. He will position us as the head rather than the tail; we will ascend to the top, never sinking to the bottom!

The focus lies in adhering diligently to God's commands.

Joseph, serving in an officer's house in Egypt, refused his master's wife, declaring, "How then can I do this great wickedness, and sin against God?" He promptly fled from her advances. Consequently, God elevated him to a position of authority beside the king of Egypt.

Mordecai, a Jew in Babylonian captivity, stood firm against worshiping Haman, a high official in the palace. Consequently, God elevated Mordecai to a position next to the Babylonian king.

Similarly, Daniel and his friends, captives from Jerusalem in Babylon, refused to consume the king's food, prioritizing their fear of God over earthly authority. In turn, God exalted them to high positions within the Babylonian kingdom.

The promise of being "the head and not the tail" found fulfillment in their lives as they diligently followed God's commands. God remains faithful to His promises when we obey His commandments.

We have a friend in God

You are my friends if you do what I command. I no longer call you servants because a servant does not know his master's business. Instead, I have called you friends, for everything that I learned from my Father I have made known to you. John 15:14, 15

In the Garden of Eden, God regularly conversed with Adam and Eve in a friendly manner. Similarly, Enoch enjoyed daily walks and conversations with God. These instances illustrate God's desire for a close friendship with humanity.

Years ago, during my youth, I experienced a severe road accident. Through God's mercies, I not only survived but also fully recovered within months. However, during that time, a visiting acquaintance suggested that my ordeal was a result of some wrongdoing, interpreting it as God's judgment. Curious about my relationship with God, he questioned me further. I responded candidly, affirming that God is my friend, and the incident was a testament to His grace rather than judgment. My response seemed to surprise him, revealing that he viewed God more as a stern judge than a friend. This encounter highlighted the danger of obeying God's commands out of fear rather than love. Although I wasn't familiar with the specific scripture at the time, I had always known God as my friend. Indeed, He is our greatest ally, always working for our good.

Jesus frequently referred to His disciples as His friends, demonstrating a deep sense of camaraderie and closeness. He used the term "My friend" when addressing them, illustrating the bond they shared. Even in challenging situations, like Lazarus' illness and Judas' betrayal, Jesus referred to them as friends, revealing His compassion and forgiveness (John 11:11, Matthew 26:50).

Greater love has no one than this: to lay down one's life for one's friends. John 15:13

He demonstrated His friendship by sacrificing His life for us. If you haven't already, accept His friendship today. In Him, we find solace in our lows and joy in our highs. Praise the Lord!

What is man that God Almighty
is mindful of him?

What is mankind that you are mindful of them, human beings that you care for them? Psalm 8:4

What is man that You should exalt him, that You should set Your heart upon him? Job 7:17

O Lord, what is man, that You regard him, the son of man that You think of him? Psalm 144:3

Sometimes, we may feel it is presumptuous to believe that God cares for us. However, considering that parents provide for their children, it is reasonable to believe that God, who created us, cares for us even more. Just as artists are meticulous about their creations, we are God's masterpiece. He is mindful of all humanity, including the poor and needy, and continually does great things for them.

He raises the poor from the dust and lifts the needy from the ash heap; he seats them with princes and has them inherit a throne of honor. 1 Samuel 2:8

He was mindful of the slave Hagar who roamed in the wilderness with a little boy and lifted her up to be a mother of a great nation. He was mindful of Joseph who was in prison and lifted him up to the highest position next to the king in Egypt. God was mindful of the little shepherd boy, David, and lifted him up to become a king.

There are many examples recorded in the Bible about God being mindful of man. He remembered them in their lowly status and lifted them to higher positions. God is always mindful of man. He is near to them who call upon His name. We are amazed at His love, and we wonder what we are, that God should be mindful of us. Though we are poor and needy, the Lord remembers us in His mercies.

Who remembered us in our lowly state, For His mercy endures forever. Psalm 136:23

HE HOLDS OUR RIGHT HAND

For I am the Lord, your God, who takes hold of your right hand and says to you, Do not fear; I will help you. Isaiah 41:13

Did you notice something profound in this Scripture? It is not us who grasp His right hand, but rather, it is the Lord who holds our right hand. This demonstrates His protective nature towards us.

It is akin to how we safeguard our young children. We instinctively hold their hands, understanding that they may easily wander off if left unattended. We recognize the potential for accidents if they're not guided. We are aware of the risks of abduction if they are not closely watched and protected.

Similarly, our Lord does not require us to cling to Him; rather, He holds onto us. Isn't it reassuring to know that the Lord firmly grasps our right hand?

Children may resist when parents hold their hands; they crave independence and freedom. Yet, as long as they remain under their parents' guidance, they are safe.

Similarly, it is due to God's immense love for us that He grasps our right hand, assuring us not to fear and promising His assistance. Whatever challenges we face today—be it an interview, a crucial decision, a medical diagnosis, or a relocation—remember that God firmly holds your right hand.

King David's declaration in Psalm 16:8 underscores the assurance that with the Lord at our right hand, we remain steadfast and unshaken. Acknowledging that God holds our right hand and reassures us, *"Do not fear, I will help you,"* let us embrace this truth without resisting His guidance. Our security lies in humbly submitting ourselves under the mighty hand of God, as articulated in *1 Peter 5:6*.

Humble yourselves under the mighty hand of God that He may exalt you in due time. 1 Peter 5:6

I HAVE CALLED YOU BY NAME; YOU ARE MINE

He counts the number of the stars; He calls them all by names. Psalm 147:4

He calls for the waters of the sea and pours them out upon the face of the earth: The Lord is His name. Amos 9:6

The Lord called me before my birth; from within the womb, He called me by name. Isaiah 49:1

I have called you by name; you are mine. Isaiah 43:1

I have also called you by your name; I have given you a title of honor though you have not known Me. Isaiah 45:4

I believe there is nothing as magnificent as a starry night sky or an endless ocean. These wonders clearly demonstrate the magnificence of God Almighty, the creator of heaven and earth. Knowing that our Lord calls each star by name and commands the waters of the sea is simply awe-inspiring! The same Lord also calls you and me by name, even before our birth, which is beyond our imagination. There is absolutely no doubt about it; there are countless scriptures we can read that confirm He has called us by name. I encourage each one of us today to claim these promises personally and strive to fulfill our calling.

God's calling upon us by name, even before our birth, serves multiple purposes as outlined in the scriptures. We are summoned to follow Jesus, equipped with the authority to confront unclean spirits, sickness, and disease (Matthew 4:19, 10:1). This calling extends to fellowship with Jesus Christ, offering an intimate communion (1 Corinthians 1:9), and urges us towards a life of holiness, guiding us to walk in purity and righteousness (1 Thessalonians 4:7). Furthermore, we are invited to Jesus to find rest in Him, embracing the peace He promises to those who seek Him (Matthew 11:28), and directed to Him to receive the abundance of living water overflowing from within us (John 7:37, 38). Amidst these divine callings, we find assurance in the faithfulness of the One who calls us (1 Thessalonians 5:24).

GOD CARES FOR YOU

Cast your cares on the Lord and He will sustain you; he will never let the righteous fall. Psalm 55:22

Cast all your anxiety on Him because He cares for you. 1 Peter 5:7

I am the one who answers your prayers and cares for you. Hosea 14:8

And if God cares so wonderfully for wildflowers those are here today and thrown into the fire tomorrow, He will certainly care for you. Matthew 6:30

You saw how the Lord your God cared for you all along the way as you traveled through the wilderness, just as a father cares for his child. Deuteronomy 1:31

The aforementioned verses extend an invitation for us to abandon the weight of our worries, casting them upon the Lord God who promises to care for us. In our moments of difficulty, He assures us of sustenance and support. It is a profound comfort to know that 'God cares for us.' Casting our cares on the Lord entails bringing our burdens to His feet and entrusting them to Him, surrendering our worries. As Jesus inquires, "Which of you by worrying can add one cubit to his stature?" (Matthew 6:27), we are reminded of the futility of fretting and the wisdom of placing our trust in Him who sustains us.

Jesus reassures us, saying, *"Are not five sparrows sold for two copper coins? And not one of them is forgotten before God. But the very hairs of your head are all numbered. Do not fear, therefore; you are of more value than many sparrows" (Luke 12:6-7).* These words highlight God's care for even the seemingly insignificant sparrows, ensuring not one is overlooked. How much more, then, will He care for us, if only we place our trust in Him?

When God offers us a place in His kingdom *(Luke 12:32),* why worry? Entrust everything to Him. Cast your cares upon Him, for He cares for you.

ON THE MOUNTAIN OF THE LORD, IT WILL BE PROVIDED

And Abraham called the name of that place Jehovah-Jireh in the mount of the Lord it shall be seen. Genesis 22:14

We are all familiar with Abraham's journey with Isaac to one of the mountains in Moriah. Abraham, initially childless, received God's promise at the age of seventy-five that his descendants would be as numerous as the stars in the sky and the sand on the seashore. He patiently waited twenty-five years for this promise to be fulfilled, and at the age of one hundred, his promised son, Isaac, was born.

Then, God instructed Abraham to sacrifice his promised son. Isaac, old enough to carry the firewood, questioned his father about the sacrificial animal. Abraham steadfastly believed in God's promise to bless his descendants through Isaac. God, acknowledging Abraham's unwavering faith, provided a sacrificial lamb in place of Isaac. In gratitude, Abraham named the place Jehovah-Jireh, signifying God's provision on His mountain.

Through faith, Abraham, when tested by God, embraced His promises and was prepared to sacrifice his only son, Isaac, believing that through Isaac his descendants would come *(Hebrews 11:17-19)*. Abraham's trust in God was such that he reasoned God could even raise the dead, and in a sense, he received Isaac back from death. Therefore, let us believe in God's promises and trust in Jehovah-Jireh. From His mountain, God will provide for all our needs.

Let us unite with the Psalmist and echo this statement of faith:

"I will lift up my eyes to the hills—From whence comes my help? My help comes from the Lord, Who made heaven and earth." (Psalm 121:1-2)

By my God, I have leaped over a wall

For by you, I have advanced against a troop; and by my God, I have leaped over a wall. Psalm 18:29

King David sang Psalm 18 when the Lord delivered him from the hands of all his enemies and from the hands of Saul.

If there's one lesson we can glean from King David, it is the essence of true humility. Despite being a victorious king who had triumphed in numerous battles, David embodied a remarkable humility. His life, from humble beginnings to remarkable success, could have warranted self-glorification, yet he chose differently. Instead of claiming credit for his achievements, David consistently attributed them to the mercy of God.

As a king, openly expressing dependency on God might have invited disapproval from his advisers, mockery from adversaries, and deemed politically incorrect by his inner circle. Nevertheless, David paid little heed to public opinion and consistently praised the Lord for his elevated position. Unashamedly, he discussed the dangers and emotional turmoil he faced, acknowledging, *"The cords of the grave coiled around me; the snares of death confronted me. In my distress I called to the Lord; I cried to my God for help. From his temple he heard my voice; my cry came before him, into his ears" (Psalm 18:5-6).*

Do we, like King David, recognize that it is solely by God's grace that we are not overwhelmed? It is only with God by our side that we can surmount the mountainous problems and barriers in our lives, and conquer our primary adversary, the devil, along with all other adversaries, relying solely on His help and guidance. As the word of the Lord declares, *"Not by might nor by power, but by my Spirit" (Zechariah 4:6),* and as Jesus Himself has said, *"Apart from me, you can do nothing"* (John 15:5). Indeed, with us is the Lord our God to help us and to fight our battles *(2 Chronicles 32:8).*

This is an easy thing in the eyes of the Lord

This is an easy thing in the eyes of the Lord. 2 Kings 3:18

Whatever your need may be, no matter how daunting it appears, remember that in the eyes of the Lord, it is effortless.

Jehoram, the king of Israel, Jehoshaphat, the king of Judah, and the king of Edom united to confront the King of Moab, who had rebelled against Israel. However, as they journeyed to battle, they faced a dire shortage of water for their armies and livestock. Seeking divine guidance, they consulted Prophet Elisha. God instructed them through Elisha to dig ditches in the valley. Despite the absence of wind or rain, the valley would be filled with water, providing for all their needs *(2 Kings 3:9, 10, 16, 17)*.

The Lord assured that filling the ditches with water and delivering the Moabites into their hands would be an easy task for Him, and indeed, He fulfilled His promise. Even what seems most challenging for humans is effortless for the Lord God. Despite the absence of wind or rain, the ditches were miraculously filled with water, showcasing the Lord's power and faithfulness.

The concerns about debts, job searches, family tensions, aging parents' health, and housing challenges are all effortlessly manageable for our Lord, working for our benefit. Like Prophet Elisha, who sought musical worship before hearing God's word, let us also engage in worship, shifting our focus beyond our current circumstances—beyond financial struggles, medical reports, and societal statistics.

With hearts filled with praise and voices lifted in song, let us worship the Lord. As we do so, let us lay all our burdens at His feet, firmly believing that it is effortless for our Lord to transform our negative situations. His promises are steadfast and true for those who have faith!

Let us boldly claim this assurance: *"This is an easy thing in the eyes of the Lord."*

WE ARE GOD'S MASTERPIECE

For we are God's workmanship, created in Christ Jesus to do good works,
which God prepared in advance for us to do. Ephesians 2:10

We are created as a new creation in Christ by God. *Therefore, if any man be in Christ, He is a new creature: old things are passed away; behold, all things have become new. 2 Corinthians 5:17*

We are His handiwork. We are His masterpieces. The apostle Paul declares that we are created in Christ Jesus for good works. How do we discern and perform these good works? The answer lies in the verse mentioned above: God Himself has prepared them for us. What a profound truth! God is crafting us as His masterpieces and simultaneously orchestrating the good works we are called to accomplish.

For instance, Queen Esther, an ordinary Jewish girl, was raised by God to the position of queen, a testament to His handiwork. He orchestrated a significant task for her—to thwart an enemy's plot to massacre the Jews. Esther's royal position uniquely positioned her to accomplish this crucial deed, ultimately saving her people and defeating their adversaries.

The Holy Spirit guides us in discerning and executing good works. He prompts us to act in situations that require our intervention, leading to inner joy when we respond. However, ignoring this guidance leads to a loss of peace. God's plans cannot be hindered, but if we fail to act, He ensures the task is completed by someone else, though we forfeit the opportunity to contribute to the good and lose our inner peace. Therefore, when you hear the voice of the Lord, do not harden your heart.

Withhold not good from them to whom it is due, when it is in the power of your hand to do it. Proverbs 3:27

REPAYING GOD FOR HIS GOODNESS TO US

What shall I return to the Lord for all His goodness to me?

I will lift up the cup of salvation and call on the name of the Lord. Psalm 116:12, 13

Lord, you have assigned me my portion and my cup; you have made my lot secure. Psalm 16:5

You prepare a table before me in the presence of my enemies. You anoint my head with oil, my cup overflows. Psalm 23:5

The Psalmist expresses his intention to lift up the cup of salvation and invoke the name of the Lord in gratitude for all that God has done in his life. This cup of salvation, a gift from God, is prepared for us even in the presence of our enemies. Therefore, we are encouraged to continuously hold up this cup of salvation, brimming with praises, magnifying the name of the Lord.

In this context, the 'cup' symbolizes our hearts or way of life, filled by God with His blessings until overflowing. To repay God's abundant goodness, we lift up our 'cups of salvation' in gratitude, magnifying His name through praise and living in constant thankfulness for His blessings.

> *"My heart is stirred by a noble theme as I recite my verses for the king; my tongue is the pen of a skillful writer." (Psalm 45:1)*

> *"A good man brings good things out of the good stored up in his heart. For the mouth speaks what the heart is full of." (Luke 6:45)*

Our hearts, like cups filled with God's blessings, overflow with goodness. When we speak from this inner abundance, we glorify God, and living water springs from within us. This is how we repay God for His goodness.

GOD'S THOUGHTS ARE NOT OUR THOUGHTS

'My thoughts are not your thoughts, neither are your ways my ways,' declares the Lord. Isaiah 55:8

When God created man, He made him in His own image and likeness, endowing him with the ability to reason and choose between right and wrong. However, when man sinned, his thoughts became corrupted, leading him away from God.

In comparing God and humanity, significant disparities emerge. God embodies unconditional love, forgiving completely and forgetting sins, while humans struggle to extend such forgiveness. The sacrificial nature of divine love, exemplified in Christ's sacrifice, contrasts sharply with human behavior. Additionally, God's standard of holiness far exceeds human righteousness, and His power and wisdom surpass human understanding and strength.

Isaiah 55:9 reminds us, *"As the Heavens are higher than the earth, so are My ways higher than your ways and My thoughts than your thoughts."* Despite our expectations for things to unfold in a particular manner, God's superior understanding enables Him to redirect the course of our actions for the better.

Speak, Lord, for Your Servant is Listening

And the Lord came and stood, and called as at other times, Samuel, Samuel.
Then Samuel answered, Speak; for thy servant hears. 1 Samuel 3:10

Eli served as the priest in the temple of the Lord, while ninety-eight-year-old, and the child Samuel ministered to the Lord under his guidance. In those days, divine revelations were scarce, and there was no clear vision from the Lord. Despite this scarcity, the Lord found young Samuel worthy of being His messenger.

One night, the Lord called Samuel, leading him to repeatedly run to Eli, believing it was him calling. Eventually, Eli recognized it was the Lord calling Samuel and instructed him to respond, "Speak, Lord, for your servant hears." Obediently, Samuel responded as instructed, becoming the conduit through which the Word of the Lord reached the people.

Samuel, nurtured from childhood in the Temple of God under the care of the aged priest Eli, continued to mature in both stature and favor with the Lord and people (1 Samuel 2:26). Despite being separated from his parents and dwelling in the temple, Samuel displayed remarkable patience and diligence in fulfilling his duties. His devout life earned favor with both God and humanity. Recognizing Samuel's faithful heart, God chose him to be a prophet to His people.

Do we recognize the voice of the Lord? It resonates through sermons, Bible verses, prophetic messages, inner promptings, and various other avenues. As followers of our Shepherd, we are assured to discern His voice, for Jesus assures, *'My sheep listen to my voice; I know them, and they follow me' (John 10:27).*

When we recognize God's voice, let us not resist but respond like Samuel: 'Speak, Lord, for your servant hears'. By doing so, we position ourselves to be vessels for God's message, just as He used Samuel as His messenger.

Thus far the Lord has helped us

Then Samuel took a stone and set it and named it Ebenezer, saying, 'Thus far the Lord has helped us.' 1 Samuel 7:12

After the Israelites emerged victorious in a battle against the Philistines, thanks to the Lord's intervention with thunder, Samuel erected a memorial stone and named it Ebenezer, signifying *'God has helped us so far'*. Throughout the Bible, there are numerous instances where people set up such memorial stones to commemorate significant events.

While fleeing from his brother's wrath, Jacob rested with a stone for a pillow and experienced a divine vision of angels ascending and descending a ladder connecting heaven and earth. God appeared to Jacob at the top of the ladder. In remembrance of this encounter, Jacob erected his stone pillow as a pillar and named the place Bethel, meaning 'house of God' *(Genesis 28:17-19)*. Upon his return to his father's house, Jacob once again encountered God near Bethel, where he received a blessing. In commemoration of this event, Jacob erected a stone pillar *(Genesis 35:14)*.

Similarly, Joshua placed twelve stones in the Jordan River, marking the spot where the priests carrying the Ark of the Covenant stood when the river parted for the Israelites' entry into Canaan *(Joshua 4:9)*. Joshua then established a covenant with the Israelites, instructing them to serve only the Lord their God and forsake all other gods. He recorded this covenant in the book of the Law of God and set up a great stone under an oak tree near the sanctuary of the Lord as a witness *(Joshua 24:26-27)*.

Do we have tangible reminders, like these monuments, that constantly prompt us to recall God's deliverance and mighty deeds in our lives?

I will remember the works of the Lord; Surely I will remember Your wonders of old. Psalm 77:11 Bless the Lord, O my soul, and forget not all his benefits. Psalm 103:2

JESHURUN GREW FAT AND KICKED

Jeshurun grew fat and kicked; filled with food, he became heavy and sleek.
He abandoned the God who made him and rejected the Rock his Savior.
Deuteronomy 32:15

Jeshurun, also known as Jacob or Israel, grew fat and rebellious, forsaking the God who had nurtured and guided him. Despite Moses referring to Jacob as "upright" or "beloved," he emphasizes Jacob's waywardness rather than his righteousness. Moses recalls how God had lovingly cared for Jacob, leading him through the wilderness and providing abundantly for him. Yet, despite God's faithfulness, Jeshurun turned away, neglecting the Rock of his salvation and failing to live up to his name, "upright."

We may wonder how Jeshurun could have strayed after all that God had done for him, but we are not much different from him. Are we truly grateful to God for all that He has done for us? He has chosen us to be His children, guiding us in goodness, and bestowing countless blessings upon us. He has instilled faith within us through His Word, extending forgiveness for our sins and providing fellowship among believers. Yet, in moments of prosperity, we often lose sight of Him, prioritizing His blessings over our relationship with Him. When we seek His aid, we are fervent, but once blessed, we neglect our connection with Him. Despite this, it is essential to cling to our Rock and Savior. Ultimately, a grateful heart is all we can offer, and it is all that is expected of us.

I WILL MAKE YOU LIKE MY SIGNET RING

I will make you like my signet ring, for I have chosen you. Haggai 2:23

A signet ring is a finger ring bearing an engraved emblem or seal, often worn by kings and nobles. They would entrust their signet rings to trusted ministers and officials for official use. For instance, Pharaoh, the king of Egypt, bestowed his signet ring upon Joseph, appointing him ruler over all the land of Egypt (Genesis 41:42). Similarly, King Ahasuerus granted his signet ring to Mordecai, a Jew, enabling him to issue decrees in the king's name to avert a planned massacre against the Jews in the kingdom, instead authorizing them to defend themselves *(Esther 8:2-8)*.

God has chosen us to be His signet ring, symbolizing His desire to grant us authority to act on His behalf. This authority extends over various domains. As believers, we inherit Jesus' promises, including power over the nations for those who overcome and keep His works until the end *(Revelation 2:26)*. He also bestows upon us the power to cast out evil and unclean spirits, along with the ability to heal all kinds of sickness and disease *(Matthew 10:1)*. Furthermore, Jesus assures us that we will have authority over the power of the enemy, allowing us to trample on serpents and scorpions without harm *(Luke 10:19)*. Additionally, believers are entrusted with the authority to preach the gospel *(Mark 16:15-18)*. This comprehensive authority reflects God's intention for His chosen ones to represent Him with power and purpose in the world.

We are like signet rings in God's hands, entrusted with the authority to execute His power for His glory. However, we must use this power wisely, solely for bringing honor to God, not for self-glorification. Remembering that we hold this authority on behalf of God, we must avoid misuse, as seen in the case of Coniah, the king of Judah, whom God removed from his position for failing to fulfill His will (Jeremiah 22:24).

A BRUISED REED HE WILL NOT BREAK

A bruised reed he will not break and a smoldering wick he will not snuff out. In faithfulness, he will bring forth justice. Isaiah 42:3

The imagery of the reed represents the weak and fragile among us, those easily swayed by life's trials. A bruised reed, therefore, signifies someone greatly afflicted yet not entirely broken. Similarly, a smoldering wick suggests little strength to endure. This scripture illustrates God's compassionate and gentle nature, showing that He does not further harm those who are already weakened or struggling. Isaiah 40:11, depicts God's nurturing care for his flock, likening him to a gentle shepherd who gathers the lambs and guides them tenderly.

The Lord, our shepherd, is not harsh; He is gentle, handling us with care and love. He does not further break a bruised reed with anger; instead, He soothes with gentle words, allowing healing and strength to grow. Similarly, if a wick burns dimly, Jesus does not snuff it out; rather, He restores its brightness by removing soot and replenishing with oil. God deals gently with our weaknesses, nurturing us with loving kindness to become strong and radiant. His comforting words and encouragement heal us, enabling us to withstand life's challenges. In instances of injustice, the Lord faithfully fights for our cause, bringing forth justice on our behalf.

Hagar, Sarah, Hannah, and the woman caught in adultery were all considered bruised reeds in society, yet God lifted them up without breaking them. Hagar and Sarah became mothers of great nations, while Hannah became the mother of the prophet Samuel. The woman caught in adultery was forgiven by Jesus and urged to "sin no more," a testament to His saving grace for all. Jesus' mission was to heal the brokenhearted, comfort the mourning, and exchange ashes for beauty, mourning for joy, and heaviness for praise (Isaiah 61:1-3). Indeed, He does not break a bruised reed. If you find yourself akin to a bruised reed, take solace in God's promise to strengthen and uplift you.

WHAT I SAY WILL COME TRUE FOR YOU

Is the Lord's arm too short? Now you will see whether or not what I say will come true for you. Numbers 11:23

Moses led the Israelites from Egypt to the land promised by God, a great multitude estimated to exceed 1.5 million people. Providing food and water for such a multitude daily was a monumental task. Miraculously, God provided for them by sending manna, described as the food of angels, which fell from heaven each day.

However, the Israelites grew weary of this provision and longed for the variety they had in Egypt, lamenting the monotony of manna. Moses, troubled by their complaints, appealed to God, who assured him that meat would be provided not just for a day or two, but for an entire month. Aware of the logistical challenges, Moses doubted the feasibility of such a feat, but God reassured him of His limitless power, affirming that His ability to perform miracles knew no bounds *(Numbers 11:23)*. A wind from the Lord brought quails from the sea and let them fall by the camp of the Israelites up to a length of a day's journey on every side of their camp up to a height of three feet upon the face of the earth, as recorded in Numbers 11:31.

Although God granted their request for meat, He was displeased with their complaints, murmuring, and weeping in their tents, as they longed for the food of Egypt. They should have made their desires known to God in prayer, believing that His hands would never grow short and were capable of performing miracles.

Let us take note and not doubt the miracle-working power of our Lord.

Is not Ephraim my dear son, the child in whom I delight?

Is not Ephraim my dear son, the child in whom I delight? Though I often speak against him, I still remember him. Therefore, my heart yearns for him; I have great compassion for him, declares the Lord. Jeremiah 31:20

Ephraim, Joseph's second son, was born in Egypt before Jacob and his brothers arrived during the famine. Upon meeting them, Jacob adopted both Ephraim and his brother Manasseh as his own, but he showed favoritism towards Ephraim. This preference may have stemmed from Jacob's own experiences as a second son, possibly seeing himself reflected in Ephraim.

A noteworthy aspect is that Ephraim became a common blessing in Israel, with people wishing, "May God make you like Ephraim and Manasseh" *(Genesis 48:20)*. Despite being Joseph's second son and the youngest of the twelve tribes as an adopted child of Jacob, Ephraim held a special place as God's "firstborn" *(Jeremiah 31:9)*. However, when Ephraim transgressed against God by failing to completely displace the Canaanites from his land as commanded, he incurred divine chastisement. This disobedience led to idolatry and disgrace, as the people turned to worship foreign gods *(Hosea 13:1; 10:6)*. Despite this, God, in His mercy, calls Ephraim to repentance, promising healing and unconditional love, with His anger turned away *(Hosea 14:4)*. Ephraim responds by renouncing idols, declaring, "What have I to do anymore with idols?" *(Hosea 14:8)*.

We may cling to certain "Canaanites" in our lives—activities and things prohibited by our Lord God. While we are undoubtedly cherished by God, disobedience and rebellion against His law provoke His anger. Yet, when we repent, He graciously heals our backsliding and loves us unconditionally.

THE LORD IS MY PORTION

Lord, you alone are my portion and my cup; you make my lot secure.
The boundary lines have fallen for me in pleasant places; surely I have a
delightful inheritance. Psalm 16:5, 6

A portion or share represents a part of the whole, often denoting an inheritance. It may encompass a share of the spoils of war, or the land apportioned in an estate division. To say "The Lord is our portion" implies that all blessings in our lives are gifts from God, our divine allotment. Placing our trust in the Lord ensures that we receive our rightful inheritance, which includes the joy in our hearts, the peace of our minds, and confidence in our Lord. Ultimately, the greatest inheritance we have, both in this life and for eternity, is the Lord Himself.

Our portion, allotted by God, includes believing in His saving grace, accepting His Word, experiencing His constant presence, being surrounded by songs of salvation, offering praises to Him, and enjoying worldly blessings. It is imperative that we safeguard this inheritance from corruption and strive to deepen our knowledge of Christ.

The Apostle Paul confidently declares that the crown of righteousness awaits him, underscoring his assurance of a future inheritance *(2 Timothy 4:8)*. God assures a great inheritance to all who seek Him, ensuring no shame for those who come. We must share the truth of God's mercy and declare "God is my portion," signifying His presence even in darkness and guarding against corruption. Let all receive their rightful portion from the Lord, safeguarding it diligently.

RECONCILING FATHERS AND SONS

Behold, I will send you Elijah the prophet before the coming of the great and dreadful day of the Lord. And He shall turn the heart of the fathers to the children, and the heart of the children to their fathers, lest I come and smite the earth with a curse. Malachi 4:5, 6

This prophetic message foresaw the arrival of John the Baptist, who preceded Christ to prepare the way for the Lord. John's mission was to preach repentance and administer baptism to the people. When John's birth was announced to his father Zachariah, the angel reiterated these words, stating that John would go before the Lord *"in the spirit and power of Elijah"* to reconcile familial relationships and lead the disobedient to the wisdom of the just, thus preparing the people for the Lord. *(Luke 1:17)*

John the Baptist paved the way for Jesus by proclaiming, *"Repent, for the Kingdom of God is at hand" (Mark 1:15)*. His preaching led people to confess their sins and undergo baptism, fostering reconciliation between parents and children, which was essential before Jesus commenced His ministry.

In God's kingdom, reconciliation among family members, neighbors, and brethren holds great significance. Repentance often precedes such reconciliation. Jesus emphasized this by instructing, *"First be reconciled to your brother, and then come and offer your gift" (Matthew 5:24)*.

God will commission messengers to carry out the ministry of reconciliation prior to the second coming of Jesus. It is imperative for His people to reconcile with others before meeting Him, as enmity cannot coexist with entry into the kingdom of God. This promise extends to every family, with messengers sent by God to bring His Word and foster peace and reconciliation among family members and others. It is vital to heed and obey these messages of reconciliation.

Through prayer and holding onto this promise, the Prince of Peace will mend broken hearts and facilitate reconciliation.

IT IS NOT BY THE SWORD THAT THE LORD SAVES

This is the word of the Lord unto Zerubbabel, saying, not by might, nor by power, but by My Spirit, says, the Lord of hosts. Zechariah 4:6

It is not by sword or spear that the Lord saves... 1 Samuel 17:47

The race is not to the swift or the battle to the strong, nor does food come to the wise or wealth to the brilliant or favor to the learned, but time and chance happen to them all. Ecclesiastes 9:11

The Scriptures above emphasize that our victory does not stem from our own strength, wisdom, or resources. Rather, it is solely through the power of the Spirit of God, working through time and circumstance. Therefore, our triumph ultimately belongs to the Lord. In comparison to the Spirit of the Lord, our own might and power pale in significance. Neither our swords nor our spears can save us; it is through the Word of God that victory is commanded.

There is no assurance that the swift will win a race, the strong will conquer in battle, or that the wise will always be provided for, the brilliant will be wealthy, or the educated will be favored. Success and favor are ultimately determined by the will and providence of God. It is God who endows us with swiftness, strength, wisdom, brilliance, and education. However, these qualities alone are insufficient for victory; they must be utilized in conjunction with God's guidance to be effective. In essence, nothing within us is inherently valuable in meeting our needs; it is solely by God's grace that we endure. While we often attribute our livelihood to our own efforts, the reality is that numerous external factors, beyond our comprehension and control, must align for our lives to flourish. No amount of wealth, beauty, or education can purchase love, affection, comfort, joy, peace, health, or any other truly valuable thing.

But by the grace of God, I am what I am, and His grace toward me was not in vain; but I labored more abundantly than they all, yet not I, but the grace of God which was with me. 1 Corinthians 15:10

God's plan for us

For I know the plans I have for you, declares the Lord, plans to prosper you and not to harm you, plans to give you hope and a future. Jeremiah 29:11

This verse holds special significance for many, including myself. I believe that when God repeatedly presents a particular verse to us, it is His way of speaking directly to our hearts. In times of uncertainty, this verse has been a source of comfort and assurance for me. I remember a moment when I was feeling disheartened due to unemployment, and I encountered this very Scripture multiple times in a Christian bookstore.

First, it caught my eye on a journal, then again on a coffee cup. When I encountered the same verse for the second time, I couldn't ignore the significance of it. Pausing, I read it again, feeling a sense of gratitude towards the Lord. I made a silent vow that if I encountered the verse once more that day, I would take it as a direct message from God. As I hurriedly made my way out of the bookstore, trying not to actively search for the verse, I was startled to see it once more, this time on an accent boat: *"For I know the plans I have for you," declares the Lord, "plans to prosper you and not to harm you, plans to give you hope and a future."*

In that moment, my heart skipped a beat and tears welled up in my eyes. I felt certain that God was speaking directly to me through this verse, assuring me of His plans to prosper me, to give me hope and a future. It renewed my hope instantly, and I couldn't help but praise the Lord for His faithfulness. Each sighting felt like a timely reminder of God's promise to prosper me, to give me hope, and a future. It was a reassuring sign that I was not alone, and that God had a plan for me, despite the challenges I faced.

Now, blessed with a fine job, I confess that it is by His grace alone. As I share this testimony, I repeat the verse three times, encouraging you to claim it as a promise from God for your own life. Keep praising Him for His plans to prosper you, give you hope, and a future.

Gladness and Joy will overtake you

*And a highway shall be there, and it shall be called the way of holiness;
the unclean shall not pass over it; the wayfaring men, though fools, shall
not go astray. No lion shall be there, nor any ravenous beast shall go up
thereon, but the redeemed shall walk there. The ransomed of the Lord will
return. They will enter Zion with singing; everlasting joy will crown their
heads. Gladness and joy will overtake them, and sorrow and sighing will
flee away. Isaiah 35:8-10*

The Prophet Isaiah describes a highway known as the way of holiness, where the redeemed will journey from their Babylonian captivity to Zion. This signifies the return of the Israelites to Judea and the believers' journey from this world to heaven. Isaiah prophesies about the path where the redeemed will travel, free from danger and guided by God's protection.

We were once held captive by the devil and the world, but God has redeemed us, and now we journey towards heaven. God has promised us a highway called the way of holiness. While Jesus described the way to life as narrow and straight, God calls it a highway, symbolizing the clear and direct path He has prepared for us. How can a highway also be narrow and straight? The path to Eternal Life is known as the way of holiness. It requires us to forsake worldly pleasures and sinful desires. Along this journey towards heaven, we will encounter trials, tribulations, and persecutions, making the path narrow and straight. However, God transforms this challenging path into a highway, allowing us to traverse it with gladness, joy, and songs of praise until we reach our destination.

We are guided along the highway of holiness by the Word of God, the teachings of Jesus, and the prompting of the Holy Spirit. Whenever we stray from this path, God's voice redirects us back onto the right track. We are accompanied by the fellowship of saints and the comforting presence of God as we journey in righteousness, experiencing peace along the way.

The journey of the redeemed culminates in the crown of everlasting joy, free from sorrow or sighing, brimming with gladness and joy.

GOD WILL NOT DESPISE A BROKEN
AND CONTRITE HEART

*My sacrifice, O God, is a broken spirit; a broken and contrite heart you,
God, will not despise. Psalm 51:17*

King David's heart shattered when he realized the gravity of his sin with a married woman. Overwhelmed with remorse, he turned to God as the only source of healing. Pouring out his plea for forgiveness, he offered his broken and contrite heart as a sacrifice to God, acknowledging his wrongdoing and pleading for a clean heart. In His mercy, God answered David's prayers, restoring his broken heart and filling him with joy. David rejoices, proclaiming, *"The Lord is close to the brokenhearted and saves those who are crushed in spirit." Psalm 34:18.*

We read about Hagar, Hannah, Naomi, Apostle Peter, and many others who, in their brokenness, found mercy from God when they turned to Him. Is your heart broken? Perhaps you have suffered an irreplaceable personal loss or faced rejection in love. Maybe you have committed a sin against God or carry an unfulfilled longing. In your despair, pour out your broken and contrite heart to God. He will not despise you. The Scripture assures us:, *"He heals the brokenhearted and binds up their wounds." Psalm 147:3*

We have a God who can heal our broken hearts and renew our spirits. He can wash away our sins and restore our hearts. All we need to do is pour out our hearts before Him as a sacrifice. We can echo the prayer of David, saying: *My God, on whom I can rely. God will go before me and will let me gloat over those who slander me. But do not kill them, Lord our shield, or my people will forget. In your might uproot them and bring them down. Psalm 59:10, 11*

Just as God answered David and restored to him the joy of his salvation, He will also forgive our sins and fill our hearts with the joy of salvation.

Come, all you who are thirsty

*Come, all you who are thirsty, come to the waters; and you who have no
money, come, buy and eat! Come; buy wine and milk without money and
without cost. Isaiah 55:1*

*On the last and greatest day of the festival, Jesus stood and said in a loud
voice, 'Let anyone who is thirsty come to me and drink.' John 7:37*

*The Spirit and the bride say, 'Come!' And let the one who hears say, 'Come!'
Let the one who is thirsty come and let the one who wishes take the free
gift of the water of life. Revelation 22:17*

God the Father calls all those who thirst to eat and drink without
paying any money. Jesus invites anyone who is thirsty to come
to Him and drink. The Holy Spirit, the Church, and all who have
heard the call are echoing the invitation for those desiring living water
to come and drink freely. This persistent call reflects the great love of
God, extended through God the Father, Jesus Christ the Son, and the
Holy Spirit, all inviting the thirsty to come and drink the living water
they offer freely.

Salvation and Eternal Life are freely offered to humanity; one
simply needs to approach God to receive them. The offer comes at
no cost. Where do we go to receive this gift from God? Jesus answers,
'Come to Me.' Close your eyes, call upon the name of Jesus, and express
your acceptance of His invitation to come to Him. He will surely fulfill
His promise and provide you with living water.

Those who have already accepted this invitation and are drinking
from the living waters should also join with God, Jesus, and the Holy
Spirit in inviting others who are thirsty. We must inform them that by
believing in Jesus, rivers of living water will flow from within them too
(John 7:38). We must guide people to Jesus, who declared, 'I am the
bread of life. Whoever comes to me will never go hungry, and whoever
believes in me will never be thirsty' (John 6:35). Those who heed this
call to satisfy their thirst without cost will never be ashamed. God will
surely cause living waters to flow from within them.

THE FEAR OF THE LORD IS THE BEGINNING OF WISDOM

"The fear of the Lord is the beginning of wisdom, and knowledge of the Holy One is understanding." Proverbs 9:10

This verse emphasizes that the initial indication of wisdom is having reverence and respect for the Lord. Without this reverence, it is unlikely that we have acquired wisdom. When we hold the Lord in reverence, we are on the path to wisdom. He provides us with the divine wisdom necessary to make sound decisions, whether big or small, each day.

When we hold the fear of the Lord, our lives are distinguished from the crowd; our thoughts are centered on godliness, and our spirits are in communion with the Holy Spirit, guiding us in discerning right from wrong. Reverence for the Lord becomes inherent in our nature. Amen!

Let us guard against being swayed by what the world deems as 'wisdom.' The world questions God's existence, rejects His grace demonstrated on the cross, deems trust in the Lord as foolishness, doubts the divine birth and resurrection of Christ, and scoffs at His second coming as King, among other biblical truths. This constitutes worldly wisdom, cautioned against in the Bible. Instead, we should pursue godly wisdom that aligns with God's Word.

Do not deceive yourselves. *"Let no one deceive himself. If anyone among you seems to be wise in this age, let him become a fool that he may become wise. For the wisdom of this world is foolishness with God." 1 Corinthians 3:18, 19*

Do not be wise in your own eyes; Fear the Lord and depart from evil. Proverbs 3:7

ONE WHO FEARS THE LORD IS TO BE PRAISED

Charm is deceptive, and beauty is fleeting, but a woman who fears the Lord is to be praised. Proverbs 31:30

This verse emphasizes that fearing God holds greater significance than outward charm and beauty, which are transient. Therefore, rather than placing undue emphasis on charm and beauty, we should esteem those who demonstrate reverence for the Lord. In today's world, considerable effort, including costly plastic surgeries and photo-editing applications, is devoted to enhancing external appearances. However, such endeavors can deceive others, as the resulting beauty is artificial and short-lived.

What is truly essential is reverence for our Lord God. *Proverbs 22:4* states, *"Humility is the fear of the Lord."* Therefore, possessing a humble spirit is the key to genuine beauty, contrary to the world's definition. While the world admires loud, proud, and fearless personalities, God values calmness, composure, and humility. This presents a stark contrast, prompting us to consider whose call we will heed.

The Apostle Paul urges us not to conform to worldly patterns but to undergo a transformation through the renewal of our minds *(Romans 12:2).* By doing so, we can discern and embrace God's good, pleasing, and perfect will. As God's chosen ones, dearly loved and holy, we are instructed to clothe ourselves with qualities such as compassion, kindness, humility, gentleness, and patience *(Colossians 3:23).* Additionally, we are encouraged to avoid selfish ambition and vain conceit, instead valuing others above ourselves with humility *(Philippians 2:3).*

Embracing humility and simplicity reflects true beauty in the eyes of our Maker. While outward beauty fades, inner beauty, cultivated through reverence for the Lord, endures and allows us to stand blameless before Him.

HE WILL SUSTAIN YOU TO THE END

He who began a good work in you will continue to perfect it until the day of Christ Jesus. Philippians 1:6

For those feeling anxious about completing their tasks in various aspects of life, be it work, studies, marriage, or general life, take heart in God's promise. He who initiated your journey is faithful to see you through to the end. So, continue to praise the Lord and remain steadfast in your course. He will sustain you until the day of Christ Jesus, ensuring you are blameless. *(1 Corinthians 1:8)*

Even in old age, God remains our support. As we age, it is natural to feel concerned about our declining health and strength, potentially leading to dependence on others for even simple tasks. In times like these, we can relate to the sentiments expressed in the Scriptures below, making them our own prayers and placing our trust in God's promise:

"Do not discard me in my old age; do not forsake me when my strength fails."
"Even when I am old and gray, do not forsake me, O God, until I proclaim Your power to the next generation, Your might to all who are to come."
Psalm 71: 9, 18

"Listen to Me, O house of Jacob, all the remnant of the house of Israel, who have been sustained from the womb, carried along since birth. Even to your old age, I will be the same, and I will bear you up when you turn gray. I have made you, and I will carry you; I will sustain you and deliver you." (Isaiah 46:3, 4)

Let us find comfort in God's promise. He has declared it, and He will fulfill it in our lives. Amen! Our God will indeed guide us through the remainder of our days, so there is no need to fear growing old.

THERE ARE SEVEN THINGS THE LORD HATES

*P*roverbs *6:16-19* outlines seven things that the Lord finds detestable, such as: haughty eyes; a lying tongue; hands that shed innocent blood; a heart that devises wicked schemes; feet that are quick to rush into evil; a false witness who pours out lies; and a person who stirs up conflict in the community.

Combining a lying tongue and a false witness who lies, we have six detestable actions our Lord hates. Haughty eyes stem from pride, where we elevate ourselves above others and look down upon them. Prophet Isaiah warns that human pride will be humbled, and only the Lord will be exalted (*Isaiah 2:11*).

According to the Apostle John, a liar is someone who denies that Jesus is the Christ *(1 John 2:22)*. Additionally, if a person claims to love God but hates their brother, they are also considered a liar *(1 John 4:20)*. God detests lies, so it is crucial not to deny the truth of Jesus Christ as our Savior and to refrain from harboring hatred towards our brother or neighbor.

While we may not have hands that shed innocent blood, a heart that devises wicked schemes, or feet that rush to do evil, many of us may have a tendency to stir up conflict in our community. As Proverbs 16:28 states, *"A perverse person stirs up conflict, and gossip separates close friends." Proverbs 16:28*

Let us strive to abhor what displeases God. May we pray earnestly: *"Teach me to do your will, for you are my God; may your good Spirit lead me on level ground." (Psalm 143:10)*

I WILL REPAY YOU FOR THE YEARS THE LOCUSTS HAVE EATEN

I will repay you for the years the locusts have eaten – the great locust and the young locust, the other locusts and the locust swarm – my great army that I sent among you. You will have plenty to eat until you are full, and you will praise the name of the Lord your God, who has worked wonders for you; never again will my people be shamed." Joel 2:25, 26

Several years ago, my family faced challenging times. We were dealing with various difficulties, including financial struggles and job insecurity. One day, in a moment of despair, I knelt beside my bed and resolved to read the Bible until I heard from the Lord. As I immersed myself in scripture, I came across *Joel 2:25-26*, where God promises restoration after loss. These verses spoke directly to my situation, filling me with peace and assurance.

Embracing God's promise, we continued to seek His guidance through prayer and scripture. In the following months, our circumstances began to turn around. Challenges were overcome, and blessings began to flow into our lives. Looking back, I am grateful for the experience and for the lesson it taught me about the power of seeking God's guidance through His word. I share this story as a reminder of the importance of listening for God's voice amidst life's trials and tribulations.

Next time you read your Bible, keep your heart open to hear Him speak. Also, claim these promises for your lives today: May the Lord repay you for everything you have lost over the years. May you have plenty to eat until you are full, and praise the name of the Lord your God, who has worked wonders for you. Never again may you be shamed. Amen!

THE LORD BLESS YOU AND KEEP YOU

The Lord bless you and keep you; The Lord make His face shine upon you And be gracious to you; The Lord lift up His countenance upon you, And give you peace." Numbers 6:24-26

These words were conveyed by God to Moses, instructing him to share them with Aaron, the High Priest, and his sons. They were to bless the people of Israel using these divine words. Our God is a God of blessings. From the creation of humanity, He has bestowed His blessings upon us.

He called Abraham to bless him and make him a blessing to many. Jacob, Abraham's grandson, eagerly sought his father Isaac's blessings, even resorting to deception to obtain them. However, Jacob understood that his father's blessings were not sufficient. We know the story of how Jacob wrestled with God Himself to secure divine blessings. As a result, God bestowed upon him a new name, Israel, and blessed him. His descendants are known by this name.

During the Israelites' journey from Egypt to the promised land of Canaan, a king encountered them and sought a seer named Balaam to curse Israel, fearing they would conquer his kingdom. However, God revealed to Balaam that it pleased the Lord to bless Israel. As a result, Balaam received only words of blessing from God for Israel (Numbers 24:1). What a loving God we serve! Despite His people's shortcomings, He desires only to bless them. He even guides His priests on the words to use when bestowing blessings upon the Israelites.

During Jesus' ministry, He dispatched His twelve disciples to various cities to spread the gospel of the kingdom of heaven. He instructed them to bless the houses they entered. If a house proved worthy, the blessing would remain; if not, it would return to them (Matthew 10:5, 12, 13). In the same way, we are called to bless others. God will supply us with the appropriate words for blessing, and He will bless us through others who speak words of blessing over us. However, it is essential for us to be worthy of receiving these blessings.

GOD GOES OVER AHEAD OF YOU

Hear, O Israel: You are to cross over the Jordan today, and go in to dispossess nations greater and mightier than yourself, great cities fortified up to heaven, a people great and tall, the descendants of the Anakim, whom you know, and of whom you heard it said, 'Who can stand before the descendants of Anak?' Therefore, understand today that the Lord your God is He who goes over before you as a consuming fire. He will destroy them and bring them down before you; so, you shall drive them out and destroy them quickly, as the Lord has said to you. Deuteronomy 9:1-3

After forty years of wandering in the desert, the Israelites stood on the brink of entering the Promised Land of Canaan. Moses, aware of his impending death and Joshua's leadership, gathered the people to remind them of God's miraculous guidance and promises throughout their journey. Despite their fears about crossing the Jordan River, facing new battles, and uncertain futures, Moses reassured them that God would precede them as a consuming fire, ensuring victory over their enemies. He encouraged the people, describing the land they were about to possess as a place of abundance, nourished by rain from heaven and continuously watched over by the Lord. (Deuteronomy 11:11, 12)

Similarly, we may find ourselves apprehensive about the uncertainties of our future, particularly the transition from earthly life to our heavenly home. Yet, we are urged to trust in God's promise to go before us, just as He did for the Israelites, consuming our enemy, the devil.

Jesus reassures us, saying, *"Fear not, little flock; for it is your Father's good pleasure to give you the kingdom." (Luke 12:32)*

Crossing over the flooding Jordan

Now the Jordan is at flood stage all during harvest. Yet as soon as the priests who carried the ark reached the Jordan and their feet touched the water's edge, the water from upstream stopped flowing. It piled up in a heap a great distance away, at a town called Adam in the vicinity of Zarethan, while the water flowing down to the Sea of the Arabah (that is, the Dead Sea) was completely cut off. So, the people crossed over opposite Jericho. The priests who carried the ark of the covenant of the Lord stopped in the middle of the Jordan and stood on dry ground, while all Israel passed by until the whole nation had completed the crossing on dry ground. Joshua 3:15-17

We stand in awe of God's mighty hand as He orchestrated the crossing of the flooding Jordan River for the Israelites. Against all odds, God stopped the river that day. Let us closely examine the passage: The Jordan was flooding due to harvest time. Instantly, when the priests' feet touched the water's edge, the upstream flow ceased. The water piled up in a heap far away from the people to allay their fears. Downstream flow to the sea was entirely cut off. The priests remained on dry ground in the middle of the Jordan. The entire nation crossed over on dry ground.

Certainly, there have been similar 'flooding Jordan' situations that we have passed through in our lives. If we look back now we will realize how the 'upstream water' had stopped flowing in and the 'downstream river' was completely cut off and how we had passed through 'dry land' as if there was no trace of a 'flooding river'. I can testify to it in my own life and am sure each one of you can do so too.

Let us give praises to God Almighty every time we think of His wonders. From what we know of our deliverances in the past, we can fully trust Him for our future too. Amen.

NAAMAN'S HEALING OF BODY, MIND, AND SOUL

Naaman's healing is documented in 2 Kings 5:1-17. He was a captain in the army of the king of Syria, esteemed and honorable, but afflicted with leprosy. A captive girl from Israel, serving Naaman's wife, suggested seeking the prophet in Samaria for his healing. Naaman journeyed to Israel with a letter from the Syrian king to his counterpart, the king of Israel. Upon reading the letter, the king of Israel was distressed, feeling powerless to cure leprosy and fearing a quarrel.

When Elisha, the prophet in Samaria, heard about this, he sent a message to the king, asking why he had torn his clothes. He requested that Naaman be sent to him so that Naaman would recognize there was a prophet in Israel. So Naaman arrived with his horses and chariots and stood at Elisha's door. Elisha then sent a messenger to Naaman, instructing him to wash seven times in the Jordan River, promising that his flesh would be restored, and he would be cleansed. However, Naaman was furious and left in anger, expecting Elisha to come out and perform a dramatic healing ritual. He questioned why he couldn't have washed in the rivers of Damascus instead.

Naaman's servants persuaded him to follow Elisha's instructions and wash himself in the Jordan River. He complied, dipping himself seven times as instructed. Miraculously, his flesh was restored, becoming as healthy as that of a child, and he was cleansed of his leprosy. Deeply moved by this experience, Naaman acknowledged the God of Israel as the one true God. Returning to Elisha, he expressed his newfound faith. Elisha blessed him, saying, "Go in peace," signifying healing not only of his **body** but also of his **soul**.

HE LURED YOU AWAY FROM THE JAWS OF TROUBLE

Yes, he lured you away from the jaws of trouble into an open area where you were not restrained, and your table was covered with rich food." Job 36:16

These words were spoken by Elihu to Job, suggesting that Job's suffering might be a consequence of his iniquities. According to Elihu, if Job were to turn to God and forsake his wrongdoing, God would rescue him from trouble and provide abundance. While Elihu accused Job of sin, it is important to note that God Himself testified to Job's integrity. Nevertheless, Elihu's assertion holds true in the broader sense that it is indeed God who delivers us from trouble and blesses us

King David echoes a similar testimony, declaring, *"He brought me out into a spacious place; he rescued me because he delighted in me" (Psalm 18:19)*. David attributes his deliverance to his earnest cry for help in distress, affirming, *"In my distress, I called to the Lord; I cried to my God for help. From His Temple He heard my voice; my cry came before Him, into His ears" (Psalm 18:6)*. Other references emphasize God's faithfulness in leading His people from adversity to abundance and liberation, such as *Psalm 66:12 and Psalm 118:5*.

Therefore, let us cast off anything that entangles us—sin, fear, guilt, addiction, temptation, doubt, or any other hindrance from our past. Trust that our Lord and Savior Jesus Christ has rescued us from these troubles and prepared a rich banquet for us in the wide open! Amen!

By His blood, we have overcome! Amen!

WELLS OF SALVATION

With joy, you will draw water from the wells of salvation. Isaiah 12:3

*On the last day, that great day of the feast, Jesus stood and cried out, saying,
"If anyone thirsts, let him come to Me and drink. He who believes in Me,
as the Scripture has said, out of his heart will flow rivers of living water."
John 7:37, 38*

In the encounter between Jesus and a Samaritan woman at a well, Jesus asked her for water to drink. Surprised, she questioned how a Jew could request water from a Samaritan. Jesus responded by telling her that if she knew the gift of God and who He was, she would have asked Him for living water, and He would have freely given it to her *(John 4:10)*.

Jesus extends a heartfelt invitation to all humanity, urging us to believe in Him so that streams of living water may flow from within us. This invitation, offered with love and concern for our souls, is open to everyone. To accept it, we need only to believe that Jesus died on the cross for the forgiveness of our sins and was raised from the dead to make us righteous. This belief triggers the flow of living water from within us. God's promise in *Isaiah 41:18* assures us that He will transform barren places into flourishing ones, with rivers and fountains in abundance. Additionally, Isaiah 55:1 beckons all who are thirsty to come to the waters and partake freely, regardless of their financial status.

Salvation fills us with an enduring joy that surpasses any circumstance we may face. To partake of this joy and drink from the wells of salvation, let us pray:

I come before You as a sinner burdened by my transgressions. My sins weigh heavily upon me, and as a result, I struggle to experience true joy. I humbly ask for Your forgiveness, Lord, and I plead for the cleansing power of the blood of Your Son, Jesus Christ, who sacrificed Himself for my redemption. I pray that You would fill me with the profound joy of salvation that comes only from You. Accept my prayer, O Lord, in the name of Jesus. Amen!

THE STREAMS OF GOD ARE FILLED WITH WATER

You care for the land and water it; you enrich it abundantly. The streams of God are filled with water to provide the people with grain, for so you have ordained it. Psalm 65:9

God's care for the land, as evidenced by His provision of water and nourishment, is a testament to His care for His people. His blessings are abundant and immeasurable, surpassing human comprehension. In His provision, God bestows upon us all that we need and more, including the intangible blessings of salvation, peace, faith, hope, and the well-being of our families. From the joy of knowing His truth to the opportunities to share His message, every aspect of our lives is enriched by His blessings. Let us offer praise and gratitude to God for His countless and incomparable blessings bestowed upon us.

Let us offer praise and gratitude to God for the abundance of material blessings bestowed upon us. From our homes and jobs to our families, friends, and cherished moments of leisure, every aspect of our lives reflects His generosity. We are blessed with the beauty of nature, the company of loved ones, and the joy of everyday experiences, from the sight of birds at our windowsill to the vast expanse of the sky. God ensures that His streams are filled with water, providing sustenance and abundance for His people, ensuring that we never go thirsty or lacking in His provision. Let us rejoice in His abundance and offer Him our heartfelt thanks for all these blessings.

They shall still bear fruit in old age; They shall be fresh and flourishing. Psalm 92:14

I will pour water on him who is thirsty and floods on the dry ground. I will pour My Spirit on your descendants and My blessing on your offspring. Isaiah 44:3

God abundantly blesses those who earnestly seek His favor. Like Jacob, let us persevere in seeking His favor, knowing that He hears the cries of His children and delights in blessing them.

His handiwork

Three cups shaped like almond flowers with buds and blossoms are to be on one branch, three on the next branch, and the same for all six branches extending from the lamp stand. Exodus 25:33

It always astonishes me when I read the meticulous instructions God gave Moses for building the Tabernacle, including every detail from measurements to materials, colors, and designs. God's attention to detail is truly remarkable, and I admire His artistic sense. It is incredible to see how He cares about every single aspect. In fact, everywhere we look, we can find evidence of God's mastery as a Designer.

The beauty and intricacy of nature are a testament to the glory and craftsmanship of God. Just as the heavens declare His magnificence and the skies proclaim His handiwork *(Psalm 19:1)*, so too do the birds of the air and the lilies of the field showcase His provision and creativity *(Matthew 6:26, 28-29)*. We, too, are His masterpieces, lovingly crafted by His hands. In Isaiah, we are likened to clay in the hands of a potter, molded and shaped according to His design *(Isaiah 64:8)*. Similarly, in Psalms, we are reminded that God intricately formed us in our mother's womb, and we are fearfully and wonderfully made *(Psalm 139:13-14)*.

Let us offer gratitude to God for the beauty that surrounds us, acknowledging His glory alone. As Ecclesiastes reminds us, He has made everything beautiful in its time *(Ecclesiastes 3:11)*. Furthermore, let us ensure that all things are conducted decently and in order, as instructed in *1 Corinthians 14:40.*

VICTORY RESTS WITH THE LORD

The horse is made ready for the day of battle, but victory rests with the Lord. Proverbs 21:31

Are you anxious about exams, promotions, studies, or your future? Take comfort, for your victory belongs to the Lord. Just as a horse prepares for battle, we also equip ourselves to face challenges, but our ultimate triumph lies in the hands of the Lord. Amen.

Here are a few additional scriptures affirming this truth. God bless you!

Fear not, for I am with you; be not dismayed, for I am your God; I will strengthen you, I will help you, I will uphold you with my righteous right hand. Isaiah 41:10

But He said to me, "My grace is sufficient for you, for my power is made perfect in weakness." Therefore, I will boast all the more gladly of my weaknesses, so that the power of Christ may rest upon me. For the sake of Christ, then, I am content with weaknesses, insults, hardships, persecutions, and calamities. For when I am weak, then I am strong. 2 Corinthians 12:9, 10

Be strong and courageous. Do not fear or be in dread of them, for it is the Lord your God who goes with you. He will not leave you or forsake you. Deuteronomy 31:6

In every battle we face, it is essential to prepare thoroughly. Just as a horse must be ready for the battlefield and an army must train and sharpen their weapons, we too must not be negligent in our preparations, even though victory ultimately comes from the Lord. Our efforts in preparing for battle are the foundation upon which God intervenes and grants us victory.

We should not boast of victory as if it were solely the result of our preparations. Instead, we recognize that any success we achieve is a blessing from God, making the victory rightfully His.

FEASTING ON THE WORD OF GOD

*When your words came, I ate them; they were my joy and my heart's delight,
for I bear your name, O Lord God Almighty. Jeremiah 15:16*

Jeremiah, the prophet, found delight and joy in consuming God's words as they were revealed to him. Do we share in this experience? God continues to send His words to us, but do we feast upon them with eagerness and delight? Can we relate to the joy and fulfillment that comes from immersing ourselves in His Word?

The Psalmist joyfully proclaims, *"How sweet are Your words to my taste, Sweeter than honey to my mouth!" (Psalm 119:103).* King David extols the truth of God's judgments, declaring them to be more desirable than gold and sweeter than honey *(Psalm 19:9-10).* Job expresses his commitment to God's commands, valuing them even more than his daily sustenance *(Job 23:12).* Jesus reaffirms the importance of God's Word, stating that life is sustained not just by bread, but by every word from God *(Matthew 4:4).* Peter encourages believers to crave spiritual nourishment, likening it to pure milk essential for growth in salvation *(1 Peter 2:2).* Ultimately, the invitation is extended to *"Taste and see that the Lord is good" (Psalm 34:8),* highlighting the richness and satisfaction found in God's Word.

Our gracious God continually prepares a banquet for us whenever we gather in His name. He eagerly anticipates our participation in this feast, whether it be through communal worship or the reading of His Word, tailored to meet our spiritual needs. With open arms, He invites us to partake in these divine banquets. Let us gratefully accept His invitation to feast with Him and find nourishment for our souls.

Behold, I stand at the door and knock. If anyone hears My voice and opens the door, I will come into him and dine with him, and he with Me. Revelation 3:20

Abundant blessings

How abundant are the good things that you have stored up for those who fear you, that you bestow in the sight of all, on those who take refuge in you? Psalm 31:19

The abundant blessings that God has prepared for those who fear Him are beyond measure! Praise the Lord! To receive these blessings, we must fulfill our part: fear God and take refuge in Him.

"Fearing God" entails obeying His commandments, while "taking refuge in the Lord" means finding safety and shelter in Him during times of trouble or pursuit. Whenever we face fear or trouble, we must seek His presence. Let us always bear in mind that God has abundant blessings in store for us. Above all, let us remember to fear God and seek refuge in Him, thus making ourselves worthy to receive the blessings He has prepared for us. In Leviticus 26:1-13, God outlines several promised blessings along with the requirements for receiving them. Firstly, He emphasizes the importance of avoiding idolatry, instructing not to make idols, set up images, or worship carved stones. Additionally, God emphasizes the significance of Sabbath observance and reverence for His sanctuary. Furthermore, He underscores the necessity of obedience to His decrees and commands.

God promises to provide rain in its season, ensuring fertile land and bountiful harvests. This abundance extends to food security and a life lived in safety on their own land. Additionally, God guarantees peace within the land, alleviating fear and providing a sense of security. Moreover, He pledges to rid the land of savage beasts, eliminating threats to physical safety. The absence of conflict is also assured, as the sword will not pass through the country. Furthermore, God promises to look upon His people with favor, bestowing His grace upon them. Finally, He vows to dwell among His people, offering His presence and protection.

These blessings are contingent upon obedience to God's commands and adherence to His decrees. Let us be careful to obey God's commands and follow His decrees so that all these promised blessings will be ours!

I WILL HELP YOU SPEAK AND WILL
TEACH YOU WHAT TO SAY

Now go; I will help you speak and will teach you what to say. Exodus 4:12

We would think Moses, having been raised by the princess of Egypt in the Palace of the Pharaoh, would be well with words. He might have learned to speak well and would have got special training to improve his communication skills. It is said of him, *"Moses was learned in all the wisdom of the Egyptians and was mighty in words and deeds." Acts 7:22*

When God called Moses to lead His people from the slavery of Egypt to the promised land of Canaan, he initially tried to evade God's call. He offered the excuse of poor communication skills, citing a stutter or stammer as a speech disorder. Although God could have healed Moses of his disability, He instead provided Aaron, Moses' brother, to serve as his mouthpiece. This act may have served to demonstrate that even with a disability, individuals can accomplish great things with God's assistance.

Despite Moses' continued pleas to be excused from the great commission, God grants him a helper, Aaron. Moreover, in *Exodus 4:15*, the Lord promises Moses: *"Now you shall speak to him and put the words in his mouth. And I will be with your mouth and with his mouth, and I will teach you what you shall do."* It is indeed remarkable how both Moses, despite his speech disorder, and Aaron, with presumably good communication skills, still relied on God's instruction on what to speak.

This underscores the importance of trusting in the Lord's guidance regardless of our abilities or limitations. Whether we are hesitant due to fear or uncertainty about our skills, we can find reassurance in God's promise to guide us and provide wisdom when we open our mouths to share His message, present our ideas, or proclaim our faith. Let us draw strength from God's assurance that God will teach us what to say.

Jesus has promised us the Holy Spirit, who will speak through us.

CROWN OF SPLENDOR IN THE LORD'S HAND

You will be a crown of splendor in the Lord's hand, a royal diadem in the hand of your God. Isaiah 62:3

A crown of splendor and a royal diadem in the hands of our Lord God signifies our magnificence and preciousness in His sight. Just as a crown glorifies a king, we are esteemed and valued by God. Defeating a king in battle involves claiming his crown. When we were sinners, we were under Satan's control. However, Jesus fought against Satan, paying the price with His own blood to redeem us from his grasp. Now, we are securely held in God's hands, and He is fashioning us into a magnificent crown.

A king cherishes his crown and guards it against any adversary. Similarly, we are securely held in God's hands, safe from any threat. Our Redeemer ensures that Satan will never reclaim us. Therefore, we need not fear anything or anyone, as we are precious to God, and He will glorify His name through us.

In the Old Testament, the high priest wore a crown inscribed with "Holy unto the Lord" as a symbol of his consecration (Leviticus 8:9). The anointing oil on the high priest's head also served as a crown (Leviticus 21:12). However, when the Israelites sinned and were taken captive to Babylon, Jeremiah lamented that their crown had fallen due to their transgressions (Lamentations 5:16).

God has bestowed upon us the titles of kings and priests, crowning us with the symbols of holiness and anointing. However, when we transgress against Him, we risk losing these crowns. The apostle Paul, in 2 Timothy 4:8, speaks of the "crown of righteousness" awaiting him, which the Lord, the righteous Judge, will grant not only to him but also to all who eagerly anticipate His return. This assurance confirms that we, too, will receive our "crown of righteousness."

This is how we can love God

If you love me, keep my commands. John 14:15

Whoever has my commandments and keeps them is the one who loves me. John 14:21

If anyone loves me, he will keep my word. John 14:23

If you keep my commandments, you will remain in my love. John 15:10

For this is the love of God, that we keep His commandments. 1 John 5:3

And this is love that we walk according to His commandments. This is the very commandment you have heard from the beginning that you must walk in love. 2 John 1:6

Indeed, the Apostle John, often referred to as "the disciple whom Jesus loved," emphasizes the correlation between loving God and obeying His commandments in his writings. This recurring theme underscores the significance of adhering to God's commandments as an expression of love towards Him.

Jesus taught that the entirety of God's commandments can be summarized in two fundamental principles: to love God with all our being and to love our neighbor as ourselves *(Matthew 22:37, 38, 40)*. These commandments encompass the essence of all moral and ethical teachings found in the Law and the Prophets.

Therefore, our love for God is demonstrated through obedience to His commandments and adherence to the teachings of Jesus. Loving God is achievable solely by obeying His commandments.

Do Not

Do not remember the former things

*Do not remember the former things, nor consider the things of old. Behold,
I will do a new thing, now it shall spring forth; shall you not know it? I will
even make a road in the wilderness and rivers in the desert. Isaiah 43:18, 19*

*If anyone is in Christ, he is a new creation. The old has passed away. Behold,
the new has come! 2 Corinthians 5:17*

Often, our minds gravitate towards past experiences, whether losses,
failures, or nostalgic memories, hindering our ability to embrace
the present and God's providence. However, God calls us to release the
burdens of the past and trust in His guidance for the present and future.

Even if we are burdened by past hurts, bad decisions, or injus-
tices, God invites us to relinquish these burdens and move forward in
His grace. *Isaiah 65:17* reassures us that the former things will not be
remembered, emphasizing God's promise of renewal. As believers, we
are encouraged to rejoice in the present, trusting in God's unchanging
nature and His plans for us, as stated in *Hebrews 13:8*.

Let us embrace the newness of being in Christ, and trust in His
unchanging nature as we journey forward with hope and faith.

Do not forsake your friends

Do not forsake your friend or a friend of your family, and do not go to your relative's house when disaster strikes you—better a neighbor nearby than a relative far away. Proverbs 27:10

A friend loves at all times, and a brother is born for adversity. Proverbs 17:17

These Scriptures from Proverbs underscore the paramount importance of friendship and provide practical guidance on how to nurture these relationships. It encourages us to actively embody friendship by being there for others, showing affection, and offering support in times of need.

We are reminded not to forsake our friends, family, or even the acquaintances of our parents, emphasizing the value of maintaining connections with those close to us, both in our immediate circles and within our extended networks. Central to this is the command to love our friends unconditionally and to extend the bond of brotherhood/ sisterhood to them, demonstrating care and compassion in all our interactions.

Moreover, we are urged to be a reliable source of assistance and encouragement, always ready to lend a helping hand when our friends require it. As we reflect on these principles, let us commit to being true friends, cultivating meaningful relationships built on love, loyalty, and mutual support, enriching our lives and the lives of those around us.

Just as Jesus has welcomed us as His friends, let us reciprocate by maintaining a close relationship with Him through prayer and obedience to His teachings. In doing so, we strengthen our bond with the ultimate Friend, finding solace and support in His unfailing love.

A man that has friends must show himself friendly: and there is a friend that sticks closer than a brother. Proverbs 18:24

Do not be afraid; you will not suffer shame

You will have plenty to eat until you are full, and you will praise the name of the Lord your God, who has worked wonders for you; never again will my people be shamed. Joel 2:26

Do not be afraid; you will not suffer shame. Do not fear disgrace; you will not be humiliated. You will forget the shame of your youth. Isaiah 54:4

Dignity is an important motivation. When we think that we are losing our dignity, we fear disgrace and we lose all hope in life. However, if our pride is in our Lord, we will not be put to shame.

Our dignity, when rooted in Him, shields us from despair even in the face of disgraceful situations. Despite moments of apparent disgrace, we can trust in God's grace, which ultimately lifts us from the depths of despair to positions of honor. Just as 1 Samuel 2:8 illustrates, God raises the downtrodden and blesses them with glory beyond measure. Therefore, in times of disgrace, we must turn to the Lord, knowing that He hears our cries and delivers us from fear. As Psalm 34:5 proclaims, those who seek the Lord radiate with His glory, unashamed in His presence.

Reflecting on the sufferings of Christ, we find solace in the assurance of future glory. Romans 8:18 reminds us that the present shame and disgrace pale in comparison to the glory that awaits us. Just as God elevated Jesus from the depths of shame to the highest seat of honor, He will likewise exalt us in due time. Therefore, let us not be consumed by present indignities but fix our gaze on the promise of eternal glory, trusting in the Lord's faithfulness to redeem and restore us.

The sufferings of this present time are not worthy to be compared with the glory which shall be revealed to us. Romans 8:18

Do not boast about tomorrow

Do not boast about tomorrow, for you do not know what a day may bring.
Proverbs 27:1

Come now, you who say, 'Today or tomorrow we will go to such and such
a city, spend a year there, buy and sell, and make a profit;'...Whereas you
do not know what will happen tomorrow. For what is your life? It is even
a vapor that appears for a little time and then vanishes away. Instead,
you ought to say, 'If the Lord wills, we shall live and do this or that.' But
now you boast in your arrogance. All such boasting is evil. James 4:13-16

In the accounts of Joshua and Esther, we see the profound impact of
preparing for tomorrow. In Joshua's time, the unexpected defeat at
the hands of their enemies revealed a need for sanctification. Through
God's guidance, they were instructed to rid themselves of any accursed
thing among them, paving the way for victory the next day. Similarly,
in Esther's story, the sinister plot of Haman backfired, leading to his
own demise and the exaltation of Mordecai. These narratives underscore the importance of addressing present issues to secure a better
future.

Jesus' words in Matthew 6:34 echo this sentiment, urging us not to
be consumed by worry about tomorrow. Instead, we are called to focus
on the present, dealing with the challenges of today while trusting in
God's provision for the future. Joshua's exhortation to "sanctify yourselves, for tomorrow the Lord will do wonders among you" reinforces
this principle. By aligning our lives with God's Word and seeking
sanctification today, we position ourselves to embrace the blessings
and victories that tomorrow holds.

As believers, we are called to anticipate a glorious future marked by
God's wonders and blessings. However, this future is intricately linked
to our actions and attitudes today. Therefore, let us commit ourselves
to sanctification, living according to the Word of God and walking
in obedience each day. By doing so, we can approach tomorrow with
confidence and joy, knowing that we have prepared ourselves to receive
all that God has in store for us.

Do not grieve, for the joy of the Lord is your strength

Nehemiah said, 'God and enjoy choice food and sweet drinks, and send some to those who have nothing prepared. This day is holy to our Lord. Do not grieve, for the Lord is your strength.' Nehemiah 8:10

Nehemiah's words in the Scripture above serve as a powerful reminder of the connection between joy and strength. As Nehemiah returned to Jerusalem from Babylon to rebuild the city's walls, he encountered a moment of solemnity when the people wept upon hearing the words of the Law read by Ezra. However, Nehemiah encouraged them to set aside their grief and instead rejoice in the Lord, emphasizing that this day was holy and that the joy of the Lord would be their strength.

Indeed, there are times when circumstances may lead us to sorrow, but it is in those moments that we must cling to God's grace, which sustains us and empowers us to overcome weakness. Our ability to find joy in the Lord, even amidst trials, is a testament to His faithfulness and goodness.

Furthermore, Nehemiah's directive to share with the less fortunate underscores the importance of not only experiencing joy ourselves but also extending it to others. By sharing our blessings with those in need, we not only alleviate their suffering but also provide them with a reason to rejoice in the Lord alongside us.

Let us heed Nehemiah's exhortation to embrace joy and share it with others, recognizing that the joy of the Lord is our strength. May we not only hear these words but also put them into action, knowing that it is through living out God's Word that we find true justification in His sight (Romans 2:13).

Do not slander one another

Brothers and sisters, do not slander one another. Anyone who speaks against a brother or sister or judges them speaks against the law and judges it. When you judge the law, you are not keeping it, but sitting in judgment on it. James 4:11

A straightforward directive to heed: "Abstain from slander." But what does it truly mean to slander someone? Slandering involves making false or damaging statements about others, tarnishing their reputation and causing harm. Even if the statements are not entirely false, they can still be damaging, leading to defamation and a negative perception of the person being discussed. So, why engage in such behavior? Isn't it akin to passing judgment?

The Bible explicitly warns against judging others, emphasizing that when we do so, we are not upholding the law but rather sitting in judgment of it *(Matthew 7:1)*. Who are we to pass judgment on someone else's servant? Ultimately, it is before the Lord that they stand or fall, as He alone has the authority to judge *(Romans 14:4)*.

We must be mindful of our words, knowing that we will be held accountable for each one uttered. Every word is recorded, and when they are replayed at the end of our earthly journey, may they reflect kindness and grace rather than slander and backbiting *(Matthew 12:37)*.

As believers, we are called to rid ourselves of all forms of negative speech, including anger, rage, malice, and slander *(Colossians 3:8)*. Instead, our conversations should be characterized by grace, seasoned with salt, uplifting and edifying those around us *(Colossians 4:6)*. In our interactions with others, let us focus on what is true, noble, right, pure, lovely, admirable, excellent, and praiseworthy, as urged in *Philippians 4:8*. By dwelling on such virtues, we cultivate a spirit of positivity and encouragement, fostering unity and harmony within the body of Christ.

For by your words, you will be acquitted, and by your words, you will be condemned. Matthew 12:37

Do not fear, little flock

Fear not, little flock, for it is your Father's good pleasure to give you the kingdom. Luke 12:32

In these words, Jesus assures us of the loving care and provision of our Heavenly Father. He knows the concerns that weigh on our hearts and the challenges we face. Whether it is the anxiety of a pending job interview, the worry over a test result, or the stress of daily life, He offers us His comforting presence and assurance.

As our Good Shepherd, Jesus understands our fears and anxieties, and He invites us to bring our burdens to Him. With tender care, He assures us of His provision and protection. No matter how small or insignificant we may feel, He reminds us that we are precious in His sight, and He delights in blessing us with His kingdom.

Despite our human limitations and vulnerabilities, we can take refuge in the promise that our Shepherd is also a King, and His kingdom knows no bounds. He leads us in paths of righteousness, protects us from harm, and grants us rest for our souls. With Him as our Shepherd-King, we lack nothing and have every reason to trust in His provision and care.

Even in the face of adversity, we can find comfort in knowing that we belong to God's kingdom. With His loving guidance and provision, we need not fear what tomorrow may bring. Instead, let us rest in the assurance that our Heavenly Father delights in granting us His kingdom and all the blessings that come with it. So, fear not, for our God is pleased to give us the kingdom, and in His kingdom, we find true peace and security. Amen! Praise the Lord!

Do not despise

As the ark of the Lord was entering the City of David, Michal, daughter
of Saul watched from a window. And when she saw King David leaping
and dancing before the Lord, she despised him in her heart. 2 Samuel 6:16

The Scriptures do not delve into whether King David held Michal's contempt against her, but it is clear that God did not view her attitude favorably. Michal, daughter of Saul, remained childless until her death—a poignant reminder for us today *(2 Samuel 6:23)*.

How often do we let contempt fester in our hearts towards our spouses, leading to discord and bitterness in our relationships? It is vital to recognize that harboring such feelings can hinder the blessings in our families. Instead, let us honor and respect our spouses, using our words and actions to build them up.

Moreover, the Scriptures warn us against despising others in various circumstances. We are cautioned not to scorn a thief compelled by hunger to steal for survival *(Proverbs 6:30)*, nor to reject the discipline or rebuke of the Lord *(Proverbs 3:11)*. Neglecting the care of our elderly mothers *(Proverbs 23:22)* or underestimating the significance of children *(Matthew 18:10)* are also admonished. Additionally, we are urged not to disregard prophecies and spiritual insights *(1 Thessalonians 5:20)*. These teachings emphasize compassion, empathy, and open-mindedness in our interactions.

Armed with these teachings, let us strive to cultivate hearts free from contempt and bitterness, embracing humility and love in our relationships. By doing so, we honor God and one another.

DO NOT SEEK REVENGE

It is mine to avenge; I will repay. Deuteronomy 32:35

"Tit for tat" is a common approach in our interactions. If someone doesn't invite us to an event, we might conveniently "forget" to include them when we host our own. When calls go unanswered, we reciprocate the silence. It is a basic form of retaliation ingrained in us, however small. Some might argue it is only natural, but should we not strive to rise above such instincts, which Jesus's sacrifice has redeemed us from? As believers, what difference do we make if we behave just like everyone else?

Yes, we've been wronged at times, but dwelling on thoughts of revenge only gives power to those who hurt us. Instead, let us move forward, releasing any desire for payback. The Scriptures repeatedly assure us that vengeance belongs to the Lord. Yet, there are moments when His timing seems slow, prompting us to cry out, like the Psalmist, *"O Lord, the God who avenges, shine forth" (Psalm 94:1)*.

Occasionally, vengeance seems within our grasp, tempting us to take matters into our own hands. Consider King Saul, whom David spared despite ample opportunity for revenge. David trusted in God's justice, refusing to harm the Lord's anointed *(1 Samuel 26:10-11)*. Similarly, we're urged not to retaliate but to leave room for God's wrath *(Romans 12:19)*. In fact, we're called to love our neighbors and refrain from seeking revenge *(Leviticus 19:18)*. Let us heed these reminders and resist the lure of retribution.

Do not seek revenge or bear a grudge against one of your people but love your neighbor as yourself. Leviticus 19:18

Do not fear the Egyptians

"Do not be afraid. Stand firm and you will see the deliverance the Lord will bring you today. The Egyptians you see today you will never see again."
Exodus 14:13

These words spoken to the Israelites echo through the ages, offering reassurance in moments of fear and uncertainty. When the Israelites fled Egypt, they faced imminent danger as Pharaoh's army pursued them. Fear gripped their hearts, leading to murmurs and complaints against Moses. But in the midst of their distress, God intervened, instructing them not to fear but to stand firm and witness His deliverance. He promised that the Egyptians they saw that day would vanish forever.

Similar trials confront us in life's journey. My spouse and I encountered our own "Egyptians" when we migrated to the US without jobs or insurance for eight months. The looming uncertainties weighed heavily on us, especially with a child on the way and the fragility of my husband's temporary job. Yet, in a moment of divine clarity during our family meditation, God spoke to us through *Exodus 14:13*. It became our anchor amidst the storm of fears—fears of job loss, financial strain, returning home empty-handed, and more. Clinging to God's promise, we prayed fervently, trusting in His faithfulness.

Remarkably, as we held fast to His word, our fears dissolved. His promise proved true, and we never faced those "Egyptians" again. Our testimony serves as a beacon of hope for those grappling with their own fears. Just as God assured the Israelites,

He assures us today: *"Do not be afraid. Stand firm and you will see the deliverance the Lord will bring you today. The Egyptians you see today you will never see again."* All His promises are Yea and Amen!

Do not let Him go unless He blesses you

Then the man said, 'Let me go, for it is daybreak.' But Jacob replied, 'I will not let you go unless you bless me.' Genesis 32:26

The passage depicts a profound moment in Jacob's life, where he wrestles with God Himself, refusing to let go until he receives a blessing. Despite his past actions of deceit and cunning to secure blessings, Jacob finds himself in a situation of fear and uncertainty, facing the imminent threat of his brother Esau's vengeance. In desperation, Jacob seeks God's intervention, acknowledging his need for divine favor to reconcile with his brother.

Throughout the night, Jacob wrestles with God, pouring out his heart in prayer, pleading for deliverance from his fears. As dawn approaches and God urges Jacob to release Him, Jacob resolutely declares, *"I will not let you go unless you bless me."* This poignant moment symbolizes Jacob's unwavering determination to receive God's blessing, regardless of the cost.

In response, God confronts Jacob's identity, making him acknowledge his past as a "cheater" by revealing his name's meaning. Yet, despite Jacob's flaws, God grants him the blessing he seeks, albeit with a physical reminder of his encounter—a lifelong limp. Jacob's tenacity in pursuing God's blessing serves as a poignant reminder for us today.

Just as Jacob wrestled with God, we are called to wrestle with Him in prayer, refusing to relent until we receive the blessings we need. Whether facing personal struggles or uncertainties about the future, we are encouraged to hold fast to God's promises, declaring, *"I will not let you go unless you bless me."* In doing so, we find assurance that God will indeed bless us according to His will, empowering us to face the challenges ahead with confidence and faith.

Do not be carried away by strange teachings

Do not be carried away by all kinds of strange teachings. Hebrews 13:9

This Scripture warns against being swayed by various strange teachings, emphasizing the importance of grounding ourselves in the foundational truths of our Christian faith *(2 Timothy 3:14-16)*. To discern these teachings, we must immerse ourselves in the Word of God through reading, meditation, study, and attentive listening.

Our faith should stand firm on the unshakable foundation of God's Word, not on human teachings. When discussing our beliefs, we should firmly root our responses in Scripture, asserting with confidence. Paul's counsel to Timothy underscores the necessity of continuing in the truths learned and assuring ourselves through a deep knowledge of the Scriptures *(2 Timothy 3:14-15)*. The Word of God serves as a source of wisdom, guiding us to salvation through faith in Christ Jesus *(John 5:39)*.

Indeed, all Scripture is inspired by God and profitable for teaching, rebuking, correcting, and training in righteousness *(2 Timothy 3:16)*. Confident in his faith, Paul declares, *"I am not ashamed, for I know whom I have believed" (2 Timothy 1:12)*.

We are urged to cling steadfastly to the doctrines we have embraced, mindful of teachings that distort the grace of God into worldliness *(Jude 1:4)*. At the core of our Christian foundation lies repentance, faith in God and Jesus Christ, water baptism, baptism in the Holy Spirit, and the hope of resurrection and eternal judgment *(Hebrews 6:1-2)*. Having established this foundation in our lives, let us press on toward maturity, striving to manifest the character of Christ within us *(Philippians 3:13-14)*.

With a firm grasp of God's Word, we are equipped to discern truth from error and to walk confidently in the path of righteousness.

Do not worry about your life

Therefore, I tell you, do not worry about your life, what you will eat or drink; or about your body, what you will wear. Is not life more important than food, and the body more important than clothes? Matthew 6:25

God's words above remind us not to be consumed by worry regarding our basic needs such as food, drink, and clothing. God, who is mindful of our fundamental necessities, has consistently provided for His creation. From the beginning, He clothed Adam and Eve and sustained the Israelites during their wilderness journey with miraculous provisions of food and water.

Throughout His ministry, Jesus emphasized the importance of spiritual sustenance over material concerns. He identified Himself as the Living Bread and Living Water, offering eternal nourishment to those who seek Him. Therefore, Jesus encourages us to trust in God's provision for our physical needs, knowing that He cares for us deeply.

Moreover, Jesus highlights the primacy of life and the body, underscoring the value of gratitude for the blessings of health and existence. While we acknowledge our basic needs, our primary focus should be on seeking God's Kingdom and spreading the gospel. By prioritizing spiritual matters, we align ourselves with God's will, and He graciously provides for our earthly needs *(Matthew 6:33)*.

Therefore, let us trust in God's abundant provision and devote ourselves to His Kingdom's advancement, knowing that He will supply all our needs according to His riches in glory.

Seek first the kingdom of God and His righteousness, and all these things shall be added to you. Matthew 6:33

DO NOT MERELY LISTEN TO THE WORD. DO WHAT IT SAYS

But be you doers of the word, and not hearers only, deceiving your own selves. James 1:22

For if any be a hearer of the word and not a doer, He is like unto a man beholding his natural face in a glass: For He beholds himself, and goes his way, and straightway forgets what manner of man He was. But whoso is not a forgetful hearer, but a doer of the work, this man shall be blessed in his deed. James 1:23-25

These Scriptures admonish us not to deceive ourselves by merely listening to the Word without putting it into action. It likens a mere hearer to someone who glances at their reflection in a mirror and then forgets what they look like. Conversely, a doer of the Word is likened to someone who looks intently into the perfect law of liberty and continues in it, being blessed in their deeds.

In his epistle, James provides practical instructions for Christian living, urging believers to respond actively to the Word they receive. These instructions include rejoicing in trials, seeking wisdom from God in faith, showing humility in both poverty and wealth, resisting temptation, exercising restraint in speech and anger, embracing the Word with meekness, controlling the tongue, caring for the vulnerable, and maintaining spiritual purity.

As recipients of God's Word, we are called not just to hear but to act upon its teachings. Let us heed James's exhortation to be doers of the Word, applying its principles to our lives with the help of God's grace. Through obedience to His Word, may we experience His blessings and fulfill His purposes in our lives.

DO NOT BE LIKE THE CHILDREN
IN THE MARKETPLACE

But whereunto shall I liken this generation? It is like unto children sitting in the markets, and calling unto their fellows, and saying, We have piped unto you, and you have not danced; we have mourned unto you, and you have not lamented. Matthew 11:16, 17

Jesus illustrates this point by highlighting the contrasting responses to John the Baptist and Himself. While John lived an ascetic lifestyle, abstaining from food and drink, some criticized him for being possessed by a demon. In contrast, when Jesus embraced a more sociable approach, eating and drinking with others, He was criticized for being a glutton and a drunkard.

Just as the children in the marketplace refused to participate in the games of their peers, some individuals exhibit a similar discontented spirit, finding fault with various expressions of religious practice. From traditional orthodox worship to lively praise and worship, they criticize every form of worship and show no desire to engage with fellow believers.

Jesus admonishes against such critical attitudes, emphasizing that both the stern warnings of John the Baptist and the teachings of love exemplified by Himself are essential aspects of proclaiming the Kingdom of God. He asserts that true wisdom will be recognized and accepted by all who are truly seeking God.

Therefore, instead of criticizing different approaches to faith, let us embrace the diversity of worship styles and unite in our common goal of repentance and experiencing the Kingdom of God.

DO NOT REVILE THE KING EVEN IN YOUR THOUGHTS

Do not revile the king even in your thoughts, or curse the rich in your bedroom, because a bird in the sky may carry your words, and a bird on the wing may report what you say. Ecclesiastes 10:20

For there is nothing covered, that shall not be revealed; neither hid, that shall not be known. What you have said in the dark will be heard in the daylight, and what you have whispered in the ear in the inner rooms will be proclaimed from the roofs. Luke 12:12, 13

The stone shall cry out of the wall, and the beam out of the timber shall answer it. Habakkuk 2:11

These Scriptures counsel against reviling authority figures and speaking ill of others, even in private, as our words may be heard and reported. They emphasize the accountability for our actions and words, cautioning that what is hidden will eventually be revealed. Even inanimate objects may bear witness to our deeds. The message extends to respecting and submitting to authority, recognizing that all power is ordained by God (*Romans 13:1, 2*).

Jesus serves as an example of humility and endurance, as depicted in *Isaiah 53:7*, where He endured oppression and affliction without complaint. Acknowledging our own unworthiness, we are urged to abstain from criticizing or complaining against God, both in our thoughts and deeds. Rather, let us adopt an attitude of appreciation and respect for our King. Despite life's challenges, let us trust in God's plan, knowing that His intentions are for our benefit.

"Come, let us bow down in worship, let us kneel before the Lord our Maker."
Psalm 95:6

Do not be yoked together with unbelievers

Do not be unequally yoked together with unbelievers. For what fellowship has righteousness with lawlessness? And what communion has light with darkness? And what accord has Christ with Belial? Or what part has a believer with an unbeliever? And what agreement has the temple of God with idols? You are the temple of the living God and He has said 'I will dwell in them.' 'Come out from among them and be separate, says the Lord. Do not touch what is unclean, and I will receive you.' 2 Corinthians 6:14-17

The passage questions the compatibility of righteousness with law-lessness, light with darkness, and Christ with Belial. It emphasizes the separation between believers and unbelievers, urging believers to avoid association with idolatry and impurity. Paul's letter to the Corinthians extends this principle beyond marriage, cautioning against being yoked with unbelievers in all relationships. The passage underscores the importance of maintaining distinctiveness from the world, as exemplified by the Israelites and Jews who dwelled apart from other nations due to their unique laws and customs.

In *1 Corinthians 7:16*, Paul advises against entering into marriages with unbelievers under the assumption of saving them through good conduct, highlighting the uncertainty of such endeavors. Similarly, *Acts 2:40* urges believers to separate themselves from the untoward generation, aligning with the biblical narrative of God's people being distinct in their way of life. *Numbers 23:9* and *Esther 3:8* further highlight the Israelites' and Jews' distinctiveness..

As God's chosen people, we are called to uphold our identity as a holy nation, proclaiming God's praises and remaining faithful to our calling as God's own special people (1 Peter 2:9).

But you are a chosen generation, a royal priesthood, a holy nation, His own special people, that you may proclaim the praises of Him who called you out of darkness into His marvelous light. 1 Peter 2:9

Do not let your heart envy

"Do not let your heart envy sinners, but always be zealous for the fear of the Lord. There is surely a future hope for you, and your hope will not be cut off." Proverbs 23:17, 18

Do not fret because of evildoers, Nor be envious of the workers of iniquity. For they shall soon be cut down like the grass, And wither as the green herb. Trust in the Lord, and do good. Psalm 37:1-3

Throughout the Bible, various passages warn against the dangers of envy: Psalm 37:1 cautions against envying the wicked, Proverbs 3:31 advises against envying oppressors, Proverbs 23:17 counsels against envy of sinners, 1 Corinthians 13:4 highlights that love is not envious, and Galatians 5:26 urges us not to seek vain glory or provoke envy in one another.

Instead of allowing envy to consume us, we are encouraged to appreciate the blessings bestowed upon us by God and to trust in His plan for our lives. Ultimately, the prosperity of the wicked and the challenges faced by the righteous are temporary, and those who remain blameless and upright find peace in the future (Psalm 37:37). Furthermore, loving our neighbors as ourselves plays a pivotal role in eliminating the space for envy, underscoring the significance of love in our relationship with others and with God.

Mark the blameless man, and observe the upright; For the future of that man is peace. Psalm 37:37

Do not be conformed to this world

And do not be conformed to this world, but be transformed by the renewing of your mind, that you may prove what is that good and acceptable and perfect will of God. Romans 12:2

Many of us wonder how to discern God's will in our lives. The Scripture above teaches that by resisting conformity to the world and allowing our minds to be transformed, we will understand God's perfect will for us.

Ephesians 4:17-32 serves as a call to action, urging us to live differently from the world around us. We are reminded to shed our old selves, characterized by deceitful desires and indulgence in impurity, and to embrace our new identity in Christ. As members of one body, we are called to truthfulness, righteous anger, and productive labor, rather than giving in to sinful tendencies or allowing bitterness and malice to take root in our hearts. Instead, we are encouraged to speak words that build others up and to cultivate a spirit of forgiveness and compassion, reflecting the love and forgiveness we have received from God.

These instructions guide us toward a transformed mindset, aligned with the will of God, and away from conformity to worldly patterns. Let us heed this call to action, striving for renewed minds to live lives that honor God.

Do not give free rein to your complaint

For the arrows of the Almighty are within me; My spirit drinks in their poison; The terrors of God are arrayed against me. Does the wild donkey bray when it has grass, Or does the ox low over its fodder? Job 6:4, 5

My soul loathes my life; I will give free course to my complaint; I will speak in the bitterness of my soul. Job 10:1

Job, known for his blamelessness and fear of God, voiced his complaints to God when faced with unimaginable trials. While we may empathize with Job's plight, it is essential to acknowledge that our own situation pales in comparison, and thus we cannot justify our complaints.

Some people appear to find fault in every facet of life—be it the weather, timing, abundance, scarcity, or relationships. The litany of their grievances seems never-ending. What sorts of grievances do we commonly voice? And does complaining fulfill any meaningful purpose or provide any tangible benefits?

No! Often, those who incessantly complain are labeled as whiners, grumps, or moaners. They become irritable, snappy, and discontented. Regardless of favorable circumstances, some remain entrenched in a melancholic state, always finding something to gripe about. Such an attitude is contrary to godliness. Scripture instructs us to be grateful in all circumstances, to cultivate contentment.

"In everything give thanks; for this is the will of God in Christ Jesus for you" (1 Thessalonians 5:18).

"Do all things without complaining and disputing, that you may become blameless and harmless, children of God without fault in the midst of a crooked and perverse generation, among whom you shine as lights in the world" (Philippians 2:14-15).

Let us strive for contentment and gratitude, reflecting God's will.

DO NOT FEAR; FOR YOU WILL NOT BE PUT TO SHAME

"Fear not, for you will not be put to shame; And do not feel humiliated, for you will not be disgraced; But you will forget the shame of your youth, And the reproach of your widowhood you will remember no more." Isaiah 54:4

Fear, shame, humiliation, and disgrace are indeed formidable experiences. Many of us can recount moments when we've endured such trials. For some, these incidents leave lasting scars, instilling a perpetual fear of further shame or disgrace.

This verse speaks directly to those of us who harbor constant apprehension of humiliation. It signifies a lack of confidence, intimidation, and a reluctance to advocate for our rights, faith, or beliefs. We fear being singled out, criticized, or ostracized. Eventually, this fear can manifest as anger, leading us to withdraw from social circles and distance ourselves from loved ones, often succumbing to depression.

This is undoubtedly one of Satan's cunning tactics, as he understands that by instilling even a hint of doubt, he can lead some of us away from the life we've found in Christ. His efforts are made easier if we are unaware of the promises outlined in the Word of God. Armed with knowledge of Scripture, we can stand firm and rebuke him in the Name of Jesus!

It is imperative that we immerse ourselves in Scripture and commit key verses to memory for everyday use. Doing so equips us to thwart the devil's attempts to instill fear in us.

Let us personalize the above verse: I will not succumb to fear, for I will not be put to shame. I refuse to feel humiliated, as I will not be disgraced. I choose to forget the shame of my past and will no longer remember the reproach I have endured.

Do not love the world and the
things in the world

Love is not the world, nor the things that are in the world. If any man loves the world, the love of the Father is not in him. For all that is in the world, the lust of the flesh, and the lust of the eyes, and the pride of life, is not of the Father but is of the world. And the world passes away, and the lust thereof: but he that does the will of God stays forever. 1 John 2:15-17

Upon reflection, it is clear that many of us are drawn to worldly possessions. Whether it is shoes, bags, watches, or other material goods, we often find ourselves desiring more. However, these desires are fleeting, as described in the scripture. They represent vain pursuits that require restraint.

The counsel given by the Apostle Paul to Timothy reinforces this idea: *"Godliness with contentment is great gain. We brought nothing into the world, and we can take nothing out of it. But if we have food and clothing, we will be content with that" (1 Timothy 6:6-8).* It is evident that the lust of the flesh, the lust of the eyes, and the pride of life are pursuits of the world, not aligned with the Father's will.

To truly love the Father, we must acknowledge and renounce our attachment to worldly things. Let us reflect on this conviction, seeking forgiveness for our transgressions and guidance to resist the allure of material possessions. May we use the resources bestowed upon us in a manner that pleases God, avoiding the repetition of these mistakes. Let us collectively seek strength and guidance to prioritize our love for God above all else, resisting the temptations of worldly possessions.

Do not fret

Do not fret because of evildoers, Nor be envious of the workers of iniquity.
Psalm 37:1

Many individuals find themselves consumed by worry over the misdeeds of others. They fret and grieve, unable to shake the thoughts from their minds. This verse advises against allowing the actions of evildoers to disturb our own lives. Instead, we are encouraged to show concern and offer prayers for them. Dwelling on the wickedness of others leaves us little room for joy and distracts us from living in harmony with God.

Psalms 37 further emphasizes, *"Fret not thyself because of him who prospereth in his way, because of the man who bringeth wicked devices to pass"*. Even if evildoers appear to prosper while the righteous face challenges, we are reminded not to fret over this discrepancy. While it is natural to feel concern and earnestly pray for God's intervention, there is no need to lose our peace of mind. Jesus himself urged, *"Let not your heart be troubled; you believe in God, believe also in Me" (John 14:1)*. Fretting contradicts the peace God intends for us, as He desires us to remain calm and composed even amidst trials.

Fretting achieves nothing and only undermines our peace. Instead, strive to find happiness despite the challenges posed by enemies. Trust that God will assist you—His support is more than sufficient. When we fret, we question God's care for us. Remember the promise of *Psalm 55:22: "Cast your cares on the Lord and he will sustain you; he will never let the righteous be shaken"*. Let us endeavor to relinquish fretting and find solace in God's promise to sustain us through all challenges.

BEAUTY REGIMEN

BEAUTY REGIMEN – A GENTLE AND QUIET SPIRIT

Your beauty should not come from outward adornment, such as braided hair and the wearing of gold jewelry and fine clothes. Instead, it should be that of your inner self, the unfading beauty of a gentle and quiet spirit, which is of great worth in God's sight. 1 Peter 3:3, 4

The scripture from *1 Peter 3:3-4* reminds us that true beauty stems not from outward adornments, such as elaborate hairstyles or extravagant jewelry and clothing, but rather from the inner self—a beauty that is enduring and precious in the eyes of God. Let us, therefore, take a moment to examine ourselves and see if we have indeed adorned ourselves with the *"unfading beauty of a gentle and quiet spirit."*

Regrettably, upon this reflection, many of us may find ourselves lacking in this quality. Too often, we find ourselves responding defensively, engaging in arguments, or resorting to conflict and chaos. Contrastingly, our Lord Jesus Christ stands as the epitome of this unfading beauty. Described in *Isaiah 53:7* as oppressed and afflicted, He remained silent, displaying a serene composure akin to a lamb before its shearers. The Gospel accounts further attest to His quiet strength in the face of accusation and interrogation, where He chose silence over defense, leaving even Pilate astonished.

Apostle Paul, in *Philippians 4:5*, exhorts believers to let their gentle spirit be known to all. Indeed, this gentle spirit bears its own reward, as *Proverbs 22:4* tells us—the reward of wealth, honor, and life, in addition to its intrinsic beauty. Furthermore, a gentle spirit offers us the gift of rest—a serene and tranquil beauty that rejuvenates the soul. Why not earnestly desire this rest with all our hearts?

Cultivating inner beauty demands intentional effort in nurturing a gentle and quiet spirit, as urged by Jesus in *Matthew 11:28-29*. As we ready ourselves to meet our Bridegroom, Jesus Christ, let us prioritize this development alongside our outward adornment. Let us aim to reflect His likeness by adorning ourselves with the enduring beauty of gentleness and tranquility.

BEAUTY REGIMEN – FEAR OF THE LORD

Charm is deceptive, and beauty is fleeting, but a woman who fears the Lord is to be praised. Proverbs 31:30

Let us delve into how embracing the fear of the Lord enhances our beauty. Similar to how a beauty regimen entails a planned routine for our physical appearance, our spiritual beauty thrives through humility and reverence for God, as stated in *Proverbs 22:4: "By humility and the fear of the Lord are riches, and honor, and life."* Furthermore, *Proverbs 1:7* emphasizes that the fear of the Lord is the cornerstone of knowledge, while *Proverbs 15:33* underscores its role as the foundation of wisdom.

So, how do we cultivate this fear of the Lord?

Proverbs 2:1-5 provides us with a clear roadmap, urging us to wholeheartedly accept and internalize God's teachings and commandments. It emphasizes the importance of actively engaging with wisdom and understanding, encouraging us to listen attentively and apply our hearts to discerning their truths. This passage motivates us to passionately seek insight and understanding, likening our quest to a diligent search for precious treasures, where every effort is dedicated to uncovering hidden riches. Through this devoted pursuit of wisdom and understanding, we are assured of developing a profound reverence for the Lord and deepening our knowledge of His ways.

By immersing ourselves in the Word of God—meditating on it, learning from it, and obediently following its commandments—we will not only acquire the fear of the Lord but also be adorned with spiritual beauty. And as we are clothed in this divine beauty, our Lord Jesus Christ will lovingly gaze upon us and declare, *"All beautiful you are, my darling; there is no flaw in you" (Song of Solomon 4:7).*

Let us, therefore, embrace this journey of spiritual enrichment and allow the fear of the Lord to transform us from within.

Beauty Regimen – Wardrobe Makeover

*As God's chosen people, holy and dearly loved, clothe yourselves with com-
passion, kindness, humility, gentleness, and patience. Bear with each other
and forgive whatever grievances you may have against one another. Forgive
as the Lord forgave you. And over all these virtues put on love, which binds
them all together in perfect unity. Colossians 3:12-14*

Today's Bible verse reminds us that as God's chosen people, we are
not only holy and dearly loved but also called to embody virtues
beyond ourselves. We are summoned to clothe ourselves with compassion, kindness, humility, gentleness, and patience. In doing so, we can
bear with one another and forgive as the Lord forgives us.

Furthermore, Apostle Paul urges us to adorn ourselves with love,
the virtue that binds all others in perfect unity. God lavishes upon
us garments of spiritual significance, dressing us to be worthy of our
union with Jesus Christ: *Isaiah 61:10* tells us that He clothes us with
the garments of salvation and covers us with the robe of righteousness.
Zechariah 3:4 illustrates how God removes our iniquitous garments
and replaces them with rich robes. *Revelation 3:5* promises that those
who triumph in Christ will be clothed in white garments. *Revelation
19:8* speaks of fine linen, symbolizing the righteous deeds of the saints.

To be pleasing to our bridegroom, Jesus, let us clothe ourselves
not only with these virtues but also with the garments God provides:
salvation, righteousness, deliverance, victory, and the righteousness
of our actions.

When adorned in this divine attire, Jesus will look upon us and
declare, *"You are all fair, my love; there is no spot in thee." (Song of Solomon 4:7)*

Let us, therefore, heed this call to action: Let us makeover our
wardrobe, filled with these beautiful bridal garments, and become the
bride of our Lord and Savior, Jesus Christ.

How to clothe ourselves with Jesus Christ?

Clothe yourselves with the Lord Jesus Christ, and do not think about how to gratify the desires of the sinful nature. Romans 13:14

Clothing ourselves with the Lord Jesus Christ entails more than a physical act; it involves adopting His mindset, emulating His behavior, and aligning ourselves with His values. Clarke's commentary on the Bible suggests that being clothed with a person means embracing their perspective, living in accordance with their principles, and standing firmly with them.

In *Galatians 3:27*, Scripture symbolically portrays baptism as being clothed with Christ. This signifies our commitment to live for Him, imitating His example, and growing in likeness to Him each day. In essence, wearing Christ means striving to live as He lived and to reflect His character in all aspects of our lives.

In Colossians chapter 3, the Apostle Paul provides guidance on living a Christ-centered life. He advises believers to focus on heavenly things, put to death earthly desires, and embrace virtues such as compassion and forgiveness. Paul emphasizes the importance of reflecting Christ's love in all aspects of life, urging believers to live in gratitude and obedience to God.

Finally, Paul emphasizes that whatever we do, whether in word or deed, should be done in the name of the Lord Jesus, with a heart filled with gratitude to God. This highlights the overarching principle of living a life that honors and glorifies God in every aspect, acknowledging His sovereignty and goodness in all things.

Let us prioritize heavenly things, forsake earthly desires, and reflect Christ's love in all we do. May we live each day clothed in Jesus Christ.

FLAWLESS BEAUTY

You are altogether beautiful, my love; there is no flaw in you. Song of Solomon 4:7

This verse holds a universal truth that speaks to the intrinsic beauty and perfection within each individual. It conveys a message of unconditional love and acceptance from God, affirming the inherent worthiness of every person. It is a reminder of the beauty that resides within us all, despite any perceived flaws or imperfections.

While we may easily enumerate our flaws, God's love transcends our imperfections. One might wonder if these are the very words Jesus speaks as He advocates for us before the Father, asserting our flawlessness. Though we may see our flaws, Jesus sees the sanctification process and the ultimate perfection we will attain. Our journey involves submitting to Jesus for sanctification.

In *Malachi 3:3*, we're likened to precious metals refined by fire. Just as a refiner purifies gold or silver to reflect his image, Jesus refines us through the trials we face until we reflect His character. When we become more like Jesus, we become flawless.

Consider Esther, who underwent an extensive purification process before meeting the earthly king. If such preparation was necessary for an earthly bride, how much more should we, the bride of Jesus, undergo sanctification? Only through this process can we be accepted by Jesus as His beloved, flawless bride.

Let us embrace the sanctification journey, knowing that through it, we become more beautiful and flawless in the eyes of our loving Savior.

BEAUTY FOR ASHES

Provide for those who grieve in Zion--to bestow on them a crown of beauty instead of ashes, the oil of gladness instead of mourning, and a garment of praise instead of a spirit of despair. Isaiah 61:3

As humanity faces various crises and upheavals, whether global, regional, or personal, the aftermath often leaves lives changed forever. Many endure loss of stability, livelihoods, and loved ones, their pain seemingly insurmountable.

Yet, for those who find solace in their faith, there remains hope amid adversity. Through prayer and meditation, they seek refuge at the feet of the Divine, finding comfort and peace beyond comprehension in His words.

In times of distress, the call to *"put on our strength and our beautiful garments"* echoes through the ages. Our strength, derived from God, sustains us through the darkest hours. Like King David, we declare, *"The Lord is the strength of my life; of whom shall I be afraid?" (Psalms 27:1)* To *"put on our strength"* is to anchor ourselves in God, finding hope and confidence in His presence.

Traditionally, mourners would clothe themselves in sackcloth and sit among ashes. However, God promises transformation for His grieving people—a crown of beauty instead of ashes, the oil of gladness instead of mourning, and a garment of praise instead of a spirit of despair.

The prophet Isaiah rejoices in the Lord, acknowledging that God clothes His people with the garments of salvation and righteousness *(Isaiah 61:10).* It is God who adorns us with these beautiful garments.

When we lean on the Lord as our strength and embrace the garments of praise, salvation, and righteousness bestowed by Him, we exchange ashes for beauty, mourning for gladness, and despair for praise. Amen!

ARE WE BEAUTIFUL?

*You are altogether beautiful, my darling; there is no flaw in you. Song of
Solomon 4:7*

Throughout the Bible, we encounter accounts of women celebrated for their beauty, such as Sarah, Abigail, Rachel, Tamar,
and Queen Vashti. Undoubtedly, beauty holds significance for every
woman, prompting us to invest time and effort in our appearance.

Yet, as we aspire for beauty, it is vital to align our standards with
those set by the Lord. Scripture reminds us that true beauty transcends
external adornments like elaborate hairstyles, gold jewelry, or fine
clothing. Instead, it emanates from within—the unfading beauty of
a gentle and quiet spirit, esteemed greatly in God's eyes *(1 Peter 3:3-4)*.

In *Proverbs 31:30*, we learn that charm is deceitful, and beauty is
transient. However, a woman who fears the Lord merits praise. Thus,
the essence of beauty lies in our reverence for God and the cultivation
of inner virtues.

Let us reflect: Do we possess the enduring beauty of a gentle and
quiet spirit? Do we truly fear the Lord? If so, then indeed, we embody
true beauty. But if uncertainty lingers, let us embark on a 'beauty
regimen' focused on nurturing a gentle spirit and cultivating the fear
of the Lord in our hearts. For in doing so, we embrace the beauty that
surpasses fleeting outward appearances and reflects the heart's true
radiance in God's sight.

A WOMAN WHO FEARS THE LORD IS TO BE PRAISED

Charm is deceitful and beauty is passing, but a woman who fears the Lord, she shall be praised. Proverbs 31:30

In a world where beauty standards often prioritize external appearances, this verse serves as a poignant reminder of true beauty's foundation: the fear of the Lord. While many invest considerable time, energy, and resources in enhancing physical appearance, Scripture emphasizes the enduring value of a woman who reveres God.

Humility and the fear of the Lord are linked, as noted in *Proverbs 22:4*, highlighting the significance of a humble spirit in cultivating inner beauty. This stands in contrast to societal norms that often celebrate boldness and assertiveness. However, the Word of God calls for a demeanor characterized by calmness, composure, and humility.

Apostle Paul urges believers to reject conformity to worldly standards and instead embrace transformation through the renewal of the mind *(Romans 12:2)*. He further emphasizes virtues such as compassion, kindness, humility, gentleness, and patience *(Colossians 3:12)*, underscoring the importance of inner qualities over external adornments.

Indeed, the Scriptures remind us that true beauty emanates from within, specifically from a gentle and quiet spirit, which holds immense value in God's sight *(1 Peter 3:3-4)*. Rather than focusing on outward embellishments like hairstyles, jewelry, or clothing, the emphasis is placed on nurturing a character marked by gentleness and tranquility.

As we navigate the pressures of societal beauty standards, let us prioritize cultivating the inner beauty that stems from reverence for the Lord. By embracing humility, gentleness, and a quiet spirit, we reflect the beauty that truly matters in God's eyes.

RESTORATION

I will restore you that you may serve Me

This is what the Lord says: 'If you repent, I will restore you that you may serve me...' Jeremiah 15:19

The Lord declares, 'If you repent, I will restore you so that you may serve me.' This promise signifies that God pledges to revive us for His service, contingent upon our repentance.

Implicit in the promise of restoration is the acknowledgment that we once served Him but have since faltered. Pride, doubt, fear, unbelief, and impenitence have hindered our service. However, God assures us that upon recognizing our faults and repenting, He will reinstate us for His service. Serving the Lord is the ultimate honor; thus, prompt repentance is urged.

The story of the prodigal son, found in Luke 15:12-24, illustrates this principle vividly. The son squandered his inheritance in reckless living, only to repent when he had nothing left. Despite feeling unworthy, his father's love and compassion led to a joyous reunion and restoration of his status as a beloved son.

The father's boundless love mirrors the infinite grace of our Heavenly Father, who eagerly welcomes us back when we repent and seek forgiveness. Our relationship with God is renewed, and we regain the privilege and blessing of serving Him. Let us rejoice in His mercy and grace. Praise the Lord.

I will restore David's fallen tent

I will restore David's fallen tent. I will repair its broken places, restore its ruins, and build it as it used to be. Amos 9:11

In our contemporary era, many families are fracturing due to the pressures of work, sinful behavior, addictions, and selfishness. These are the devil's strategies, slowly corroding the harmony and peace within family units. His aim is to dismantle the family nucleus, making it easier to lead its members away from the Lord. While the devil seeks to sow discord in families, our Lord specializes in restoring broken families and reestablishing what has fallen. *Isaiah 58:12* depicts our Lord as the *"Repairer of Broken Walls, Restorer of Streets with Dwellings."*

Reflecting on Israel's history, we witness the fall of David's tent during the Babylonian captivity, resulting in the dissolution of Judah's kingdom. Even upon the Jews' return from Babylon and the reconstruction of the Temple, the kingdom of David remained elusive. However, the promise of God awaits the Restorer of David's tent, Jesus Christ.

Though some anticipated Jesus to revive David's earthly kingdom, His divine plan transcended earthly realms. As Jesus explained to His disciples, His kingdom was not of this world. While born into David's lineage, crucified and resurrected as the King of all humanity, Jesus inaugurated a new kingdom during His earthly ministry—the Church, over which He reigns as King, building and restoring this unseen kingdom. Upon His return, Jesus will reign over the earthly kingdom of David alongside His Church, ushering in an era of peace and righteousness. This fulfills God's promise: *"I will restore David's fallen tent."*

This promise extends to our broken families. Let us fervently pray for peace and restoration within our households, assured that He will mend our brokenness, repair our shattered places, and rebuild what has been lost. All praise, glory, and honor belong to Jesus Christ, our ultimate Restorer.

I WILL RESTORE TWICE AS MUCH TO YOU

Even now I announce that I will restore twice as much to you. Zechariah 9:12

Instead of their shame, my people will receive a double portion, and instead of disgrace they will rejoice in their inheritance, and so they will inherit a double portion in their land, and everlasting joy will be theirs. Isaiah 61:7

Consider the story of Job, a man of great wealth and honor, known for his righteousness and compassion towards others. Suddenly, tragedy struck. He lost all his possessions, his children, and his health. Despite enduring immense suffering and being ostracized by those around him, Job remained faithful. In the end, God not only delivered him from his afflictions but also bestowed upon him double the blessings he had before.

Similarly, Joseph's journey was fraught with adversity. Sold into slavery by his own brothers, he rose to prominence in Egypt. Despite facing seemingly insurmountable odds, God orchestrated events that reunited him with his family and granted him a double portion of blessings.

These stories exemplify God's faithfulness to those who trust in Him. Today, we can claim the promise of restoration and receive a double portion of blessings. Just as Elisha desired double the spiritual gifts of Elijah and saw his request fulfilled, we too can personalize and claim today's promise of restoration.

God's promises are unwavering—always *"yes"* and *"Amen."* Let us trust in His faithfulness and embrace the abundant blessings He has in store for us.

Restoring the Sabbath of our Lord

'Remember the Sabbath day, to keep it holy.' Exodus 20:8

Nehemiah, having returned from Babylonian captivity, under-took the monumental task of rebuilding the walls of Jerusalem. Despite the challenges he faced, Nehemiah was committed to restoring obedience to the Lord's commandments among the people.

Upon observing that the Sabbath was being disregarded, with merchants conducting business as usual, Nehemiah took decisive action. *Nehemiah 13:15-22* details how Nehemiah ordered the city gates to be closed before the Sabbath, preventing traders from entering or leaving. Nehemiah confronted the nobles engaged in trading on the Sabbath, reminding them of the consequences their forefathers faced for desecrating the Sabbath. Nehemiah stationed servants at the gates to enforce Sabbath observance and instructed the Levites to purify themselves and serve as gatekeepers, sanctifying the Sabbath day.

As believers today, we should reflect on whether we are truly observing God's designated day for worship or merely debating whether the Sabbath falls on Saturday or Sunday. Regardless of the day, *Psalm 118:24* reminds us to rejoice and be glad in it, dedicating it to worshiping God. *Leviticus 23:3* emphasizes the Sabbath as a day of rest, distinct from the other six days of labor.

Let us honor the Lord by abstaining from our own work, seeking our own pleasure, and refraining from idle talk on the sacred Sabbath day, as instructed *in Isaiah 58:13-14.*

I WILL RESTORE JUDGES AS IN THE DAYS OF OLD

I will restore your judges as at the first and your counselors as at the beginning. Afterward, you shall be called the city of righteousness, the faithful city. Isaiah 1:26

When the Israelites inherited the land of Canaan, Joshua divided it among the twelve tribes, without kings to rule over them. In times of conflict, God raised judges to lead and deliver His people from their enemies *(Judges 2:18)*. This period lasted for roughly 500 years until the time of Prophet Samuel. Subsequently, the people, desiring a monarchy, sought a king to rule over them, leading to a transition from judges to kingship that endured for approximately 160 years.

Following the Babylonian captivity, however, Israel found itself without judges or kings. Yet, amidst this uncertainty, God's promise echoed through Isaiah, assuring the Israelites of the restoration of judges as in times past. In the New Testament, Jesus imparted a profound promise to His twelve disciples, declaring, *'You who have followed Me will also sit on twelve thrones, judging the twelve tribes of Israel.' (Matthew 19:28)* Apostle Paul also proclaimed the role of saints in judging the world. *(1 Corinthians 6:2)*

Jesus Christ Himself embodies the ultimate Judge, as evidenced by various Scriptures. In *2 Timothy 4:8,* we are reminded of the righteous judgment of the Lord, who will award the crown of righteousness to those who await His return. Likewise, *Revelation 22:12* emphasizes Jesus' imminent return, bringing rewards according to individuals' deeds. Acting as a reminder of God's sovereignty, Acts 17:31 speaks of a future day of judgment, where God, through Jesus, will judge the world in righteousness. In essence, the judges appointed by God, whether human or divine, hold a significant role in guiding and assessing His people throughout history.

As we ponder the legacy of judges, including Christ, let us embrace our duty to uphold righteousness and justice, advancing God's kingdom on earth as it is in heaven.

HE WILL RESTORE THE FORTUNES OF JACOB'S TENTS

This is what the Lord says: 'I will restore the fortunes of Jacob's tents and have compassion on his dwellings...' Jeremiah 30:18

Jeremiah prophesied the return of Israel from Babylonian captivity, envisioning the rebuilding of the Temple and the restoration of Jerusalem's walls. God promises to bring the Israelites back from Babylon, reestablishing them in their dwellings and reviving worship in the Temple. Reflecting on the beauty of Jacob's tents, as proclaimed by Balaam in *Numbers 24:5*, God assures that He will show compassion and restore their fortunes.

Today's message echoes this promise of restoration for our own lives. In times of economic downturn or uncertainty, trusting in the Lord alleviates panic. Just as Scripture promises, God cares for our dwellings and will restore our fortunes.

Our faith lies in the Lord, our eternal Supplier, whose abundance never runs dry *(Psalm 104:28)*. *Matthew 6:25-34* reminds us that our heavenly Father knows our needs and urges us not to worry. As Peter instructs, we are encouraged to cast all our anxiety on Him, for He cares for us *(1 Peter 5:7)*.

The tents of the righteous resound with rejoicing and salvation *(Psalm 118:15)*. Let us reflect on these verses and pray for the restoration of our faith and the prosperity of our homes. Shall we?

I WILL RESTORE YOU TO HEALTH
AND HEAL YOUR WOUNDS

'I will restore you to health and heal your wounds,' declares the Lord, 'because you are called an outcast Zion for whom no one cares.' Jeremiah 30:17

This message brings hope to the sick among us. Take heart, for the Lord has promised to restore our health and heal our wounds. As Prophet Isaiah foretold concerning Christ the Lord, *"He was pierced for our transgressions, he was crushed for our iniquities; the punishment that brought us peace was upon him, and by His wounds, we are healed."* *(Isaiah 53:5)* Amen! By His wounds, we are healed.

When interceding for loved ones who are ill, we can envision the power of the blood shed on the cross, applying it over them. Likewise, in prayers for our households, we can visualize the cleansing and protection offered by the shed blood of Jesus Christ, covering doorsteps, rooms, territories, and beyond.

What good is our Christian faith if we merely speak of healing without truly believing it for ourselves? Would we not eagerly seek out and apply a new ointment promising healing? Then why hesitate to embrace the healing power of Christ our Lord with even greater fervor?

Reflect on the parable of the Good Samaritan *(Luke 10:32-33)*. Just as the Samaritan showed compassion by binding the wounds of the injured man, pouring oil and wine, and caring for him, Jesus Christ, our Good Samaritan, binds and heals our wounds. Amen.

In *Jeremiah 3:22*, God promises to cure us of backsliding, considering it a wound as well. He declares, *"I will bring health and healing to it; I will heal my people and will let them enjoy abundant peace and security."* *(Jeremiah 33:6)*

Let us echo the prayer of Jeremiah: *"Heal me, O Lord, and I will be healed."* *(Jeremiah 17:14)*

LET US

LET US GO TO THE HOUSE OF THE LORD

I rejoiced with those who said to me, 'Let us go to the house of the Lord.'
Psalm 122:1

One thing I ask of the Lord, this is what I seek: that I may dwell in the
house of the Lord all the days of my life, to gaze upon the beauty of the
Lord and to seek him in his temple. Psalm 27:4

The call to gather in the house of the Lord resonates deeply with believers worldwide, reflecting the shared joy and privilege of coming together as God's people. While the house of the Lord extends beyond physical buildings to encompass the assembly of believers, the promise of Jesus to be present where two or three gather in His name underscores the significance of communal worship *(Matthew 18:20)*.

Neglecting the fellowship of believers is to overlook a divine privilege, for in coming together, we invite the tangible presence of God to fill our midst and usher in a sense of joy beyond measure. This gathering transcends physical boundaries, encompassing the unseen Church that God builds daily—a spiritual house where believers are likened to living stones, collectively forming a holy priesthood *(1 Peter 2:5)*.

Indeed, each believer is a temple of God, indwelt by His Spirit, calling us to maintain the sanctity of this dwelling place for the Divine. As we respond to the call to gather with gladness and singing, we embrace not only the fellowship of believers but also the sacred responsibility of honoring God's presence within us. Therefore, let us heed the invitation with hearts filled with gladness, joining together in worship and unity as we enter into the house of the Lord.

Enter his gates with thanksgiving and his courts with praise; give thanks
to him and praise his name. Psalm 100:4

LET US LOVE OUR ENEMIES

But I say to you who hear: Love your enemies, do good to those who hate you, bless those who curse you, and pray for those who spitefully use you. To him who strikes you on the one cheek, offer the other also. And from him who takes away your cloak, do not withhold your tunic either. Give to everyone who asks of you...Luke 6:27-36

The command to love our enemies, as articulated by Jesus, challenges the very essence of human nature. It calls for a radical shift in perspective—one rooted not in reciprocity but in unconditional love and grace. Despite its inherent difficulty, Jesus assures us that with God's help, loving our enemies is not only possible but also transformative.

In demonstrating love to our enemies, we mirror the divine love exemplified by Jesus Himself, who willingly sacrificed His life for those who opposed Him. His prayer for forgiveness even in the face of crucifixion underscores the depth of His love and serves as a model for our own actions.

By loving our enemies and praying for those who persecute us, we align ourselves with the character of our heavenly Father, who extends blessings without discrimination, showering both the righteous and the unrighteous with His provision and care. This divine love knows no bounds, transcending human understanding and expectations.

In striving to love our enemies, we aspire toward perfection, reflecting the boundless love of our heavenly Father. As we allow God to fill our hearts with His love, may we become vessels of His grace, extending forgiveness and compassion even to those who oppose us.

LET US REMEMBER THIS WHEN WE HARVEST

When you reap your harvest in your field, and forget a sheaf in the field, you shall not go back to get it; it shall be for the stranger, the fatherless, and the widow, that the Lord your God may bless you in all the work of your hands. When you beat your olive trees, you shall not go over the boughs again; it shall be for the stranger, the fatherless, and the widow. Deuteronomy 24:19, 20

Do not go over your vineyard a second time or pick up the grapes that have fallen. Leave them for the poor and the alien. I am the Lord your God. Leviticus 19:10

The verses remind us of God's compassion for the vulnerable, urging us to share our blessings with the less fortunate. We're called to ensure our harvest benefits others, not just ourselves. Generosity brings abundant blessings, reflecting our attitude towards God. Helping the poor honors Him and yields blessings, even if it seems uncertain at first. Let us be mindful of the needy in our abundance, knowing our kindness reverberates blessings.

The principle of giving and receiving, emphasized in *Luke 6:38* and *2 Corinthians 9:6*, reveals the reciprocal nature of generosity. By generously giving to those in need, we invite abundant blessings from God—a cycle reflecting His own generosity towards us. Additionally, our treatment of the poor mirrors our attitude towards God Himself. Proverbs 14:31 stresses that kindness towards the needy honors God, whereas neglecting them displays contempt for their Maker.

While assisting the poor may seem extravagant or impractical to some, Ecclesiastes 11:1 encourages us to have faith in God's provision. Just as casting bread upon the waters may appear uncertain, our acts of generosity ultimately lead to blessings in due time. Therefore, as we reflect on our harvest and financial blessings, let us remember to be generous toward the less fortunate, recognizing that our kindness honors God and results in abundant blessings.

He who is kind to the poor lends to the Lord, and he will reward him for what he has done. Proverbs 19:17

LET OUR WORDS BE A FEW

Do not be quick with your mouth, do not be hasty in your heart to utter anything before God. God is in heaven, and you are on earth, so let your words be few. Ecclesiastes 5:2

When words are many, sin is not absent, but he who holds his tongue is wise. Proverbs 10:19

Often, we tend to use more words than necessary when expressing ourselves, whether in prayer or conversation, believing that verbosity ensures our message is heard. However, Jesus cautioned against this in Matthew 6:7, warning against vain repetitions. Similarly, God rebuked Job for speaking without knowledge in Job 38:2. Jesus reassured His disciples that the Holy Spirit would speak for them, advising them not to worry about what to say in Mark 13:11.

The Holy Spirit advocates for us, conveying our prayers to God and speaking on our behalf. Rather than relying on our own multitude of words, we should trust in the Holy Spirit is guidance. By seeking the Holy Spirit is filling, we allow Him to speak through us both to others and to God. Let us pray for the Holy Spirit is presence in our lives, remembering the Psalmist's plea in *Psalm 19:14* for words acceptable to God. Those who fear the Lord converse with sincerity, knowing that He listens attentively *(Malachi 3:16).*

Lord, let the words of my mouth be acceptable in thy sight. Psalm 19:14

Those who fear the Lord speak one to another. The Lord listens to them. Malachi 3:16

LET US BE STILL AND KNOW THAT HE IS THE LORD

"Be still and know that I am Lord." Psalm 46:10

God calls us to be calm and still, trusting that He is actively working on our behalf. However, we often rush to solve our problems independently, only turning to God in desperation when our efforts fail. Yet, His message remains unchanged: "Be still," allowing Him to demonstrate His sovereignty.

Just as we would ask a child to be still when removing a thorn, God asks us to trust Him to alleviate our pain and fears. *Psalm 55:22* reassures us that if we cast our burdens upon the Lord, He will sustain us and keep us steadfast.

In *Luke 10:40*, Jesus reminds Martha that Mary chose the one necessary thing: sitting calmly at His feet and listening to His words. Similarly, we are encouraged to be still in God's presence, awaiting His guidance and comfort.

Let us pray for the wisdom to be still and witness God's glory unfolding in our lives. For the Lord of Hosts is our refuge *(Psalm 46:11)*, and He promises to fight for us if we remain still *(Exodus 14:14)*.

The Lord of Hosts is with us; The God of Jacob is our refuge. Psalm 46:11

The Lord will fight for you; you need only to be still. Exodus 14:14

LET US RESIST THE DEVIL

Resist the devil, and he will flee from you. James 4:7

The devil often operates with cunning subtlety, manifesting in various forms such as self-pity, temptation, depression, and weariness to erode our joy, faith, and spiritual well-being. It can be challenging to recognize his influence, but anything that detracts from our experience of salvation can be attributed to his schemes. Thus, it is crucial to resist his tactics promptly.

To resist the devil effectively, we must first submit ourselves to God, acknowledging His authority and sovereignty *(James 4:7)*. We should also remain self-controlled, alert, and vigilant, recognizing that the devil prowls around like a roaring lion, seeking to devour those who are vulnerable *(1 Peter 5:8)*. It is essential to stand firm in our faith, refusing to succumb to his lies and deceptions *(1 Peter 5:9)*.

Furthermore, we are encouraged to clothe ourselves with the full armor of God, which equips us to withstand the devil's attacks and schemes *(Ephesians 6:11)*. This spiritual armor includes elements such as truth, righteousness, faith, salvation, and the Word of God.

In resisting the devil, we can engage in practices such as prayer, fasting, and quoting Scripture. Jesus Himself exemplified this resistance during His temptation in the wilderness, where He countered the devil's lies with the truth of God's Word (Matthew 4:4, 7, 10). Additionally, certain kinds of spiritual strongholds can only be overcome through prayer and fasting *(Matthew 17:21)*.

Ultimately, we can overcome the devil's influence by relying on the power of the blood of the Lamb, Jesus Christ, and by testifying to His victory in our lives *(Revelation 12:11)*. Through prayer, the Word of God, and the indwelling presence of the Holy Spirit, we can stand firm against the devil's schemes and emerge victorious in spiritual warfare.

LET US GIVE CAREFUL THOUGHT TO OUR WAYS

Now, therefore, thus says the Lord of hosts: "Consider your ways! "You have sown much, and bring in little; You eat, but do not have enough; You drink, but you are not filled with drink; You clothe yourselves, but no one is warm; And he who earns wages, earns wages to put into a bag with holes." Haggai 1:5, 6

The destruction of the Temple in Jerusalem by the Babylonian king led to a period of captivity for the Jews. Upon their return after 70 years, Ezra laid the foundation to rebuild the Temple. However, after two years, the work halted. In response, God raised prophets like Haggai to encourage the people to resume building.

The lack of blessings in their lives was attributed to their neglect of building God's Temple. God pointed out their meager harvests, unfulfilled satisfaction, and fleeting wealth as consequences of their indifference towards His dwelling place. Instead, they prioritized their own comfort, dwelling in well-furnished homes while neglecting the House of God.

Drawing a parallel, Paul reminds us that we are temples of God, with His Spirit dwelling within us *(1 Corinthians 3:16)*. This spiritual foundation, laid by the apostles, necessitates careful building upon. Similarly, Peter describes believers as living stones forming a spiritual house, offering sacrifices to God through Jesus Christ *(1 Peter 2:5.)*.

Reflecting on our ways, we should assess whether we are truly blessed in our endeavors. If not, it may stem from neglecting our spiritual growth and involvement in building up the Church. Just as the Jews were urged to prioritize God's Temple, we too should prioritize our spiritual development and the collective growth of our faith community.

LET US NOT CONCEAL OUR SINS

"He who conceals his sins does not prosper, but whoever confesses and renounces them finds mercy." Proverbs 28:13

The verse from *Proverbs 28:13* underscores a fundamental principle of salvation: acknowledging and renouncing one's sins leads to finding mercy. This process of conviction, repentance, and discontinuation of sin is essential for genuine salvation, reflecting a heart transformed by grace.

As we grow in Christ, we may become increasingly aware of overlooked sins from our past, prompting ongoing repentance and forgiveness. There's no shame in this continuous cycle; rather, it is a testament to the renewing work of salvation in our lives, inviting us to embrace the joy of redemption anew.

The parable of the humble tax collector in *Luke 18:13, 14* illustrates the power of genuine repentance, as he found justification through a sincere plea for mercy. Similarly, the thief on the cross, acknowledging his guilt and recognizing Jesus' innocence, received a promise of paradise in *Luke 23:40-43*.

The repentance of Nineveh, as recounted in Jonah 3:10, further emphasizes the transformative impact of confession, leading to divine forgiveness and sparing of judgment.

In essence, confessing our sins leads to spiritual prosperity, as it reflects a heart humbled before God and open to His mercy and grace.

Let us do good works of serving others

Each of you should use whatever gift you have received to serve others, as faithful stewards of God's grace in its various forms. 1 Peter 4:10

We are called to utilize our gifts and talents not for personal gratification, but to serve one another within the body of believers, complementing each other's efforts. Ephesians 2:10 emphasizes that we are God's handiwork, created for the purpose of advancing His Kingdom through good works.

These good works have eternal significance, shaping our legacy beyond this life. Just as Jesus came to fulfill the ultimate good work of salvation, we are entrusted with specific tasks to further His kingdom. Matthew 5:16 urges us to let our light shine through good deeds, glorifying God. Romans 2:7 promises eternal life to those who persist in doing good, seeking God's glory.

Galatians 6:9 encourages us not to grow weary in doing good, assuring that a harvest awaits those who persevere. Likewise, Titus 3:14 underscores the importance of devoting ourselves to good works, meeting urgent needs and avoiding unproductive lives. And Hebrews 6:10 assures us that God acknowledges and rewards our labor of love in service to His name and His people.

Let us, therefore, heed the call to action. Let us utilize our gifts, talents, and resources to serve one another and advance God's Kingdom through good works. May we persist in doing good, knowing that our efforts have eternal significance, and that God sees and rewards our labor of love.

LET US NOT BECOME WEARY OF DOING GOOD

Let us not become weary in doing good, for at the proper time we will reap a harvest if we do not give up. Galatians 6:9

The passage from Matthew 25:31-40 highlights the importance of compassion and kindness in the Christian faith. It emphasizes that acts of goodwill, no matter how small they may seem, are significant in the eyes of God. Even if these acts go unnoticed or underappreciated by others, they are not overlooked by God.

The imagery of the Son of Man coming in glory to separate the righteous from the unrighteous portrays a scene of divine judgment where the righteous are rewarded for their deeds of kindness and compassion. These deeds, such as feeding the hungry, giving drink to the thirsty, welcoming strangers, clothing the naked, visiting the sick, and ministering to those in prison, are seen as directly impacting Jesus himself.

This passage serves as a reminder to believers that their actions towards others are ultimately actions towards God. It encourages believers to continue doing good works, even when they may not receive recognition or appreciation from those around them, knowing that God sees and values their efforts. The promise of reward for these deeds, as mentioned in the passage, provides encouragement and motivation for believers to persist in their acts of kindness and service.

Therefore, let us not grow weary in our efforts to do good, for our kindness and compassion are not in vain.

LET US AWAKE AND PUT ON OUR STRENGTH

Awake, awake; put on thy strength, O Zion; put on thy beautiful garments,
O Jerusalem. Isaiah 52:1

The imagery of Jerusalem or Zion in captivity in Babylon, depicted as a woman in mourning sitting in the dust and being mocked by the people of Babylon, paints a powerful picture of the suffering and humiliation experienced by the people of God during their exile.

In this context, the call to *"Awake, awake; put on thy strength, O Zion; put on thy beautiful garments, O Jerusalem"* takes on even greater significance. It is a call for the people of God to rise up from their state of despair and oppression, to shake off the dust of mourning, and to clothe themselves with strength and beauty once again.

The mocking taunt of the Babylonians, *"Lie down that we may walk over you,"* (*Isaiah 51:23*) serves as a reminder of the humiliation and degradation experienced by the people of God in exile. But the call to awaken and put on strength is a declaration of hope and resilience in the face of adversity.

Ultimately, this message speaks to the enduring faith and perseverance of God's people, even in the midst of suffering and oppression. It is a reminder that God is faithful to deliver His people from captivity and to restore them to a place of honor and dignity. And it is a call to trust in God's promises and to stand firm in the face of adversity, knowing that He is our strength and our salvation.

Let us awaken from spiritual slumber and embrace the strength and beauty God provides. Like Jerusalem rising from dust, let us cast off despair and clothe ourselves in salvation and righteousness. As we await Christ's return, may we prepare as a radiant Bride, living faithfully and sharing His light with the world. Rise up, embrace God's strength, and shine His hope.

LET US GO SKY WATCHING

Then God said, 'Let there be lights in the firmament of the heavens to divide the day from the night; and let them be for signs and seasons and for days and years.' Genesis 1:14

The heaven, even the heavens, are the Lord's; But the earth He has given to the children of men. Psalm 115:16

God has reserved the heavens for Himself while entrusting the earth to humanity. Yet, He desires to bridge the gap between heaven and earth, between mankind and divinity. Thus, He has provided us with a ladder connecting the two realms, and it is through Jesus that this pathway has been opened for us. Through Him, heaven descends to humanity, and humanity ascends to God in heaven.

The heavens themselves declare the glory of God, showcasing His divine craftsmanship. When we gaze upon the skies, we are reminded of His greatness and our own insignificance in comparison. Scriptures such as *Isaiah 55:9, Psalm 103:11, Daniel 12:3,* and *Acts 1:11* resonate deeply as we contemplate the vastness of the heavens.

In our celestial observations, we find parallels to our faith and hope: Jesus is likened to the Sun of Righteousness *(Malachi 4:2),* while His Church serves as the moon, reflecting His light, and believers are akin to stars, each shining with varying degrees of brightness *(1 Corinthians 15:41).* As we look to the skies, let us be reminded of the majesty of our Creator and the promise of His return.

LET US CELEBRATE THE FEAST OF INGATHERING

Celebrate the Feast of Ingathering at the end of the year, when you gather in your crops from the field. Exodus 23:16

The Feast of Tabernacles, also known as the Feast of Ingathering, corresponds to the time of year when the fruits of the earth were gathered. It commemorates the Israelites' forty years of dwelling in tents or tabernacles during their wilderness journey.

In 2 Corinthians 5:4, the Apostle Paul likens our bodies to temporary dwellings or "tents," emphasizing the transient nature of our earthly existence. As we celebrate the Feast of Tabernacles, we are reminded of our temporary sojourn in our physical bodies.

During this feast, we reflect on our blessings throughout the year, symbolized by the harvest of the earth. It is a time to express gratitude to God for His abundant provision and protection in our lives.

Lasting for seven days, the Feast of Tabernacles involves the construction of temporary shelters using natural materials, signifying the impermanence of earthly dwellings. This practice reminds us of God's provision and guidance during the Israelites' journey from Egypt.

The essence of the Feast of Tabernacles underscores the transient nature of our earthly lives and the anticipation of our eternal home with God (1 Corinthians 5:1, 4, 8). It serves as a reminder to live in readiness for our ultimate gathering with God's people.

Moreover, the Feast of Ingathering points towards the second coming of Jesus, symbolized by His gathering of His harvest and treasure. As we await this event, let us strive to bear fruit and maintain readiness for our glorification and gathering with God's people in eternity.

LET LOVE AND FAITHFULNESS NEVER LEAVE US

Let love and faithfulness never leave you; bind them around your neck, write them on the tablet of your heart. Then you will win favor and a good name in the sight of God and man.

Trust in the Lord with all your heart and lean not on your own understanding; in all your ways acknowledge him and he will make your paths straight. Proverbs 3:3-6

Often in marriage, love can grow cold. Many, including believers, succumb to the notion of love's chill as a justification to abandon their commitment to their spouses. Even those who endure such trials cannot deny that the thought has crossed their minds. This subtle and cunning erosion of love is a tool used by the devil to dismantle the harmony of marriage.

Therefore, it is crucial to remain vigilant and not be deceived by the enemy's schemes. Whenever our minds dwell on unnecessary thoughts, let us redirect our focus to the virtues outlined in *Philippians 4:8*: whatever is true, noble, right, pure, lovely, admirable, excellent, or praiseworthy.

When you sense your love for your spouse waning, recall the words of *Romans 5:5: "the love of God has been poured out in our hearts by the Holy Spirit who was given to us.."* Our love grows cold when we fail to heed the voice of the Holy Spirit speaking to our hearts. By being filled with the Holy Spirit, we can renew our love for our spouse, to whom we've pledged lifelong devotion.

Even if your spouse seems unloving, remember that you are cherished in the eyes of the Lord, whose love for you never falters. You hold a special place in His heart, and He alone provides your significance and security. As *Isaiah 62:5* reassures, *"As a bridegroom rejoices over his bride, so will your God rejoice over you."*

May love and faithfulness always be your companions.

Let us walk in the light of the Lord

The people walking in darkness have seen a great light; on those living in the land of deep darkness, a light has dawned. Isaiah 9:2

Come, O house of Jacob, let us walk in the light of the Lord. Isaiah 2:5

To walk in the light of the Lord involves several key principles:

Believe in Jesus: Jesus proclaimed, *'I have come into the world as a light so that no one who believes in me should stay in darkness' (John 12:46).*

Follow Jesus: He declared, *'I am the light of the world. Whoever follows me will never walk in darkness but will have the light of life' (John 8:12).*

Love your brother: *Anyone who loves their brother and sister lives in the light, and there is nothing in them to make them stumble. 1 John 2:10*

Reject hatred: Hatred toward a fellow believer indicates one remains in darkness despite claims of being in the light (1 John 2:9).

Avoid unequal partnerships: Scripture warns against aligning with unbelievers, emphasizing the incongruity between light and darkness *(2 Corinthians 6:14).*

Lead others to righteousness: The wise will shine like stars and those who guide others to righteousness will shine forever *(Daniel 12:3).*

Engage in good works: Let your light shine through righteous actions, bringing glory to God *(Matthew 5:16).*

Clothe yourselves with Jesus: Act with decency, adorning yourself with the nature of Christ, casting off the deeds of darkness *(Romans 13:13, 14).*

Let us embrace these principles wholeheartedly and let the light of Christ illuminate every step of our journey.

LET US RESTRAIN OURSELVES
FROM WEEPING AND TEARS

This is what the Lord says: 'Restrain your voice from weeping and your eyes from tears, for your work will be rewarded,' declares the Lord.' Jeremiah 31:16.

King David's poignant words in *Psalm 56:8* remind us that God treasures our tears, keeping them in His bottle and recording them in His book. This profound revelation underscores God's deep empathy and concern for our every sorrow.

In *Revelation 21:4*, we find solace in the promise that God will wipe away every tear from our eyes, eradicating death, sorrow, crying, and pain. This assurance speaks directly to those enduring loss, broken relationships, illness, financial struggles, and various forms of suffering.

Even in moments of repentance for our transgressions, God's mercy abounds. *Psalm 30:5* assures us that while we may experience weeping in the night, joy inevitably arrives with the morning light. The narrative of King Hezekiah in *2 Kings 20:3, 5* illustrates God's attentive ear to our prayers and His willingness to heal our afflictions, as evidenced by His response to Hezekiah's tears. *Psalm 126:5, 6* offers a profound truth: those who sow in tears will reap in joy. Although we may endure seasons of weeping and toil, our labor will ultimately yield a bountiful harvest of rejoicing.

While God encourages us not to wallow in despair, there are times when tears are necessary and even sacred. Jesus Himself wept, demonstrating the authenticity of human emotion. Thus, when God bids us not to weep, He invites us to embrace hope, trusting that our present sorrows will one day give way to abundant joy. Like the sower who weeps over his seeds, let us persevere with the assurance that our tears will yield a harvest of gladness.

LET US OBEY HIS COMMANDS TO AVAIL HIS GRACE AND PEACE

If you love me, keep my commands. John 14:15

In fact, this is love for God: to keep his commands. And his commands are not burdensome. 1 John 5:3

The words of Jesus in *John 14:15* emphasize the inseparable link between love for God and obedience to His commands. Similarly, *1 John 5:3* clarifies that genuine love for God is demonstrated through obedience to His commands, which are not burdensome but liberating.

Obeying God's commands unlocks His abundant blessings, including grace and peace. According to *Leviticus 26:3-13*, adherence to His decrees brings about a cascade of blessings:

- Rain will fall in its season, yielding bountiful crops and fruitful trees.
- Safety and abundance of food will characterize life on the land.
- Peace will reign, dispelling fear and ensuring security.
- Threats from wild beasts and enemies will be nullified.
- Victory over adversaries will be assured, with remarkable displays of strength and favor.
- Fruitfulness, multiplication, and divine presence will distinguish God's people.
- The yoke of oppression will be shattered, allowing for upright and dignified living.

These promises underscore the profound benefits of obedience to God's commands. By faithfully following His precepts, we invite His favor, protection, and provision into our lives. As we align ourselves with God's will and diligently obey His commands, let us anticipate the fulfillment of His promises with confidence and gratitude. Amen!

LET US BREAK CAMP AND DEPART

The Lord our God said to us at Horeb, You have stayed long enough at this mountain. Break camp and advance into the hill country of the Amorites... and along the coast, to the land of the Canaanites. Deuteronomy 1:6, 7

As the Israelites neared the culmination of their forty-year journey in the wilderness, Moses recounted their experiences to the new generation gathered on the east side of the river Jordan. Among their significant stops was Mount Horeb, also known as Mount Sinai, where they spent about a year. During this time, God imparted His Law and statutes, directed the construction of the Tabernacle, ordained priests, instituted sacrifices, and established festivals. Once these foundational elements were established, they were instructed to break camp and continue their journey toward the Promised Land.

Similarly, in *Philippians 3:9-11*, the Apostle Paul urges believers not to be content with mere adherence to religious rituals and observances. Rather, he encourages them to pursue a deeper righteousness rooted in faith in Jesus Christ. This pursuit entails striving to know Christ intimately, experiencing the power of His resurrection, sharing in His sufferings, and ultimately attaining the resurrection of the dead.

The Christian life, Paul emphasizes, is dynamic and forward-moving (*Philippians 3:13, 14*). It is likened to a race, demanding active engagement and perseverance. Believers are called to cast aside hindrances and press on toward the goal of obtaining the Kingdom of God. Paul's own attitude reflects this ethos: he refuses to dwell on past accomplishments or setbacks but instead focuses on the future prize awaiting him in Christ Jesus.

Therefore, let us emulate Paul's determination and spiritual vigor, discarding complacency and embracing a relentless pursuit of Christlikeness. As we fix our gaze on the prize set before us, may we run the race of faith with endurance, knowing that our ultimate destination is in the presence of our Lord and Savior.

LET US PUT ASIDE THE DEEDS OF DARKNESS

The night is nearly over; the day is almost here. So let us put aside the deeds of darkness and put on the armor of light. Romans 13:12

As the night gives way to the approaching dawn, heralding the imminent return of Jesus Christ, apostle Paul implores believers to cast off the deeds of darkness. These dark deeds, as outlined in *Romans 13:13-14* and *Ephesians 5:5*, encompass various forms of immoral behavior such as carousing, drunkenness, sexual immorality, debauchery, dissension, jealousy, and the indulgence of fleshly desires.

In *Ephesians 5:8 and 11*, Paul underscores the contrast between our former state of spiritual darkness and our present status as children of light. He warns against any association with the fruitless deeds of darkness, emphasizing that even a hint of such behavior is incompatible with our new identity in Christ.

Believers are called to imitate God and live lives characterized by love, as exemplified by Christ's sacrificial love for us *(Ephesians 5:1-2)*. We are urged to awaken from spiritual lethargy and allow Christ's light to illuminate our lives, transforming us from darkness to light *(Ephesians 5:14)*.

In light of the prevailing evil in the world, believers are exhorted to live wisely, seizing every opportunity to honor God *(Ephesians 5:15-16)*. This includes edifying one another through spiritual songs and heartfelt worship *(Ephesians 5:19)*.

Now that we understand what constitutes the deeds of darkness, let us earnestly strive to put them away from our lives. By doing so, we open ourselves to the radiant presence of Jesus Christ, whose light will shine upon us and guide us on the path of righteousness.

LET OUR EYES LOOK STRAIGHT AHEAD

Let your eyes look straight ahead, fix your gaze directly before you. Proverbs 4:25

My eyes are ever toward the Lord, for He shall pluck my feet out of the net. Psalm 25:15

Your eyes will see the King in His beauty; they will see the land that is very far off. Isaiah 33:17

Our eyes look to the Lord our God until He has mercy on us. Psalm 123:2

These Bible verses urge us to maintain unwavering focus on Jesus, recognizing Him as the ultimate guide to the Kingdom of God. Emphasis is placed on adhering to His teachings and remaining steadfast on the path He has illuminated. God's Word serves as the guiding light, directing us in our journey.

Let us keep our focus on the Lord Jesus, rather than being distracted by the imperfections of others, for He alone is the Way, the Truth, and the Life. His teachings illuminate the path to the Kingdom of God, guiding us along the narrow way. Should we stray, God's Word serves as our compass, redirecting us back to the right course.

Isaiah reminds us that God's voice will guide us, urging us to walk in His ways *(Isaiah 33:17)*. We are urged not to rely on human reasoning but to remain resolute in following the path laid out by God's Word. The Apostle Paul's exhortation in Philippians 3:13-14 underscores the importance of pressing forward toward spiritual goals, leaving behind worldly distractions and focusing on the prize awaiting in Christ Jesus.

Forgetting what is behind and straining toward what is ahead, I press on toward the goal to win the prize for which God has called me heavenward in Christ Jesus. Philippians 3:13, 14

LET US WALK UPRIGHTLY AND ENTER INTO PEACE

Those who walk upright enter into peace; they find rest as they lie in death.
Isaiah 57:2

The only certainty in life is our death. Indeed, death will come one day, yet the specifics of when, where, and how remain uncertain. Even the certainty of death is not absolute, as saints alive during the return of Jesus will not experience it.

Death is a universal experience, prompting us to ponder why we fear it. Whether consciously acknowledged or not, we inherently understand that death is not the end. God has instilled this awareness within us, fostering a fear of the unknown afterlife, knowing that our sins will accompany us beyond death.

In the journey of life, let us walk upright and embrace the peace that comes from faith. Jesus, in His wisdom, assures us that those who heed His teachings will transcend death's grasp and never truly perish *(John 8:51).* He proclaims Himself as the source of resurrection and life, offering eternal solace to those who believe in Him *(John 11:25, 26).* Even to the repentant thief, He promises immediate entry into paradise *(Luke 23:43),* illustrating that upright living stems from faith in His kingdom.

By accepting Jesus' sacrifice, we open the gates to Paradise, ensuring that those who follow His guidance will find peace, even in the face of mortality. And those who walk uprightly will enter into peace, finding rest even in death. *(Isaiah 57:2)*

LET US CONTINUE WITH THE THINGS
THAT WE HAVE LEARNED

*But you must continue in the things which you have learned and been
assured of, knowing from whom you have learned them, and that from
childhood you have known the Holy Scriptures, which are able to make you
wise for salvation through faith which is in Christ Jesus. 2 Timothy 3:14, 15*

In his letter to Timothy, the Apostle Paul affirmed the inevitability
of persecution for those pursuing godly lives *(2 Timothy 3:12)*. Paul's
message to Timothy served as both a challenge and an encouragement,
urging him to persist in his ministry despite the adversities he would
encounter.

Paul also warned Timothy of the perilous nature of the last days,
describing a society characterized by self-centeredness, greed, arrogance,
blasphemy, disobedience, ingratitude, unholiness, and a disregard for
goodness. He cautioned Timothy to distance himself from such individuals *(2 Timothy 3:1-5)*. Furthermore, Paul reminded Timothy of his
teachings, conduct, purpose, faith, and endurance amid trials, urging
him to remain steadfast in those principles.

Living in the present age, we witness the persecutions and hardships
endured by followers of Jesus worldwide. Rather than be disheartened,
we should draw inspiration from their testimonies, propelling us forward in our own journey of faith.

These trials should motivate us to endure suffering for Christ, driven
by His love. For *"all Scripture is given by inspiration of God and is profitable for doctrine, for reproof, for correction, for instruction in righteousness"*
(2 Timothy 3:16). Thus, the Word of God equips us to walk the path of
righteousness and endure the challenges of the Christian life. Let us
therefore continue in our learning and application of the Scriptures,
allowing them to guide and shape our lives as we navigate the trials
and joys of our faith journey.

LET US REASON TOGETHER WITH THE LORD

'Come now, let us reason together,' says the Lord. Isaiah 1:18

*'Present your case,' says the Lord. 'Set forth your arguments,' says Jacob's
King. Isaiah 41:21*

*Review the past for me, let us argue the matter together; state the case for
your innocence. Isaiah 43:26*

These Scriptures remind us that our Lord is ready for a prolonged
dialogue with us. He beckons us to approach Him, to present
our cases, and to engage in a reasoned discussion together. Our Lord
invites us into a heartfelt conversation.

If uncertainties weigh heavy on your mind, now is the time to seek
guidance from the Lord. Surrender to Him those matters beyond your
control, those burdens beyond your grasp. Share with Him your dis-
appointments—be it concerning health, work pressures, relationships,
finances, or any other concern. Lay it all before Him. He will listen,
and in trusting Him, you will find solace.

This conversation is two-fold. God will also speak to you. He may
address actions or words He does not endorse. Yet, He will reassure you
of His love and offer guidance on rectifying missteps. His invitation
to reason with Him holds the promise: *"though your sins be as scarlet,
they shall be as white as snow; though they be red like crimson, they shall
be as wool." (Isaiah 1:18)*

Do not miss this opportunity for a one-on-one dialogue with our
Lord Jesus Christ. It will undoubtedly be a profound personal exchange.
Lay your failures and burdens at His feet. He will grant you rest, illu-
minate your path, and console and guide you with love.

God calls us to reason with Him—not to argue and quarrel but to
engage and reconcile. Let us embrace this invitation, knowing that in
our dialogue with Him, we find redemption and renewal.

LET US SERVE THE LORD WITH OUR HOUSEHOLD

Choose for yourselves this day whom you will serve, whether the gods which your fathers served that were on the other side of the River or the gods of the Amorites, in whose land you dwell. But as for me and my house, we will serve the Lord. Joshua 24:15

Joshua, the leader of the Israelites, gathered the elders, heads, judges, and officers of Israel in his old age to remind them of the Lord's deeds and to urge them to remain faithful to the Law of Moses. He warned against turning to other gods or mingling with foreign nations, emphasizing the importance of cleaving solely to the Lord. Joshua cautioned that failing to do so would result in the Lord's anger and the presence of snares and traps among them. He urged them to fear the Lord, serve Him sincerely, and cast away the gods of their ancestors.

Concluding his speech, Joshua declared, "But as for me and my house, we will serve the Lord" (Joshua 24:15). In response, the people pledged to serve the Lord and obey Him. This pivotal moment underscores the importance of making a conscious decision to serve the true God, who has bestowed His Son, Jesus Christ, upon us for salvation. It entails rejecting all idols and philosophies of other gods, focusing solely on knowing and following the path of our God and His Son, Jesus Christ, which leads to Eternal Life.

LET US BE RECONCILED TO OUR BROTHER

If you are offering your gift at the altar and there remember that your brother has something against you, leave your gift there in front of the altar. First, go and be reconciled to your brother; then come and offer your gift. Matthew 5:23, 24

When we approach God's presence with an offering, Jesus instructs us to prioritize reconciliation with anyone we've wronged before presenting our gift. Our worship should not proceed until we've made amends. The emphasis is on restoring relationships before religious rituals. Regardless of who's at fault, the key is reconciliation, not argumentation.

Loving God isn't enough; we must also love our neighbors as ourselves. Without this love, our offerings to God hold no value. As stated in *1 Corinthians 5:8*, let us approach worship with sincerity and truth, free from malice and wickedness.

Before engaging in worship or offering, let us reflect on our relationships, ensuring peace with others and love towards fellow worshippers and family. Following Jesus' directive, let us initiate reconciliation, trusting in His ability to foster peace. It is crucial to take the first step toward reconciliation, even if we're not at fault, as Jesus, the Prince of Peace, works in the hearts of all involved to bring about reconciliation.

LET US REJOICE IN THE LORD ALWAYS

Rejoice in the Lord always and again I say Rejoice. Philippians 4:4

Despite life's challenges, rejoicing always is not only possible but also instructed by Scripture.

There are countless reasons to rejoice in the Lord. We celebrate His deliverance from the bondage of sin, His adoption of us as His children, and His forgiveness and salvation through Jesus Christ. Our hope of receiving Eternal Life fills us with joy, as does the gift of each new day. We rejoice in our fellowship with God and His people, the opportunity to worship and give thanks, and the gatherings for festivals and celebrations ordained by God.

We find joy in every good thing bestowed upon us by the Lord, including the fellowship of believers, the Word of God, and the songs of salvation that uplift our spirits. Even in the face of persecution and slander, we rejoice, knowing that our reward in heaven will be great. Let us, therefore, rejoice always, finding joy in the Lord and His abundant blessings.

This is the day which the Lord has made; we will rejoice and be glad in it. Psalm 118:24

LET OUR GENTLENESS BE KNOWN TO ALL MEN

Let your gentleness be known to all men. Philippians 4:5

This verse encourages us to visibly embody gentleness in our interactions. How can we achieve this? Let us read the entire passage of Scripture, which provides guidance:

"Rejoice in the Lord always. Again, I will say, rejoice! Let your gentleness be known to all men. The Lord is at hand. Be anxious for nothing, but in everything by prayer and supplication, with thanksgiving, let your requests be made known to God; and the peace of God, which surpasses all understanding, will guard your hearts and minds through Christ Jesus."
(Philippians 4:4-6)

These verses teach us not to worry but to rejoice in the Lord always. Anxiety breeds panic, not gentleness. By eliminating anxiety, we can increase our gentleness. Presenting our requests to God through prayer and petition, accompanied by thanksgiving, results in the peace of God guarding our hearts and minds, eradicating anxiety completely.

What are the benefits of gentleness? Scripture highlights numerous blessings associated with gentleness. As *Matthew 5:5* affirms, those who display meekness are blessed, destined to inherit the earth. *Psalm 149:4* reinforces this notion, asserting that the Lord delights in His people and bestows salvation upon the meek. Similarly, *Psalm 37:11* declares that the meek will not only inherit the earth but also find joy in abundant peace. Moreover, Paul's counsel in Galatians 6:1 emphasizes the importance of gentleness in restoring those who stumble in sin, cautioning against pride and temptation. Furthermore, *Titus 3:2* underscores the virtue of gentleness by urging believers to refrain from speaking ill of others, avoiding conflicts, and instead, demonstrating gentleness and respect toward everyone.

Let us refrain from harshness in our interactions with others and instead show empathy and sympathy, especially when dealing with those less fortunate.

LET US TAKE REFUGE IN THE LORD

God is our refuge and strength, a very present help in trouble. Psalm 46:1

Seeking refuge in the Lord entails finding safety and shelter from danger or distress in His presence. Whenever fear, trouble, or danger pursue us, we can seek refuge in God's protective embrace.

Boaz, addressing Ruth, acknowledged her refuge under the wings of the Lord, promising her a full reward from the God of Israel *(Ruth 2:12)*. King David sought refuge in the Lord, expressing in song: *"The Lord has become my fortress, and my God the rock in whom I find shelter"* *(Psalm 94:22)*. He further declares, *"The Lord is my rock, my fortress, and my deliverer; my God is my rock, where I seek refuge, my shield, and the horn of my salvation, my stronghold" (Psalm 18:2)*. With unwavering trust, David proclaims, *"I will declare of the Lord, 'He is my refuge and my fortress, my God in whom I place my trust'" (Psalm 91:2)*.

Psalm 91 enumerates the blessings bestowed upon those who seek refuge under the shadow of God's wings: deliverance from the snares of the devil and pestilence, protection under His feathers, fearlessness in the face of darkness and destruction, and immunity from evil and plague. *Psalm 84:3* illustrates how the sparrow finds a home and the swallow a nest at God's altar, highlighting the shelter and refuge available for us and our children.

Can we affirm with conviction, "He is my refuge, my fortress, my God in whom I trust."?

Blessed are all who take refuge in God. Psalm 2:12

LET US PRESS ON TOWARD THE MARK

Forgetting those things which are behind and reaching forward to those things which are ahead, I press toward the goal for the prize of the high calling of God in Christ Jesus. Philippians 3:13, 14

In the pursuit of a prize, every contender exercise self-discipline, knowing that they strive for a crown that perishes. We run our race with an eye on an incorruptible crown. Therefore, let us be diligent to adhere to the rules, ensuring we do not forfeit our reward. The Apostle Paul admonishes us to run with purpose, not aimlessly, and to train rigorously for the eternal prize *(1 Corinthians 9:24-26)*.

Paul exemplifies this dedication by subjecting his body to discipline to secure victory in the race of faith. As his life draws to a close, he declares triumphantly, *"I have fought the good fight, I have finished the race, I have kept the faith" (2 Timothy 4:6-8)*. The heroes of faith chronicled in *Hebrews 11* serve as inspiration, each running their unique race with unwavering faith and emerging victorious.

Let us emulate these exemplars, laying aside every hindrance and sin, persevering with patience in the race set before us, fixing our eyes on Jesus *(Hebrews 12:1, 2)*. Just as Jesus triumphed, ascending to the right hand of God, we too will receive our eternal reward if we persevere until the end.

Therefore, let us run with endurance, encouraged by the multitude of witnesses who have gone before us and obtained the prize. With steadfast faith and perseverance, we shall inherit the ultimate prize: eternal life with God.

LET US BE ALERT

Be alert and of sober mind. Your enemy the devil prowls around like a roaring lion looking for someone to devour. 1 Peter 5:8

The Lord said to Satan, 'Where have you come from?' Satan answered the Lord, 'From roaming throughout the earth, going back and forth on it' Job 1:7

The devil continually seeks openings to ensnare and destroy us. His tactics manifest in sudden loneliness, mood swings, self-pity, and the insidious presence of depression, jealousy, anger, fear, unbelief, pride, and enmity. Without self-discipline and vigilance, we become vulnerable to his schemes.

How can we remain vigilant?

We must first submit ourselves to God and resist the devil, knowing that he will flee from us when we do so *(James 4:7)*. Through prayer, we seek God's protective shelter, trusting that He will deliver us from the traps set by the enemy *(Psalm 91:3)*. We implore God to cover us with the blood of His Son, which serves as a powerful deterrent to the devil's schemes, ensuring our safety in body, soul, and mind. Persistent prayer fortifies us against the devil's advances, as it is through prayer that we secure victory over his attacks.

Living in constant communion with God shields us from the enemy's assaults, as he cannot breach the presence of the Almighty. Memorizing Scripture equips us with the sword of truth, enabling us to counter the devil's lies with the Word of God. Avoiding association with ungodly influences prevents the corruption of our moral character, as 'Evil company corrupts good habits' *(1 Corinthians 15:33)*. Furthermore, we exercise caution in our speech, recognizing that 'In the multitude of words sin is not lacking' *(Proverbs 10:19)*.

Let us remain vigilant and resolute, resisting the devil's deceptions, for in doing so, he will flee from us, unable to gain a foothold in our lives.

LET US BUY THE TRUTH AND NOT SELL IT

*Buy the truth and do not sell it—wisdom, instruction, and insight as
well. Proverbs 23:23*

In John 14:6, Jesus declares himself as the way, the truth, and the life,
emphasizing that access to the Father is exclusively through him. He
is the embodiment of truth, and acquiring this truth entails embracing
Jesus in our lives at any cost. Believing that Jesus is the sole path to God
underscores his pivotal role in God's plan to reconcile humanity since
the fall in Eden. However, many reject Jesus due to deception by the
father of lies, who leads them astray with falsehoods.

Matthew 13:44 compares the kingdom of heaven to hidden treasure
in a field, illustrating the priceless value of discovering truth. Those
who recognize this truth willingly sacrifice everything to possess it,
echoing the sentiment to "buy the truth, and do not sell it." Countless
individuals throughout history have forsaken worldly possessions and
comforts for the sake of Jesus and his kingdom.

Jesus's words in John 8:31-32 emphasize the transformative power
of truth, indicating that abiding in his teachings leads to liberation.
Therefore, acquiring truth involves adhering to Jesus's teachings and
following them obediently.

For those who have encountered the truth, it is imperative to hold
onto it steadfastly and not trade it for anything. Conversely, for those
yet to discover the truth, the call is to acquire it at any cost. Jesus assures
in *Matthew 19:29* that those who sacrifice earthly attachments for his
sake will receive manifold blessings and inherit eternal life, affirming
the promise of abundant rewards for those who embrace the truth
wholeheartedly.

LET US MAKE EVERY EFFORT TO ADD TO OUR FAITH

Giving all diligence, add to your faith virtue, to virtue knowledge, to knowledge self-control, to self-control perseverance, to perseverance godliness, to godliness brotherly kindness, and to brotherly kindness love. For, if these things are yours and abound, you will be neither barren nor unfruitful in the knowledge of our Lord Jesus Christ. For he who lacks these things is short-sighted, even to blindness, and has forgotten that he was cleansed from his old sins. 2 Peter 1:5-9

What does it profit, my brethren, if someone says he has faith but does not have works? Can faith save him? If a brother or sister is naked and destitute of daily food, and one of you says to them, "Depart in peace, be warmed and filled," but you do not give them the things which are needed for the body, what does it profit? Thus, also faith by itself, if it does not have works, is dead. James 2:14-17

Then the King will say to those on His right hand, 'Come, you blessed of My Father, inherit the kingdom prepared for you from the foundation of the world: for I was hungry and you gave Me food; I was thirsty and you gave Me drink; I was a stranger and you took Me in; I was naked and you clothed Me; I was sick and you visited Me; I was in prison and you came to Me.' Matthew 25:34-36

These passages from the Scriptures emphasize the importance of combining faith with action. Merely professing faith without corresponding deeds is deemed ineffective. While salvation is indeed through faith and grace, true maturity in Christ requires more. Alongside faith, we're called to cultivate virtues such as goodness, knowledge of God's Word, self-control, perseverance in prayer, godliness, kindness, and above all, love for others.

When these virtues accompany our faith, we naturally extend help to the needy, feed the hungry, care for the sick, provide for the destitute, welcome strangers, love our enemies, and strive to emulate Jesus Christ. In essence, genuine faith is evidenced by our actions and the fruit it bears in our lives.

Let us accept the one whose faith is weak

Accept the one whose faith is weak, without quarreling over disputable matters. One person's faith allows them to eat anything, but another, whose faith is weak, eats only vegetables... If we live, we live for the Lord; and if we die, we die for the Lord. So, whether we live or die, we belong to the Lord. Romans 14:1-8

Romans 14:1-8 encourages believers to welcome those who are weak in faith without passing judgment on their opinions or practices. Some may choose to eat certain foods while others abstain, and each person should be fully convinced in their own mind. Regardless of differing practices, all believers serve the same Lord and are accountable to Him alone. Therefore, it is not our place to judge or condemn one another. Each believer lives and dies for the Lord, and whether we eat or abstain, we do so to honor Him. Ultimately, we belong to the Lord both in life and death, and we are called to live according to His will, recognizing that we are accountable to Him alone.

This passage serves as a timely reminder to avoid pride and judgment towards others based on differences in beliefs or practices. Rather, it promotes humility and advocates for prayer concerning both our weaknesses and strengths. It prompts us to resist the temptation to pass judgment and to aim for acceptance and understanding in our interactions.

LET US PREPARE A ROOM

Prepare a guest room for me, because I hope to be restored to you in answer to your prayers. Philemon 1:22

Throughout the Bible, there are numerous instances of preparing a room for someone or something. Paul, in his letter to Philemon, requests that a room be made ready for him. Similarly, Jesus provides detailed instructions to His disciples for preparing the Passover, known as the Last Supper.

In Luke 22:10-12, Jesus directs His followers to a specific location where they will find a furnished upper room for the Passover meal. This passage underscores the importance of meticulous preparation for significant events.

Additionally, there's the account of a wealthy woman who, recognizing the holiness of the Prophet Elisha, decides to construct a room for him in 2 Kings 4:9-10. Her gesture reflects the hospitality and reverence shown towards spiritual figures in biblical times.

Moreover, Jesus Himself speaks of preparing a place in His Father's house for believers in John 14:2, highlighting the concept of readiness and provision.

In contemporary terms, we are encouraged to prepare a room in our hearts for Jesus. Often, our hearts become cluttered with worldly concerns, leaving little space for the Savior. Worries, resentment, and distractions occupy much of our inner dwelling.

Today, let us heed the call to cleanse a corner of our hearts, making ample room for Jesus to dwell. In this sacred space, He can assist us in clearing away the debris of our lives, bringing joy and awe in His presence. Once the room is prepared, let us invite Him in, for He eagerly desires to commune with us.

LET US AVOID GOSSIP

A gossip betrays a confidence; so, avoid a man who talks too much. Proverbs 20:19

G ossip, often characterized by informal discussions about the private lives of others, tends to be unkind and frequently lacks truth. It is a behavior explicitly cautioned against in the Bible.

To abstain from participating in gossip, it is vital to promptly halt any such conversations when they arise. Though it might feel awkward, redirecting the dialogue away from gossip is crucial.

It is worth noting that listening to gossip can be just as damaging as spreading it, and those who engage in gossip with you may also gossip about you to others. As believers, it is incumbent upon us to resist the allure of gossip, even when it is disguised as sharing prayer requests.

Instead, we should prioritize maintaining confidentiality and offer prayerful support. Ultimately, there's no justification for gossip, and engaging in it is not only unproductive but also potentially harmful.

A gossip betrays a confidence, but a trustworthy man keeps a secret. Proverbs 11:13

LET US BE THE SALT OF THE EARTH
AND THE LIGHT OF THE WORLD

You are the salt of the earth; but if the salt loses its flavor, how shall it be seasoned? It is then good for nothing but to be thrown out and trampled underfoot by men. You are the light of the world. A city that is set on a hill cannot be hidden. Nor do they light a lamp and put it under a basket, but on a lamp stand, and it gives light to all who are in the house. Let your light so shine before men, that they may see your good works and glorify your Father in heaven. Matthew 5:13-16

Just as salt enhances the flavor of food and preserves it from decay, as children of God, we are called to bring goodness and positivity to society. Our presence and prayers help avert sin and contribute to the well-being of others.

Luke 6:45 reminds us that our words reflect the condition of our hearts. Therefore, let us ensure that our speech is always gracious and seasoned with wisdom, as advised in *Colossians 4:6*.

To fulfill this role effectively, we must fill our hearts abundantly with the treasures of the Word of God, joy, peace, righteousness, love, wisdom, and the fruits and gifts of the Holy Spirit. These qualities enrich our lives and make us useful instruments in God's hands.

Just as Jesus is the true Light, illuminating every heart, let us shine brightly in the world, spreading His light and truth to those around us. *Philippians 2:14-16* urges us to conduct ourselves without complaining or disputing, so that we may stand blameless and harmless in the midst of a dark and twisted generation. By holding fast to the word of life and radiating Christ's light, we become beacons of hope and truth in a world in need.

As the salt of the earth and the light of the world, let us be seasoned with the Holy Spirit and lift up the words of life to illuminate the path for others.

LET US DO IT ALL IN THE NAME OF THE LORD JESUS

Whatever you do, whether in word or deed, do it all in the name of the Lord Jesus, giving thanks to God the Father through Him. Colossians 3:17

Sing and make music in your heart to the Lord, always giving thanks to God, the Father, for everything, in the name of our Lord Jesus Christ. Ephesians 5:19, 20

Whatever we do, we are asked to do it in the name of our Lord Jesus Christ. Even the simplest acts, such as giving a cup of water to a thirsty person, should be done with Jesus in mind. Going the extra mile for someone, even when it is challenging, should be approached with the teachings of Jesus in our hearts.

When we receive and assist children, we do so in the name of Jesus, as stated in *Matthew 18:5*. Jesus promises abundant blessings to those who forsake worldly attachments for His name's sake, assuring them of eternal life *(Matthew 19:29)*.

Despite the persecution and trials, we may face for bearing the name of Jesus, we are blessed, knowing that our reward in heaven will be great. The power of the name of Jesus has saved and healed us, and our prayers are answered through His name.

God has exalted His Son Jesus Christ by giving Him a name high above any other name, *Philippians 2:5, 11*. God has glorified the name of Jesus to the extent that whatever we ask in His name, we receive. Therefore, every deed we undertake should align with Jesus' teachings, ensuring that our actions honor and glorify Him.

Believing in the name of Jesus makes us children of God *(John 3:16)*, emphasizing the immense power and significance of His name. Thus, in everything we do, let us do it in the name of Jesus. Amen.

LET US TAKE HIS YOKE UPON US AND LEARN FROM HIM

Take my yoke upon you and learn from me, for I am gentle and humble in heart, and you will find rest for your souls. Matthew 11:29

A yoke, traditionally a heavy wooden bar placed over the necks of two animals to ease their burden in pulling a plow or cart, serves as a powerful metaphor in *Matthew 11:30*. Here, Jesus invites all who are weary and burdened to come to Him and take up His yoke, which He promises is easy and light compared to the heavy burdens they bear alone.

What, then, is the yoke of Jesus? It is the noble task of preaching the gospel of the kingdom of God, calling people to repentance, and spreading the message of salvation. Jesus came to seek and save the lost, and He invites us to join Him in this mission.

How can we bear this burden of Jesus? Through prayer for those who have not yet accepted Him as their Savior, demonstrating love to all and allowing the love of Christ to shine through our lives, proclaiming the Gospel message of Jesus' sacrifice for the forgiveness of sins, and teaching and explaining the Word of God to others.

Indeed, it is a great privilege to stand alongside Jesus, sharing in His burden of seeking and saving lost souls. By taking up His yoke, we find that His burden is light, and His yoke is easy. Compared to the weight of our own struggles, His yoke offers solace and rest.

As we heed Jesus' invitation and bear His yoke, we discover the truth of His promise in *Matthew 11:30*: His yoke is indeed easy, and His burden is light.

Let us go to the potter's house

The word of God came to the prophet Jeremiah asking him to *"Arise and go down to the potter's house, and there I will cause you to hear My words." Jeremiah 18:1, 2*

Jeremiah's encounter at the potter's house serves as a vivid illustration of God's sovereignty over nations and individuals. Just as the potter molds clay into vessels according to his will, God shapes and molds us according to His divine plan.

God's message through Jeremiah emphasizes His authority to bring both judgment and blessing upon nations based on their obedience or disobedience to His will. If a nation turns from evil and obeys God, He will relent from bringing disaster upon it. Conversely, if a nation rebels and disobeys God, He may withdraw the blessings He had intended for it.

As vessels in the hands of the Potter, we are subject to God's molding and shaping. If we stray from His will, He has the prerogative to reshape us according to His purposes. Therefore, we should not take God's blessings for granted, as they are contingent upon our obedience to His will.

However, God's grace is also evident in His willingness to forgive and bless those who humble themselves and repent from their wrongdoing. A humble heart has the power to turn God's curses into blessings, whereas pride can lead to a reversal of blessings into curses.

Thus, the key lies in maintaining a humble attitude before God. Scripture teaches that humility leads to honor, and those who humble themselves under God's mighty hand will be exalted in due time. Therefore, let us heed the wisdom of Scripture and humble ourselves before God, trusting in His sovereignty and mercy.

Pride brings a person low, but the lowly in spirit gain honor.

Proverbs 29:23 Humble yourselves, therefore, under God's mighty hand, that he may lift you up in due time. 1 Peter 5:6

GODLY LIFE

FRIENDSHIP WITH THE WORLD IS
ENMITY AGAINST GOD

*Don't you know that friendship with the world means enmity against
God? Therefore, anyone who chooses to be a friend of the world becomes
an enemy of God. James 4:4*

*Do not love the world or the things in the world. If anyone loves the world,
the love of the Father is not in him. 1 John 2:15*

'Friendship with the world' and 'loving the world' means to conform to the ungodly ways of the world. The above verses warn us
that if we conform to the world then we would find ourselves at odds
with God, and the love of the Father would not dwell within us. We
cannot simultaneously be friends with both the world and God; we
must choose one over the other.

*No one can serve two masters. Either you will hate one and love the other,
or you will be devoted to the one and despise the other. You cannot serve
both God and money. Matthew 6:24*

Our focus should be directed towards heavenly aspirations, rather
than earthly pursuits. As stated in Colossians 3:1-2, having been
raised with Christ, we are encouraged to set our hearts and minds on
things above, where Christ reigns at the right hand of God. Instead
of chasing after worldly temptations such as fame, wealth, and sinful
indulgences, we are urged to seek the Kingdom of God and its righteousness. Romans 12:2 advises against conforming to the world's
standards but encourages a transformation through the renewal of our
minds, enabling us to discern and embrace God's will. Jesus offers each
of us a friendship request, which involves turning away from worldly
enticements and pleasures to accept His invitation.

*"Do not conform to the pattern of this world but be transformed by the
renewing of your mind. Then you will be able to test and approve what
God's will is—his good, pleasing, and perfect will." – Romans 12:2*

How pleasant it is when brothers live together in harmony!

Behold, how good and how pleasant it is for brethren to dwell together in unity! It is like the precious oil upon the head, running down on the beard, the beard of Aaron, running down on the edge of his garments. It is like the dew of Hermon, descending upon the mountains of Zion; for there the Lord commanded the blessing, Life forevermore. Psalm 133

God recognizes the value of His people coming together in harmony, which is why He ordained numerous festivals and feasts for the Israelites to celebrate by gathering in Jerusalem's Temple. These gatherings included the Feast of Unleavened Bread, the Lord's Passover, the Feast of Harvest, and the Feast of Tabernacles, among others.

Deuteronomy 16:14 emphasizes the inclusivity of these celebrations, welcoming all members of society to rejoice together. Jesus Himself participated in these festivals alongside His family, relatives, and later His disciples, underscoring their significance. For instance, during the Feast of Tabernacles, Jesus proclaimed a message of spiritual fulfillment to the crowds *(John 7:37)*.

Sunday, designated as the day of worship, serves as a time for God's people to assemble in His presence, experiencing His fellowship and that of fellow believers. When we gather as God's children, the oil of joy anoints us, and blessings flow from His divine presence. Let us not neglect the importance of these ordained feasts, for they are occasions of divine communion and celebration.

He brought me to the banqueting house, and his banner over me was love. Song of Solomon 2:4

WHATEVER HE DOES PROSPERS-THE KEY TO SUCCESS

Blessed is the man who walks not in the counsel of the ungodly, nor stands in the path of sinners, nor sits in the seat of the scornful. But his delight is in the law of the Lord and in His law he meditates day and night. He shall be like a tree planted by the rivers of water that bring forth its fruit in its season, whose leaf also shall not wither, and whatever he does shall prosper. Psalm 1:1-3

Each of us possesses a purpose in life, a goal we earnestly pursue. We seek to achieve our aims so that we may be deemed successful. While the world grapples with defining the key to success, Psalm 1 presents the fundamental principles we must adhere to in order to thrive in all our endeavors.

The first principle to adhere to is avoiding the counsel of the ungodly, as their guidance is often deceptive. Let us echo the prayers of Job and the Psalmist, fervently pleading, *"May the counsel of the wicked be far from me" (Job 21:16)* and *"Guide me with your counsel and afterward receive me to glory" (Psalm 73:24).*

The second guiding principle urges us to steer clear of the paths frequented by sinners, recognizing that such company inevitably leads to ruin. Proverbs 1:10 provides a solemn warning: "My son, if sinners entice you, do not consent." This caution underscores the importance of resisting the allure of sinful influences and remaining steadfast in our commitment to righteousness.

Lastly, it is crucial to avoid adopting a scornful demeanor, as it invites consequences (2 Chronicles 36:16-17). Instead, take delight in the law of the Lord and meditate on His teachings day and night. As Psalm 119:105 says, "God's Word is a lamp to our feet and a light unto our path." The Word of God holds greater value than the riches of the world.

By following these principles, we become like trees planted by rivers of water, bearing fruit in due season and prospering in all our endeavors.

THE WISE MAN BUILDS HIS HOUSE ON THE ROCK

As Jesus concluded His sermon on the mount, He drew a parallel between a wise man and a foolish one, illustrating with a metaphor. He said, *"Whoever hears these sayings of Mine, and does them, I will liken him to a wise man who built his house on the rock: and the rain descended, the floods came, and the winds blew and beat on that house, and it did not fall, for it was founded on the rock" (Matthew 7:24-25).* Conversely, Jesus warned, *"But everyone who hears these sayings of Mine and does not do them, will be like a foolish man who built his house on the sand: and the rain descended, the floods came, and the winds blew and beat on that house, and it fell. And great was its fall" (Matthew 7:26-27).*

All who come to Jesus heed His Word and embark on building their spiritual houses. Those who diligently practice His teachings are likened to wise individuals who build on a solid foundation. Conversely, those who neglect His teachings are akin to foolish individuals constructing their houses on unstable ground.

Both encounter life's storms—illness, death, loss, loneliness, financial struggles, and more. Yet, during these trials, those who have practiced Jesus' words stand firm in their faith, while those who have not falter, their faith crumbling.

Ultimately, all must face the final storm: God's judgment. Only those whose spiritual lives remain steadfast will be prepared. This steadfastness comes from wisdom gained by practicing Jesus' teachings. Conversely, those who have ignored His Word will not withstand God's judgment.

James 1:22 echoes this sentiment: *"Do not merely listen to the word, and so deceive yourselves. Do what it says."*

So, where have you built your house? Let it be on the Rock of Salvation—our Lord Jesus Christ—and His teachings.

WISDOM AND FOLLY BOTH CALL OUT

Wisdom has adorned her house with intricately carved pillars, setting a table with sumptuous provisions of meat and wine. From the highest places in the city, she calls out, saying, *"Whoever is simple, let him turn in here.' To those who lack understanding, she beckons, 'Come, partake of my bread and drink of the wine I have mixed. Forsake foolishness and embrace life, walking in the path of understanding. The fear of the Lord is the beginning of wisdom, and knowledge of the Holy One leads to understanding. Through me, your days will be multiplied, and the years of your life increased." (Proverbs 9:4-6, 10, 11)*

Contrastingly, Folly, characterized by her clamor, audacity, and lack of wisdom, takes her seat at the door of her house in the high places of the city. She too calls out to passersby, enticing them with promises of stolen pleasures and clandestine indulgences. *(Proverbs 9:13-17)*

Both Wisdom and Folly beckon us from lofty heights, each offering its own allurements. While Wisdom promises eternal life, attainable through reverent fear of the Lord, renunciation of foolishness, and adherence to divine guidance, Folly tempts with fleeting pleasures that lead to ruin.

Whom will you heed?

Jesus Himself admonishes us, *"Enter through the narrow gate. For wide is the gate and broad is the road that leads to destruction, and many enter through it. But small is the gate and narrow the road that leads to life, and only a few find it" (Matthew 7:13-14).* Many are drawn to the broad path of destruction, but only a few discover the narrow path to life.

Accept Wisdom's invitation and embrace eternal life. Close your ears to Folly's seductive words, for they lead only to destruction.

THE VIRTUES OF A NOBLE WOMAN

Who can find a virtuous woman? For her price is far above rubies. Proverbs 31:10

A mother imparts valuable advice to her son, urging him to cherish and seek a virtuous woman, one who reveres the Lord, as his life partner. The virtues of such an exemplary woman are eloquently described in Proverbs 31:1-27:

A virtuous woman brings her husband good and avoids harm all her days, diligently working with eager hands. Like a merchant ship laden with provisions, she provides abundance and rises before dawn to care for her household and servants. Discerning, she invests wisely and manages her affairs, carrying out her tasks with strength and dignity. She ensures her efforts are fruitful, even working late into the night, and generously extends her hand to the poor and needy.

Planning ahead, she provides for her family's needs and skillfully crafts fine clothing and decorates her home. Clothed with strength and honor, she speaks with wisdom and kindness, diligently overseeing her household and avoiding idleness. These virtues exemplify the ideal qualities of a woman, attainable through reverent obedience to God's Word. Children and spouses alike praise a virtuous woman, with her children calling her blessed and her husband extolling her excellence. For fleeting is favor and transient is beauty, but a woman who reveres the Lord shall be esteemed.

These are the attributes that are valued in a woman. A woman can attain these noble virtues, by fearing God, which means obeying the Word of God.

Who may dwell in the Lord's sacred tent?

Lord, who may dwell in your sacred tent? Who may live on your holy mountain? Psalm 15:1

In Psalm 15, King David poses a question to the Lord: Who may dwell in your sacred tent? Who may live on your holy mountain? (Psalm 15:1) David then provides criteria for those eligible to live in the Holy Mountain of God.

They are described as individuals whose walk is blameless and who do what is righteous, speaking the truth from their hearts and refraining from slander or wrongdoing toward their neighbors. They honor those who fear the Lord, keep their promises even when it is difficult, lend to the poor without interest, and refuse bribes against the innocent (*Psalm 15:2-5*).

To qualify to dwell in God's tent and ascend His mountain, one must strive to embody these qualities. In *1 Thessalonians 4:14-17*, it is noted that Jesus ascended to the highest heaven where God's throne resides, and upon His return, He will call believers to ascend to Him. Therefore, it is imperative that we live in accordance with the standards outlined by David to be deemed worthy

A CALL TO BE UNITED

I appeal to you, brothers, in the name of our Lord Jesus Christ, that all of you agree together, so that there may be no divisions among you and that you may be united in mind and conviction. What I mean is this: Individuals among you are saying, 'I follow Paul,' 'I follow Apollos,' 'I follow Cephas,' or 'I follow Christ.' Is Christ divided? Was Paul crucified for you? Were you baptized into the name of Paul? 1 Corinthians 1:10, 12, 13

Apostle Paul's concern over the divisions within the early church still echoes in the Church today. Despite the passage of centuries, we continue to grapple with similar issues. Can we, with the guidance of the Holy Spirit, set aside our differences and worship the Lord in unity today, as Paul instructs us?

The multitude of divisions and denominations within the Church is inevitable, as believers often align themselves with specific leaders and interpretations of Scripture that resonate with them. However, Paul reminds us of two crucial reasons to remain united: Christ, not any church leader, was crucified for us, and we are baptized in His name, not in the name of any apostle or pastor. Regardless of our varying interpretations of the Bible, the foundational truth remains unchanged: Christ died for us, and we are baptized in His name.

Let us therefore refrain from engaging in foolish and ignorant disputes, as they only foster strife (2 Timothy 2:23). Instead, let us unite, transcending denominational affiliations, in the name of the One who unites us all—our Lord Jesus Christ.

JACOB'S BLESSINGS TO HIS SON JOSEPH

In Genesis chapter 49, Jacob bestows blessings upon each of his twelve children, with these blessings carrying prophetic weight. Reuben, Jacob's first son, does not receive the firstborn's blessing of a double portion due to defiling his father's bed. Instead, the firstborn's blessing is divided among Jacob's sons.

Judah receives the blessing of kingship, foretelling the birth of the Messiah, while Levi is blessed with the priesthood. Joseph, despite not being the firstborn, receives a double portion as his two sons are adopted by Jacob, effectively adding to the tribes of Israel.

Joseph, beloved by both Jacob and God, is cherished from his childhood, especially after being thought dead but seen alive. God's blessings pour upon Joseph through Jacob's words. He is likened to a fruitful vine by a spring, with strong branches climbing over walls.

Though hostile forces may attack him, his bow remains steady, empowered by the Almighty. Joseph is promised abundant blessings from God, surpassing those of his father, including blessings from heaven, the deep, and the womb. He is foreseen to be distinguished among his brothers.

Joseph's righteousness and aversion to sin please God, earning him these blessings even before Jacob confers them. His elevation to a position next to the King of Egypt is a testament to God's favor. Rather than faulting earthly fathers for lack of wealth or inheritance, Joseph's story underscores that it is God's blessings that enrich us.

Therefore, let us strive to be worthy recipients of God's blessings by fearing Him, for He blesses those who revere Him.

Our living hope: Joy amidst our trials

In all this, you greatly rejoice, though now for a little while you may have had to suffer grief in all kinds of trials. These have come so that the proven genuineness of your faith – of greater worth than gold, which perishes even though refined by fire – may result in praise, glory, and honor when Jesus Christ is revealed. 1 Peter 1:6, 7

In the midst of our trials, Apostle Peter encourages us to find joy, understanding that these difficulties are temporary and serve to refine the authenticity of our faith. He stresses the incomparable value of this faith, likening it to precious gold that not only withstands refining fire but emerges even more valuable, leading to praise, glory, and honor upon the revelation of Christ. The Apostles themselves embodied this perspective, rejoicing even amid persecution and shame endured for the sake of Jesus' name.

Jesus Himself blessed those who faced hatred, exclusion, and reviling for His sake, instructing them to rejoice in such persecution, for their reward in heaven would be great *(Matthew 5:10-12)*. Even amidst tribulations in the world, Jesus encouraged His followers to take heart and remain cheerful *(John 16:33.)*.

In a similar vein, the Apostle Paul conveyed that the sufferings endured in the present age are insignificant compared to the future glory awaiting believers (Romans 8:18). He underscored the assurance that enduring hardships with Christ leads to sharing in His reign. Despite the pain associated with discipline, it ultimately produces righteousness and peace for those who undergo it *(Hebrews 12:11)*.

In hardships, divine discipline is revealed, negating despair. Instead, let us rejoice, confident that God's grace will eventually restore, strengthen, and establish us after enduring for a brief period.

And the God of all grace, who called you to his eternal glory in Christ, after you have suffered a little while, will himself restore you and make you strong, firm, and steadfast. 1 Peter 5:10

THE OFFER OF LIFE OR DEATH

See, I set before you today life and prosperity, death and destruction. For I command you today to love the Lord your God, to walk in obedience to him, and to keep his commands, decrees, and laws; then you will live and increase, and the Lord your God will bless you in the land you are entering to possess. But if your heart turns away and you are not obedient, and if you are drawn away to bow down to other gods and worship them, I declare to you this day that you will certainly be destroyed. You will not live long in the land you are crossing the Jordan to enter and possess.
Deuteronomy 30:15-18

After forty years of leading the people through the wilderness, Moses gathered them to reiterate God's laws and decrees. He assured them that these laws were not too difficult or distant for them to obey. Moses emphasized that God's word was accessible and within their grasp.

Calling heaven and earth as witnesses, Moses presented a choice: life and blessings vs. death and curses. To choose life, they must love the Lord, listen to His voice, and cling to Him. If they turned away to worship other gods, they would face destruction and not enjoy long days in the land.

These commandments and laws, although initially given to the Israelites, hold timeless relevance for all humanity. They serve as guiding principles for righteous living and moral conduct, transcending cultural and historical boundaries. Life and blessings remain attainable for all, regardless of background or circumstance, but their realization hinges solely upon our unwavering obedience to the commands of God.

BLESSED IS THE MAN WHO PERSEVERES UNDER TRIAL

Blessed is the man who perseveres under trial, because when he has stood the test, he will receive the crown of life that God has promised to those who love him. James 1:12

Trials can often feel overwhelming, as every individual encounters suffering in various forms. From daily decision-making to navigating relationships, balancing responsibilities, and facing health and financial challenges, the trials of life are manifold.

Yet, in the midst of adversity, many may be tempted to distance themselves from the Lord, even denying their faith to suit their own agendas. However, those who remain steadfast in their faith in God will ultimately be rewarded.

The Apostle Paul exemplifies this endurance, declaring, *"I have fought the good fight, I have finished the race, I have kept the faith. Finally, there is laid up for me the crown of righteousness, which the Lord, the righteous Judge, will give to me on that Day"* (2 Timothy 4:7-8). Jesus, too, assures us, *"In this world, you will have trouble. But take heart! I have overcome the world"* (John 16:33). Moreover, Paul reassures us that God is faithful and provides a way out when we face temptation beyond what we can bear *(1 Corinthians 10:13)*.

To handle trials and temptations with grace, we can draw inspiration from Job, who, despite immense suffering, maintained his integrity and trust in God. Even when urged to curse God and die, Job responded, *"You are talking like a foolish woman. Shall we accept good from God, and not trouble?"* (Job 2:9-10).

Therefore, let us cast aside every hindrance and sin, running with endurance the race set before us (Hebrews 12:1).

BLESSINGS ARE IN STORE FOR THE PURE-HEARTED

Pursue peace with all people, and holiness, without which no one will see the Lord. Hebrews 12:14

Blessed are the pure in heart, for they will see God. Matthew 5:8

Who may ascend the hill of the Lord? Who may stand in His holy place? He who has clean hands and a pure heart. Psalm 24:3, 4

Truly God is good to Israel, to such as are pure in heart. Psalm 73:1

These verses emphasize the importance of having a pure heart to see God and stand in His holy presence. *Proverbs 22:11* declares, *"One who loves a pure heart and who speaks with grace will have the king for a friend."* Similarly, *Colossians 4:6* advises, *"Let your speech always be with grace, seasoned with salt, that you may know how you ought to answer each one."*

Our words reflect the condition of our hearts, as *Luke 6:45* affirms, *"A good man out of the good treasure of his heart brings forth good, and an evil man out of the evil treasure of his heart brings forth evil. For out of the abundance of the heart his mouth speaks."* Likewise, *Matthew 12:34* states, *"How can you, being evil, speak good things? For out of the abundance of the heart the mouth speaks."*

Thus, to speak graciously, we must cultivate a pure heart. This is attainable through accepting Jesus as our Lord and Savior and being filled with the Holy Spirit.

A CORD OF THREE STRANDS IS NOT QUICKLY BROKEN

Two are better than one because they have a good return for their labor:
If either of them falls down, one can help the other up. Though one may
be overpowered, two can defend themselves. A cord of three strands is not
quickly broken. Ecclesiastes 4:9, 10, 12

In the beginning, God created heaven and earth, finding His creation good each day. However, upon creating man in His image, He remarked, *'It is not good that the man should be alone; I will make him a helpmate' (Genesis 2:18)*. So, the Lord God caused a deep sleep to fall upon Adam, taking one of his ribs to fashion a woman and present her to him. Adam recognized her as *'bone of my bones and flesh of my flesh' (Genesis 2:23)*.

Yet, Adam and Eve needed more than just each other to thrive. They required a third presence to strengthen their bond, to interpret their emotions and thoughts. That third person was their Creator—God Himself. Each day, God walked and talked with them in the Garden of Eden *(Genesis 3:8)*.

Similarly, in marital misunderstandings, the Holy Spirit guides and comforts, bringing healing and unity. Acting as the third cord, the Holy Spirit strengthens the marital bond, making it resilient.

Never remain as two strands, nor become a single strand. God, the third strand, unites and fortifies the relationship. In every relationship—whether between parents and children, siblings, neighbors, friends, or business partners—keeping God as the third strand binds us together.

This can be achieved by inviting God into our lives and obeying His guidance.

THE POWER OF OUR TONGUE

The tongue has the power of life and death, and those who love it will eat its fruit. Proverbs 18:21

For by your words, you will be acquitted, and by your words, you will be condemned. Matthew 12:37

When words are many, sin is not absent, but he who holds his tongue is wise. Proverbs 10:19

James vividly depicts the tongue as a destructive force, capable of wreaking havoc and shaping the course of life itself (James 3:6). In moments of frustration, do we respond with impulsiveness, or do we exercise restraint, placing our trust in the Lord's ability to resolve our issues?

When confronted with gossip or negativity from friends, do we contribute to the harmful discourse, or do we display wisdom by offering prayers for resolution? Are our words agents of healing or harm, blessings or curses? Let us intentionally choose words that bring life, blessing others rather than cursing them, as we will inevitably reap what we sow with our tongues.

A soothing tongue has the power to bring life, while a deceitful tongue crushes the spirit (Proverbs 15:4). Let us guard against hypocrisy, ensuring that our praise for God is not undermined by words of condemnation towards others (James 3:9-11). Just as fresh water and salt water cannot flow from the same source, our words should consistently reflect the goodness within our hearts.

SHOUTS OF JOY AND VICTORY RESOUND
IN THE TENTS OF THE RIGHTEOUS

Shouts of joy and victory resound in the tents of the righteous: The Lord's right hand has done mighty things! Psalm 118:15

Shouts of joy and victory echo within the tents of the righteous, proclaiming the mighty deeds of the Lord's right hand (Psalm 118:15). But what significance do these "tents of the righteous" hold? According to the Scripture, they symbolize places where constant praise and thanksgiving resound, as the Lord continually performs mighty works for His people.

Reflecting on our own homes, what kind of voices do they echo? Do we acknowledge and celebrate the powerful deeds accomplished by God's hand in our lives? Can others hear our expressions of joy and victory in the Lord?

For those facing circumstances that hinder their shouts of joy and victory, here is a word of encouragement from the Scripture: *"When the Lord restored the fortunes of Zion, we were like those who dreamed. Our mouths were filled with laughter, our tongues with songs of joy. Then it was said among the nations, 'The Lord has done great things for them'"* *(Psalm 126:1, 2).* Keep praising the Lord despite the challenges! Soon, joy and victory will be yours!

In the Gospels, we witness how houses where Jesus and His disciples were welcomed became filled with a sweet fragrance of miracles, repentance, forgiveness, and abundance. (Luke 19:1-10; Luke 5:17-26; Luke 7:36-50; John 2:1-11; Mark 2:1-12) Even as the disciples prayed in an upper room, the Holy Spirit descended with a mighty wind, drawing people to them through their loud praises. (Acts 2:1-4) Similarly, the house of Cornelius was filled with the outpouring of the Holy Spirit amidst great praise to God. (Acts 10:44-48)

Let our homes, too, be filled with the songs of salvation and praises to our Lord. Amen! Let us lift His Holy name in continuous praise.

ARE OUR MOUTHS FILLED WITH LAUGHTER?

Our mouths were filled with laughter, our tongues with songs of joy. Then it was said among the nations, 'The Lord has done great things for them.
Psalm 126:2

Yet, some of us seem perpetually serious, devoid of spontaneous laughter. With stern faces and constant complaints, joy seems elusive to those around us.

Joy, however, is an internal state reflected externally. When joy fills our hearts, laughter flows from our lips, and our tongues sing with joyous melodies. Others will notice this joy, recognizing our calm demeanor amidst adversity, a testament to the mighty works of God in our lives.

When was the last time you laughed wholeheartedly, sang with unreserved joy, or danced in thanksgiving? Can observers say that the Lord has done mighty things for you?

Consider the laughter of Sarah at the birth of Isaac, a miraculous event in her old age, prompting laughter from all who heard *(Genesis 21:6)*. Reflect on the jubilant songs sung by Moses and the Israelites at the parting of the Red Sea *(Exodus 15:1, 20)*, or the exuberant dancing of King David before the Ark of God *(1 Chronicles 13:8)*. Remember the joyous celebrations during Nehemiah's time, where the joy of Jerusalem reverberated far and wide *(Nehemiah 12:43)*.

Indeed, as Ecclesiastes proclaims, 'A feast is made for laughter' *(Ecclesiastes 10:19)*, and Paul urges us to 'Rejoice in the Lord always' *(Philippians 4:4)*. Let us embrace the joy that comes from God's mighty deeds and share it with the world.

SIGNIFICANCE OF BAPTISM

Go therefore and make disciples of all nations, baptizing them in the name of the Father and of the Son and of the Holy Spirit. Matthew 28:19

This directive from Jesus to His disciples before ascending to Heaven is known as the Great Commission.

Baptism is a sacred ordinance established by God, and to be baptized is to fulfill His commandment. Even Jesus Himself underwent baptism to set an example for those who would follow Him, stating to John the Baptist, *"It is proper for us to do this to fulfill all righteousness." (Matthew 3:15)*

The disciples, following Jesus' command, preached the Gospel and baptized those who accepted Him as their Savior. Throughout the Acts of the Apostles, around twelve baptismal ceremonies are recorded, each accompanied by great joy, signifying the fulfillment of God's Word.

Though to some observers, baptism may appear as a mere ritual, God-ordained ceremonies carry profound spiritual significance. The Apostle Paul elaborates that baptism symbolizes our participation in the death, burial, and resurrection of Jesus *(Romans 6:3, 4)*. It serves as an outward declaration of our inward faith—a bold proclamation that we belong to Jesus and believe in His redemptive work.

Jesus Himself emphasized the importance of baptism, declaring, *"He who believes and is baptized will be saved, but he who does not believe will be condemned." (Mark 16:16)*

Therefore, beloved, let us not neglect the ordinance of baptism, for it is a divine commandment ordained by God. If you believe in Jesus Christ but have not yet been baptized, I encourage you to commit to this important step as a public declaration of your faith and allegiance to Him.

PINE TREE INSTEAD OF THE THORN BUSH

Instead of the thorn bush will grow the pine tree and instead of briers, the myrtle will grow. This will be for the Lord's renown, for an everlasting sign, which will not be destroyed. Isaiah 55:13

A few years ago, my work contract unexpectedly ended, leaving me disheartened, especially since I had hoped for a permanent position. In that moment of sadness, God comforted me with this very Scripture: *"Instead of the thorn bush will grow the pine tree, and instead of briers the myrtle will grow."* The situation I faced was undoubtedly a thorn bush, riddled with internal politics.

I clung to the promise, believing that God would bless me with something better—a more enduring opportunity. It wasn't until five months later that I saw the fulfillment of that promise, my "pine tree" finally emerging. Throughout those months, I never wavered in my faith that God would keep His word. I praise Him for His faithfulness in fulfilling His promise in my life!

Today, God extends the same promise to you. If you are navigating through difficult times, I urge you to hold onto this very verse as your own promise and to keep believing in it. Surely, God will bring it to fruition, and you will soon see your pine tree replace the thorn bush! Amen!"

HE THAT WATERS SHALL BE WATERED

The liberal soul shall be made fat, and he that waters shall be watered also himself. Proverbs 11:25

The proverbial wisdom of *Proverbs 11:25* suggests that those who are generous and compassionate will themselves find abundance and refreshment. Likewise, *Luke 6:38* teaches that giving leads to receiving—a principle of divine reciprocity where the measure one uses in giving determines the measure received. In *Mark 9:41*, Jesus promises reward even for the simplest acts of kindness done in His name, emphasizing the significance of generosity. *Proverbs 19:17* further reinforces the idea that lending to the poor is akin to lending to the Lord, ensuring eventual repayment from Him.

Encouragement to give generously extends beyond material wealth; it encompasses our prayers and actions. While unseen by others, our acts of kindness are observed by God, who promises to reward them openly *(Matthew 6:3-4)*. *Hebrews 6:10* reassures believers that God does not overlook their efforts to serve others in His name but acknowledges them with love. This reciprocity is likened to the earth receiving rain and producing a bountiful harvest *(Hebrews 6:7)*. Furthermore, *Romans 2:6-7* underscores the principle that those who persist in doing good will receive honor and eternal life.

In essence, these passages emphasize the spiritual law of sowing and reaping, where acts of generosity and compassion are not only rewarded but also reflect God's character and purposes in the world. As you reflect on these verses, consider how you can embody the spirit of generosity in your own life today. Whether through financial contributions, acts of kindness, or prayers for others, let us actively seek opportunities to bless those around us and be instruments of God's love and provision in the world.

It is not like the land of Egypt

For the land which you go to possess is not like the land of Egypt from
which you have come, where you sowed your seed and watered it by foot,
as a vegetable garden; but the land which you cross over to possess is a
land of hills and valleys, which drinks water from the rain of heaven, a
land for which the Lord your God cares; the eyes of the Lord your God
are always on it, from the beginning of the year to the very end of the year.
Deuteronomy 11:10-12

The Scripture passage above draws a clear distinction between the
land of Egypt and the land the Israelites were destined to possess.
In Egypt, they endured toil and labor to earn their produce, watering
the land by foot like a mere vegetable garden. However, the promised
land they were to inherit was described as a land of abundance, with
hills and valleys nourished by the rain from heaven. Here, the Lord
their God would watch over it diligently, from the beginning to the
end of the year.

This stark contrast between past struggles and future abundance
is not confined to ancient Israel but holds significance for us today.
Just as the Israelites transitioned from laborious toil to a promised
land of ease, we too can expect God's abundant provision in our lives.
Our inheritance, like theirs, is under the loving care of the Lord, who
watches over it unfailingly.

Reflecting on this promise, we realize that every blessing we receive
is a gift from God Himself. Whether it be worldly possessions or spiritual gifts, every good thing in our lives originates from Him. As *James*
1:17 affirms, *"Every good gift and every perfect gift is from above and comes*
down from the Father of Lights."

Therefore, let us hold fast to the assurance of God's provision and
care for us. Let us trust in His promise of abundance and ease, knowing
that He is faithful to protect and sustain us throughout our lives. As
we meditate on these truths, let us also respond with gratitude and
obedience, recognizing that our generous God calls us to share His
blessings with others.

ARE YOU SAVED?

Every person should have a clear answer to the question, "Are you saved?" Understanding salvation is crucial for this response. Salvation is akin to being in a perilous situation, crying out for help, and someone coming to rescue you from danger.

King David vividly describes his rescue by God in *Psalm 40:1-3*. He was trapped in a pit of miry clay, crying out for God's intervention. God heard his plea, lifted him out of the pit, and set his feet on solid ground. David's experience is a testament to God's saving power.

Paul also shares his struggle with sin in *Romans 7:19, 20, 24, 25*. He acknowledges his inability to overcome sin on his own and cries out for deliverance. He recognizes Jesus Christ as the only one who can save him from his sinful nature.

Being saved involves acknowledging Jesus Christ as our Savior, crying out to Him for deliverance from sin, and proclaiming how He has saved us. As *Romans 10:9-10* affirms, believing in our hearts and confessing with our mouths that Jesus is Lord leads to salvation.

Let us reflect on our own salvation experience and boldly declare Jesus as our Savior. If you haven't made this confession yet, I invite you to do so now and experience the transformative power of Christ in your life.

How to know the perfect will of God?

And do not be conformed to this world, but be transformed by the renewing of your mind, that you may prove what is that good and acceptable and perfect will of God. Romans 12:2

Understanding the perfect will of God requires a transformation of our minds, as stated in *Romans 12:2*. This transformation entails rejecting conformity to the world's standards and embracing renewal. The responsibility to discern God's will is squarely upon us, emphasized by the Scriptures. While the ungodly chase after worldly pursuits, we are called to resist such conformity.

Ephesians 4:22-24 provides practical guidance for renewing our minds. We are urged to reject falsehood and speak truthfully, manage anger without sinning, guard against giving the devil a foothold, and abstain from stealing. Instead, we are encouraged to work diligently and share with others. We are also instructed to let only wholesome words proceed from our mouths, avoid grieving the Holy Spirit, and let go of bitterness, anger, and malice. Instead, we're called to show kindness and forgiveness.

By following these principles outlined by the Apostle Paul, our minds undergo transformation, aligning with God's will rather than conforming to the world's standards. Let us commit to this process of renewal, ensuring that God's perfect will is accomplished in our lives.

THE TONGUE HAS THE POWER OF LIFE AND DEATH

The tongue has the power of life and death, and those who love it will eat its fruit. Proverbs 18:21

The Scriptures emphasize the profound impact of our words. *Proverbs 18:21* reminds us that the tongue holds the power of life and death, and *Matthew 12:37* reinforces this by stating that we will be judged by our words. *Proverbs 10:19* warns against the sin that often accompanies excessive speech, highlighting the wisdom in holding one's tongue. *James 3:6* vividly depicts the destructive potential of the tongue, likening it to a fire that can corrupt and set ablaze one's entire life.

In light of these warnings, the Apostle Paul urges believers to let their speech be filled with grace, seasoned with salt, enabling them to respond to others with wisdom *(Colossians 4:6)*. We must introspect: do our words build up or tear down? Do they bring life or death? *Proverbs 15:4* extols the virtue of a wholesome tongue, likening it to a tree of life that imparts blessing.

Our confession of faith in Jesus as Lord fills our tongues with praise, echoing the sentiments of King David in *Psalm 35:28*. However, *James 1:26* cautions against hypocrisy, emphasizing the importance of controlling our tongues for genuine religious practice. Similarly, *1 Peter 3:10* admonishes us to keep our tongues from evil and our lips from deceitful speech if we desire a life filled with goodness and joy.

Let us take these Scriptures to heart and endeavor to use our tongues wisely, blessing and encouraging others while honoring God. May our words be a reflection of the life-giving grace bestowed upon us by our Lord and Savior, Jesus Christ.

How many times should we
forgive our offender?

Peter came to Jesus and asked, 'Lord, how many times shall I forgive my brother when he sins against me, up to seven times?" Jesus answered, "I tell you, not seven times, but seventy times seven.' Matthew 18:21, 22

Peter's inquiry to Jesus about forgiveness prompts a profound response: not merely seven times, but seventy times seven. Forgiving someone who repeatedly offends us challenges our human nature, as our hearts struggle to heal and our minds cling to resentment.

Yet, Jesus instructs us to extend forgiveness each time we are asked, mirroring God's forgiveness of our own transgressions. This call to forgive, even when it feels undeserved, reflects the depth of God's grace toward us. While the idea of forgiving someone countless times may seem daunting, it embodies the essence of God's unconditional love and mercy.

As recipients of God's forgiveness, we are called to extend the same grace to others, regardless of how many times they may offend us. This divine principle reminds us of the importance of forgiveness in our lives and our relationship with God. Let us embrace this challenge with humility and grace, knowing that in forgiving others, we honor God and reflect His boundless love.

"For if you forgive other people when they sin against you, your heavenly Father will also forgive you. But if you do not forgive others their sins, your Father will not forgive your sins." Matthew 6:14-15

MY JOY IN YOU MAKES YOUR JOY COMPLETE

As the Father has loved me, so have I loved you. Now remain in my love. If you obey my commands, you will remain in my love, just as I have obeyed my Father's commands and remain in His love. I have told you this so that my Joy may be in you and that your Joy may be complete. John 15:9-11

In the Scripture above, Jesus emphasizes the connection between love and joy, urging us to abide in His love to experience fullness of joy. This joy is not merely circumstantial but stems from a deep, abiding love for God and others. Salvation itself is a source of profound joy, rooted in the belief that Jesus is Lord, who sacrificially died for our sins, rose again, and intercedes for us before the Father.

It is the liberation from the guilt of sin that brings an indescribable joy, grounded in the promise of eternal life and the assurance of forgiveness. *Isaiah 43:25* reassures us of God's faithfulness in blotting out our transgressions, offering us the freedom to embrace joy without the weight of guilt.

If you haven't yet experienced this joy of salvation, I invite you to surrender your heart to Jesus. Let us pray together: Dear Lord, we rejoice in the joy of our salvation, grateful for the sacrifice of Jesus on the cross. For those who haven't experienced this joy, open their hearts to recognize Jesus as their Savior. Grant them the gift of salvation, filling them with your abundant joy. We praise and glorify your name for the joy of salvation you have bestowed upon us. Amen.

BLESSED ARE THE PURE IN HEART

Blessed are the pure in heart, for they will see God. Matthew 5:8

One who loves a pure heart and who speaks with grace will have the king for a friend. Proverbs 22:11

From these Scriptures, we glean that individuals who cherish a pure heart and communicate with grace will find favor, even with royalty. *Psalm 24:3-5* underscores that only those with clean hands and a pure heart can ascend the hill of the Lord and receive His blessings. Additionally, *Psalm 97:11* accentuates that light and joy await those who are upright in heart.

On the other hand, *Jeremiah 17:9* warns us about the deceitfulness of the heart, acknowledging its inherent wickedness. Yet, there is hope, as *Deuteronomy 30:6* assures us that God will circumcise our hearts, removing deceit and enabling us to love Him wholeheartedly. This purification process is likened to refining silver, where God purifies His children to offer righteous sacrifices *(Malachi 3:3).*

Deuteronomy 4:9 urges us to diligently keep God's teachings in our hearts, passing them down through generations. *Hebrews 12:14* underscores the importance of pursuing peace and holiness to see the Lord.

Let us echo King David's prayer in *Psalm 51:1, 7, 10*, seeking God's mercy and purification, asking Him to create in us clean hearts and renew right spirits within us. May this prayer be ours as we seek to walk in purity and grace before the Lord. Amen.

Let not your heart be troubled

"Let not your heart be troubled..." Peace I leave with you; my peace I give you. I do not give to you as the world gives. Do not let your hearts be troubled and do not be afraid. John 14:1, 27

These reassuring words from Jesus, were spoken to His disciples just before His crucifixion. In a time of impending trial and persecution, Jesus sought to comfort them, knowing the challenges they would face without His physical presence. He offered them His peace, a peace that surpasses worldly understanding and transcends circumstances.

Reflecting on these words, we realize that we are in a more fortunate position than the disciples were at that moment. We live after the resurrection, having experienced the presence of the Holy Spirit and witnessed the transformative power of salvation. Unlike the disciples, we have the assurance of Christ's victory and the support of a community of believers.

Yet, despite these blessings, we often find ourselves troubled and anxious. We worry about various aspects of life, allowing fear and uncertainty to overshadow our faith. But Jesus reminds us to take comfort in His love and to accept the peace He freely offers. As *Psalm 55:22* encourages us, we can cast our cares upon the Lord, knowing that He will sustain us.

So, when troubles arise and anxieties overwhelm us, let us remember the promise of God found in *Isaiah 41:10: "Fear not, for I am with you; Be not dismayed, for I am your God. I will strengthen you, Yes, I will help you, I will uphold you with My righteous right hand."* Let us hold fast to this promise and choose to trust in God's unfailing presence and provision. Let not our hearts be troubled, for our God is with us.

BLESSED ARE THOSE WHO MOURN

Blessed are those who mourn, for they will be comforted. Matthew 5:4

Our Lord Jesus Christ, often referred to as the "Man of sorrows," understands the depths of mourning and grief firsthand. In *Isaiah 53:3*, it is written that He was despised and forsaken, acquainted with sorrow and grief, a figure shunned by many. Therefore, He intimately relates to those who mourn, and one of His primary missions is to bring comfort to them.

As stated in *Isaiah 61:1-3*, the Lord has anointed Jesus to proclaim good news to the poor, bind up the brokenhearted, and bring freedom to captives. He is here to comfort all who mourn, offering them a crown of beauty instead of ashes, the oil of joy instead of mourning, and a garment of praise instead of despair. In our moments of grief and sorrow, we are encouraged to bring all our burdens to the feet of Jesus, knowing that He will envelop us in His comforting presence, filling us with the overwhelming peace of the Holy Spirit. Indeed, He will exchange our mourning for joy and our despair for praise. Hallelujah! Praise the Lord!

As *Revelation 7:17* assures us, the Lamb at the center of the throne will be our shepherd, leading us to springs of living water. In His loving care, God will wipe away every tear from our eyes, bringing an end to all our sorrows.

GRACE AND PEACE

My grace is sufficient for you, for my power is made perfect in weakness.
2 Corinthians 12:9

Peace I leave with you; my peace I give you. John 14:27

G od's assurance of His grace and peace, as expressed in *2 Corinthians 12:9* and *John 14:27*, is a gift readily available to us. Yet, it is
essential to consider whether we've truly embraced these gifts. When
we feel frustrated or restless, it may indicate that we haven't fully
received the peace that God's grace offers. Grace encompasses God's
love, mercy, kindness, and justice, as exemplified in instances like
Abraham's encounter with God in *Genesis 19:19*.

Peace, on the other hand, provides the rest promised by Jesus in
Matthew 11:28. So how do we receive these blessings? Firstly, through
deepening our knowledge of God and Jesus, as highlighted in *2 Peter
1:2*, achieved through Scripture study and prayer. Secondly, by obediently following God's commandments, which brings peace and favor,
as indicated in *Leviticus 26:3, 6, and 9*.

Lastly, through prayer, as outlined in *Philippians 4:6-7*, where bringing our requests to God with thanksgiving results in His peace guarding
our hearts and minds.

INVITED OR CHOSEN

The parables about the wedding feast, are narrated by Jesus. *Matthew 22:1-4*

The parable of the wedding feast, narrated by Jesus in *Matthew 22:1-14*, illustrates the Kingdom of Heaven as a king who prepares a banquet for his son's wedding. Despite many being invited, those initially invited refused to attend. The king, angered by their rejection and mistreatment of his servants, invited others from the streets to fill the banquet hall. However, one guest was found without proper attire and was cast out. Jesus concluded the parable by stating, *"For many are invited, but few are chosen."*

This parable serves as a message to the Jews, emphasizing how God has repeatedly invited them to His banquet through prophets and ministers, yet they rejected His invitation by rejecting Jesus. It underscores the importance of accepting God's invitation and undergoing a sanctification process, symbolized by wearing proper wedding garments provided by the King. Merely accepting the invitation is not enough; true participation in the wedding feast requires adherence to the King's requirements for purity and holiness.

Let us respond to God's call by coming to Him as we are, but also being willing to undergo the sanctification process He provides. May we clothe ourselves in His righteousness and prepare our hearts to enter His banquet hall. Let us not take His invitation lightly, but earnestly seek to be among the chosen few who will partake in the eternal celebration of His Kingdom.

THE PHARISEES

*Woe to you Pharisees, because you give God a tenth of your mint, rue,
and all other kinds of garden herbs, but you neglect justice and the love
of God. You should have practiced the latter without leaving the former
undone... Luke 11:42*

The Pharisees were a Jewish sect distinguished by their strict observance of traditional and written Law. They presented themselves
as self-righteous individuals, boasting of superior sanctity. However,
Jesus rebuked them as hypocrites, highlighting their neglect of justice
and genuine love for God.

Considering themselves righteous, the Pharisees viewed all other
Jews as sinners. They took pride in their self-righteousness, thanking
God for their perceived purity. Their emphasis lay in tithing, fasting,
praying, offering alms, and adhering meticulously to the rules and
rituals of the Law of Moses. Instead of attributing authority to God,
they often referenced "Moses has said" rather than "God has said."

Upon the commencement of Jesus' ministry, the Pharisees struggled
to accept the growing following He amassed. They continuously found
fault with His words, teachings, and actions. They accused Jesus of
being in league with demons when He cast them out. Questions arose
regarding His authority to forgive sins or heal on the Sabbath. They
criticized His association with tax collectors and sinners during meals,
as well as His perceived lack of adherence to rituals like washing before
meals. Even when a woman anointed His head and feet with costly
ointment, they questioned His acceptance of a sinful woman's touch.

Jesus acknowledged the righteousness of the Pharisees, yet He
asserted that true righteousness surpasses theirs for entry into the kingdom of heaven. It is the righteousness of Jesus, obtained through belief
in Him as Savior, that we need to clothe ourselves with. Let us heed
Jesus' call to a righteousness that transcends mere external observance,
embracing instead a genuine love for God and justice towards others.

THE FRAGRANCE OF THE PERFUME

Then Mary took about a pint of pure nard, an expensive perfume; she poured it on Jesus' feet and wiped his feet with her hair. And the house was filled with the fragrance of the perfume. John 12:3

Matthew and Mark recount the same incident, stating that she poured the perfume on His head (Matthew 26:7, Mark 14:3).

The act of pouring out the costly perfume carries significant symbolism. Mary demonstrated her complete devotion to the Lord by holding nothing back in her offering. She disregarded potential criticism for what some might view as wastefulness and acted without seeking approval from others, including her sister or brother. She didn't consider selling the perfume to benefit the poor; her sole focus was honoring Jesus.

The Apostle Paul, in his letter to the Philippians, echoes this sentiment, declaring that he counts all worldly gains as loss compared to the surpassing worth of knowing Christ Jesus as Lord (Philippians 3:7-8). Indeed, nothing compares to the infinite value of a relationship with Jesus.

The remarkable aspect of Mary's gesture was not just the offering itself but the fragrance that filled the house. Likewise, when we offer ourselves as living sacrifices to God, our lives become a sweet fragrance within our households.

Let us not cling to worldly possessions but surrender them at the feet of Jesus, spreading the sweet fragrance of devotion. Just as we are to God the pleasing aroma of Christ among those who are being saved (2 Corinthians 2:15).

Are we willing to offer our best to the Lord? Do we view all things as worthless compared to Christ? Have we gained Christ, considering everything else as rubbish? Can others perceive the fragrance of devotion in our lives? Let us live as fragrant offerings to God, expressing love in all we do.

No profit in gaining the whole world, yet forfeiting the soul?

Whoever wants to be my disciple must deny themselves and take up their cross and follow me. For whoever wants to save their life will lose it, but whoever loses their life for me will find it. What good will it be for someone to gain the whole world, yet forfeit their soul? Or what can anyone give in exchange for their soul? Matthew 16:24-26

A man once received a bountiful harvest from his field but failed to acknowledge God's provision. Instead of sharing his abundance with those in need, he selfishly planned to hoard it for his own comfort and enjoyment. However, God admonished him, calling him a fool, and warned that his life would end that very night, leaving behind all his amassed wealth to others (Luke 12:16-20). Jesus concluded the parable by emphasizing that accumulating treasures for oneself does not make one rich toward God (Luke 12:21).

Consider the example of King Alexander, who sought to conquer the world but died at a young age, leaving behind all his conquests. Despite his victories, what did he truly gain?

The message is clear: true wealth lies in godliness and contentment. We enter this world with nothing, and we cannot take anything with us when we depart. Therefore, let us be satisfied with having food and clothing. Those who chase after wealth often fall into temptation, leading to destruction and sorrow, *as the love of money is the root of all kinds of evil (1 Timothy 6:6-10).*

Godliness with contentment is a great gain. For we brought nothing into this world, and it is certain we can carry nothing out. And having food and raiment let us be content. But they that will be rich fall into temptation and a snare, and into many foolish and hurtful lusts, which drown men in destruction and perdition. For the love of money is the root of all evil: which while some coveted after, they have erred from the faith, and pierced themselves through with many sorrows. 1 Timothy 6:6-10

The Parable of the Wheat and the Tares

Jesus shared a parable with His disciples, likening the Kingdom of Heaven to a man who sowed good seed in his field. However, while everyone slept, an enemy came and planted weeds among the wheat. As both wheat and weeds grew, the servants questioned the owner, who explained that an adversary had sown the weeds. He instructed them not to uproot the weeds, lest they damage the wheat, but to wait until the harvest when the weeds would be separated and burned, while the wheat would be gathered into the barn *(Matthew 13:24-30)*.

Jesus then interpreted the parable, identifying Himself as the one who sows the good seed, the field as the world, the good seeds as the children of the kingdom, and the weeds as the sons of the evil one. The devil is the adversary who sows the weeds, and the harvest represents the end times when the angels will separate the righteous from the wicked *(Matthew 13:38-42)*.

Those who belong to God are like the good seed, while those under the influence of the devil are like the weeds. Though they may coexist in the world, there will come a time when they will be separated. The wheat, representing the righteous, will be gathered into God's kingdom, while the weeds, symbolizing the wicked, will face judgment.

Let us therefore surrender ourselves to be like the good seed in the hands of Jesus, bearing fruit for His kingdom.

Your faith has made you well

Jesus was passing through a village in Samaria. There, ten men who were lepers stood afar off, lifted up their voices, and said, *'Jesus, Master, have mercy on us.' Luke 17:13*

As Jesus passed through a village in Samaria, ten lepers stood at a distance, calling out to Him for mercy. Responding to their plea, Jesus instructed them to show themselves to the priests. As they obeyed and journeyed to the priests, they found themselves healed of their leprosy, becoming clean once again. However, only one of them, realizing he was healed, returned to Jesus, glorifying God with loud praises and falling at Jesus' feet in gratitude. Jesus, noticing the absence of the other nine, questioned the Samaritan, highlighting his grateful response and faith, and declaring him "well".

While all ten lepers were physically healed, the Samaritan's deeper healing came from his faith in Jesus, resulting in a transformation of his mind and soul. This contrast underscores the importance of gratitude and acknowledgment of God's blessings. We are reminded to express thankfulness not only for physical healing but also for the spiritual renewal and transformation that comes through faith in Jesus.

Are we truly grateful for the healing we've received from God, both physically and spiritually? Do we believe in Jesus' power to heal not just our bodies but also our minds and souls? True wellness encompasses both physical and spiritual wholeness, attained through faith in Jesus and expressed through praise and gratitude.

Let us not settle for mere adherence to religious rituals or worldly blessings. Instead, let us seek true wellness through faith in Jesus, acknowledging His mercy with heartfelt thanksgiving, and proclaiming His healing power to the world.

MIRROR IMAGE OF CHRIST

"We all, with open face beholding as in a glass the glory of the Lord, are changed into the same image from glory to glory, even as by the Spirit of the Lord." 2 Corinthians 3:18

In our daily lives, it is crucial that we reflect Christ's image as clearly as a mirror. Our pastor often emphasizes that for many people, we might be the only representation of Christ they encounter, and our homes may be the only semblance of a church they witness. They may not pick up a Bible, attend a church service, or listen to a sermon, but they observe us closely, witnessing how we navigate life's challenges.

Are our actions truly reflecting Christ? The verse above suggests that as we gaze upon the glory of the Lord, we are gradually transformed into His likeness by the Spirit of God.

Galatians 3:27 states that those who are baptized into Christ are clothed with Him. This implies that when others look at us, they should not see us, but rather see Christ manifested in our lives. Are we indeed mirrors reflecting Jesus? To achieve this, we must emulate His qualities and follow His teachings, as outlined in the Gospels. By living according to His example, we become transformed into mirror images of Jesus.

The Apostle Paul, in *Galatians 6:17*, speaks of bearing the marks of the Lord Jesus in his body, indicating the sufferings he endured for the sake of the Gospel. He became a mirror image of the suffering Jesus. Similarly, *1 Peter 2:23* describes how Jesus responded to suffering without retaliation, entrusting Himself to God, the righteous Judge.

Are we also following in His footsteps, responding to harm with patience and committing ourselves to the hands of God? Let us strive to be mirrors reflecting the character and love of Jesus in all that we do, so that others may see Him through us and be drawn closer to Him.

WELL DONE, GOOD AND FAITHFUL SERVANT!

'Well done, good and faithful servant! You have been faithful with a few things; I will put you in charge of many things. Come and share your master's happiness!' Matthew 25:23

Here, Jesus tells the parable of the talents, where a master entrusts his servants with different amounts of talents (a unit of currency) according to their abilities. The servants who multiplied their talents were praised and rewarded, while the one who buried his talent out of fear was rebuked.

The message is clear: we are called to make the most of the resources and abilities that God has given us. Whether it is our time, finances, skills, or spiritual gifts, we are to use them wisely and diligently for the glory of God and the advancement of His kingdom.

The parable highlights the principle that faithfulness in small things leads to greater responsibility and blessings from God. If we are faithful stewards of what God has entrusted to us, He will entrust us with more and welcome us into His joy.

We should aspire to hear our Master say to us, "Well done, good and faithful servant! Come and share your master's happiness." This can be achieved by faithfully using our talents to serve God and others, bringing glory to His name and furthering His kingdom.

Let us not squander the gifts and opportunities God has given us, but instead invest them wisely for His purposes. As *Luke 16:10* reminds us, being faithful with little will lead to greater trust and blessings from God.

Whoever can be trusted with very little can also be trusted with much and whoever is dishonest with very little will also be dishonest with much. Luke 16:10

There was a great calm

He got up, rebuked the wind, and said to the waves, 'Quiet! Be still!' Then the wind died down and it was completely calm. Mark 4:39

The story recounted in *Mark 4:39* and *Matthew 8:24-27* illustrates Jesus' authority over the elements. As Jesus and His disciples sailed across the sea, a violent storm arose, threatening to capsize their boat. Despite the chaos, Jesus remained asleep until His disciples woke Him, fearing for their lives. In response, Jesus rebuked the wind and the sea, instantly calming the storm and leaving His disciples in awe of His power.

Likewise, many of us may find ourselves in the midst of life's storms, feeling overwhelmed by challenges that seem insurmountable. Whether it is family discord, job loss, financial struggles, health issues, relational conflicts, or battles with sin, the tempests of life can leave us feeling powerless and afraid.

Yet, the same Jesus who calmed the storm for His disciples centuries ago remains with us today. His voice still carries the authority to quiet the raging winds in our lives and bring about a profound calm. We need only to call upon Him in faith, trusting that He cares for us and has the power to intervene in our circumstances.

Just as Jesus questioned His disciples' faith during the storm, He invites us to examine our own faith amidst life's challenges. Do we truly believe that Jesus is present with us in the midst of our storms? Do we trust in His ability to bring peace and deliverance?

Let us take heart in the assurance that Jesus is indeed with us, ready to rebuke the storms that threaten to overwhelm us. As we place our faith in Him, He will speak the words, "Quiet! Be still!" and bring about a great calm in our lives, filling us with His peace and marveling at His miraculous work.

Is our garden ready?

Awake, north wind, and come south wind! Blow on my garden, so that its fragrance may spread abroad. Let my lover come into his garden and taste its choice fruits. Song of Solomon 4:16

In Song of Solomon 4:16, the maiden Shulamite calls upon the winds to blow upon her garden, inviting her Lover to come and enjoy its delights. The imagery of the garden symbolizes believers preparing themselves for the presence of Jesus Christ, their beloved.

Just as the Shulamite meticulously tends to her garden, believers are called to cultivate their hearts and lives for Jesus. The enclosed garden represents a life consecrated to God, with its spring and fountain sealed, symbolizing purity and commitment. Through the planting of virtues and the cultivation of spiritual fruit, believers create a fragrant offering to their Lord.

The contrasting north and south winds signify the varied experiences believers encounter—adversity and prosperity—which shape and refine them, preparing them to bear fruit for the Lord. Ultimately, it is the Holy Spirit, depicted as the wind, who works within believers, empowering them to grow and produce spiritual fruit.

As believers eagerly anticipate the return of their Lord, they must continually assess their spiritual readiness. Just as the Shulamite desires her garden to be prepared for her Beloved, believers must ensure that their lives are characterized by spiritual vitality and fruitfulness. If they find themselves lacking, they can call upon the Holy Spirit to work within them, bringing forth the fruits of righteousness and spreading the sweet fragrance of Christ's love to those around them.

Let us, therefore, keep our gardens prepared for Jesus, cultivating lives that are pleasing to Him and ready to welcome His presence.

KEEP WATCH SINCE YOU DO NOT KNOW THE HOUR

They will see the Son of Man coming on the clouds of heaven with power and great glory. Heaven and earth shall pass away, but my words shall not pass away. Watch, therefore: for you know not what hour your Lord shall come. Matthew 24:30, 35, 42

No one knows about that day or hour of the coming of Jesus, not even the angels in heaven, nor the Son, but only the Father. Matthew 24:36

These Scriptures highlight the anticipation of Jesus Christ's return and the need for readiness among believers. Jesus emphasizes the uncertainty surrounding the exact timing of His coming, urging vigilance and preparedness at all times. The imagery of Jesus coming on the clouds with power and glory signifies His majestic return, a moment that will bring both awe and mourning to the earth. In light of this, believers are exhorted to stay vigilant, living in accordance with God's commandments and teachings, and filled with the Holy Spirit, ensuring there is no darkness within them.

As the Bridegroom, Jesus is coming for His bride, the Church, and believers are called to keep themselves pure and ready for His return. Just as a bride prepares herself eagerly for her groom, so too should believers eagerly anticipate the coming of their Lord, maintaining purity and holiness. The passage from *Malachi 3:17* reinforces the idea that believers are treasured possessions to the Lord, emphasizing the importance of living in a manner that honors Him.

Additionally, the promise of *1 Thessalonians 4:16-17* assures believers that when Christ returns, both the dead in Christ and the living believers will be caught up to meet Him in the air. This underscores the need for readiness among all believers, whether alive or deceased, to meet the Lord when He returns.

In summary, believers are urged to remain watchful and prepared, living lives that reflect purity, holiness, and obedience to God's commandments, eagerly awaiting the glorious return of Jesus Christ.

A TREE IS IDENTIFIED BY ITS FRUIT

Every good tree bears good fruit, but a bad tree bears bad fruit. A good tree cannot bear bad fruit, nor can a bad tree bear good fruit. Every tree that does not bear good fruit is cut down and thrown into the fire. Therefore, by their fruits, you will know them. Matthew 7:17-20

Jesus uses the analogy of trees and their fruit to illustrate a spiritual truth: just as a good tree naturally produces good fruit and a bad tree produces bad fruit, so too do our actions reveal the condition of our hearts. He emphasizes that a tree that fails to bear good fruit will ultimately be cut down and destroyed.

This principle is further illustrated in the parable of the barren fig tree found in *Luke 13:6-9.* Despite being given time and care to produce fruit, the fig tree remained barren, leading to its eventual condemnation. This serves as a sobering reminder that as believers, we are called to bear fruit in our lives that glorifies God.

The fruits of the Spirit outlined in *Galatians 5:22-23*—love, joy, peace, patience, kindness, goodness, faithfulness, gentleness, and self-control—serve as a benchmark for believers to evaluate their spiritual growth. These qualities should be evident in our lives as a result of being filled with the Holy Spirit.

However, Jesus also warns of the consequences of failing to bear fruit, as seen in the account of the fig tree He cursed in *Matthew 21:19.* Just as the fig tree withered due to its lack of fruit, so too will those who fail to produce spiritual fruit face spiritual consequences.

Therefore, it is essential for believers to continually submit themselves to the sanctifying work of the Holy Spirit, allowing Him to cultivate the fruits of righteousness within them. By doing so, we demonstrate our faithfulness to God and bring glory to His name through our actions and attitudes. Let us strive to bear fruit that is pleasing to the Lord, knowing that our lives will be a testament to His transformative power.

BE SURE YOU KNOW THE CONDITION OF YOUR FLOCK

Be sure you know the condition of your flocks, give careful attention to your herds. Proverbs 27:23

When Jesus asked Simon three times if he loved Him more than others. Simon answered: 'Yes Lord' – to which Jesus said, 'Feed my lambs' and 'Take care of my sheep'. *John 21:15-17*

The verse from Proverbs 27:23 emphasizes the importance of knowing and caring for one's flock or herds. In John 21:15-17, Jesus instructs Peter to feed His lambs and take care of His sheep, symbolizing the responsibility believers have to nurture and care for others, especially those under their care.

Jesus entrusts us with the task of caring for His lambs and sheep, which represent our children, students, servants, and all those who depend on us. For church leaders, this responsibility extends to the believers in their congregations.

To fulfill this duty, we must be diligent in understanding the condition of our flock. We need to know if our children and those under our care are walking with the Lord, where they are, and what they are doing. It involves setting a positive example, spending time with them, praying for them, and showing them love and affection.

Just as Jesus showed compassion to the multitude and the apostles wrote epistles to encourage believers, we are called to love and feed our flock spiritually. We should strive to ensure that none of our "lambs" go astray, seeking them out with prayer and bringing them back to the fold.

In following Jesus's example as a good shepherd, we demonstrate our love for the Lord by caring for those entrusted to us. Let us be diligent in knowing the condition of our flock and giving them the attention and care they need to thrive spiritually.

HEARD, SEEN, WITNESSED

When the angels had left them and gone into heaven, the shepherds said to one another, "Let's go to Bethlehem and see this thing that has happened, which the Lord has told us about." So, they hurried off and found Mary and Joseph, and the baby, who was lying in the manger. When they had seen him, they spread the word concerning what had been told them about this child. Luke 2:15-17

This passage recounts the shepherds' response to the angels' announcement of Jesus' birth. They immediately went to Bethlehem to see the newborn Jesus and then shared the news with others.

Similarly, we have all heard about Jesus and His mission to save us. The crucial question is whether we have personally accepted Him as our Savior and experienced the cleansing power of His blood shed for us. Once we have encountered Jesus and His saving grace, we are called to witness to others about the reality of His birth and its significance for humanity.

Jesus commissioned us to share the good news of His salvation with others, spreading the message to the ends of the earth. When we encounter Jesus and experience His forgiveness and presence in our lives, we should not keep this joy of salvation to ourselves. Instead, we should carry the light of Jesus wherever we go, demonstrating to others that He is the only way to salvation.

Just as the shepherds heard, saw, and then witnessed to others about Jesus, we too are called to hear the message of salvation, experience His presence in our lives, and share that reality with those around us.

COMFORTED BY A ROD AND A STAFF

Your rod and your staff, they comfort me. Psalm 23:4

A staff is a sturdy wooden stick with a curved end, held by the shepherd, while a rod is a thick stick typically worn in the shepherd's belt.

When considering how a shepherd's rod and staff can provide comfort to sheep, it is natural to focus on their disciplinary function, such as guiding straying sheep back to the flock. However, a deeper reflection reveals that these tools serve various other purposes:

The shepherd employs the staff to bend tree branches so the animals can access nourishing leaves, clear pathways, and untangle bushes the sheep may become ensnared in. Additionally, the rod is utilized for defense, warding off predators like snakes or dogs and ensuring the safety of the flock. It is also used to examine sick animals and provide support when needed.

Moreover, the shepherd's rod and staff signify authority and protection, establishing the shepherd's role as the leader and guardian of the flock.

In our spiritual lives, as the Lord is our Shepherd, His rod and staff provide comfort and assurance. While they may be used for correction when necessary, their primary purpose is to guide, protect, and care for us. Just as a loving earthly father disciplines his children for their benefit, our Heavenly Father's discipline is rooted in His love for us, fostering our growth and well-being. Thus, we find solace in knowing that we are under His watchful care and guidance. Amen.

In the way of righteousness is life

In the way of righteousness there is life; along that path is immortality.
Proverbs 12:28

Life is a series of choices, each one shaping our eternity. There's no middle ground – it is either black or white, the narrow path to eternal life or the broad road to destruction. Our choices determine whether we please God or the world, whether we embrace good or evil. There's no room for ambiguity.

In Deuteronomy, God presents the Israelites with a clear choice: life and prosperity or death and destruction. He commands them to love Him, walk in obedience, and keep His decrees. The consequence of disobedience is equally clear – destruction and curses.

Today, the same choice is before us. God urges us to obey His Word, to choose life and blessings. If we refuse, we are effectively choosing death and curses. The decision is ours to make, and we cannot blame anyone but ourselves.

So, what will we choose? Will we embrace God's Word and receive His blessings, or will we reject it and face the consequences? The choice is ours, and it carries eternal significance.

This day I call the heavens and the earth as witnesses against you that I have set before you life and death, blessings and curses. Now choose life, so that you and your children may live and that you may love the Lord your God, listen to his voice, and hold fast to him. For the Lord is your life, and he will give you many years in the land he swore to give to your fathers, Abraham, Isaac, and Jacob. Deuteronomy 30:15-20

Hold on to what you have

I am coming soon. Hold on to what you have, so that no one will take your crown. Revelation 3:11

Only hold on to what you have until I come. Revelation 2:25

The message is clear: "Hold on to what you have." But what exactly do we possess? Let us turn to Scripture for guidance:

We're instructed to hold on to the good *(1 Thessalonians 5:21)*, embracing what is righteous and virtuous in our lives. We're encouraged to cling unwaveringly to the hope we profess, knowing that the One who promised is faithful *(Hebrews 10:23)*. Moreover, we're reminded to grasp firmly the gift of eternal life to which we have been called *(1 Timothy 6:12)*, recognizing its profound significance.

Wisdom is likened to a tree of life, and we're urged to lay hold of it for blessings *(Proverbs 3:18)*. Additionally, we're called to hold firmly to our faith, standing steadfast in what we believe *(Hebrews 4:14)*. We're also exhorted to stand firm and cling to the teachings passed on to us *(2 Thessalonians 2:15)*, recognizing their importance in guiding our lives.

Furthermore, we're reminded to hold on to instruction and guard it diligently, recognizing its vital role in shaping our lives *(Proverbs 4:13)*.

As believers in Christ, we're called to hold on to these truths, virtues, and instructions until His return. It is through the help of the Holy Spirit that we can maintain this firm grip on what we have been given. Therefore, let us seek the Holy Spirit is guidance and strength to hold fast to what is good and true in our lives.

WHY DIE BEFORE YOUR TIME?

Do not be over wicked, and do not be a fool--why die before your time?
Ecclesiastes 7:17

The Scripture above warns against being overly wicked or foolish, as it can lead to premature death or destruction. It urges individuals to consider the consequences of their actions and to choose wisdom and righteousness instead.

God extends an invitation to those who are weary and burdened, offering them rest and relief from their struggles. This invitation is echoed in *Matthew 11:28*, where Jesus calls upon all who are weary to come to Him for rest and comfort. It emphasizes the importance of surrendering one's burdens and finding solace in the love and grace of God.

The sacrifice of Jesus on the cross provides redemption and freedom for all who believe in Him. By accepting His sacrifice and surrendering to His will, individuals can find peace, joy, and deliverance from the bondage of sin and despair.

James 4:7 encourages believers to submit themselves to God and resist the devil, knowing that through God's strength, they can overcome temptation and evil. Similarly, *James 1:12* reminds believers of the reward awaiting those who persevere under trial, emphasizing the importance of enduring faith and trust in God's promises.

By surrendering to God, resisting temptation, and persevering in faith, believers can experience the fullness of life and receive the eternal crown of life promised by God.

"Come to me, all you who are weary and burdened, and I will give you rest. Matthew 11:28

Blessed is the man who perseveres under trial because when he has stood the test, he will receive the crown of life that God has promised to those who love him. James 1:12

Will a man rob God? Yet you rob Me

"Will a man rob God? Yet you have robbed Me! But you say, 'In what way have we robbed You?' In tithes and offerings. Bring all the tithes into the storehouse, That there may be food in My house. Malachi 3:8, 10

This Scripture highlights the importance of tithing and offering in the worship of God. God admonishes His people for withholding their tithes and offerings, equating it to robbing Him of what rightfully belongs to Him. By neglecting to contribute to the work of the Lord, individuals not only deprive God but also hinder the blessings that He intends to pour out upon them.

The command to bring all tithes into the storehouse emphasizes the necessity of supporting the work of God's house, ensuring that there is provision for the needs of the ministry. God promises abundant blessings and provision for those who faithfully give, assuring them of His favor and protection.

Many individuals may find themselves at odds with this command, rationalizing their inability to tithe or give offerings. However, the Scripture makes it clear that withholding from God is a serious offense, one that not only deprives Him but also impacts the giver's own blessings and provision. It is a matter of trust and obedience, demonstrating faithfulness in honoring God with our resources.

The passage challenges believers to examine their stewardship and commitment to God's work, encouraging them to give willingly and cheerfully, knowing that God loves a cheerful giver. By embracing a spirit of generosity and obedience in their giving, believers can experience the fullness of God's blessings and provision in their lives.

Let each one give as he purposes in his heart, not grudgingly or of necessity; for God loves a cheerful giver. 2 Corinthians 9:7

Persevere under trial

*Blessed is the man who perseveres under trial because when he has stood
the test, he will receive the crown of life that God has promised to those
who love him. James 1:12*

The passage highlights the blessedness of those who endure trials
with steadfast faith, as they will ultimately receive the crown of
life promised by God. Trials are an inevitable part of life, encompassing
various challenges such as decision-making, relationships, health issues,
and financial struggles. However, instead of turning away from God
during tough times, believers are encouraged to cling closer to Him,
trusting in His faithfulness and sovereignty.

Jesus Himself acknowledges the reality of trials in the world but
offers assurance by proclaiming His victory over the world (*John 16:33*).
The Apostle Paul, in his writings, exemplifies the importance of persevering in faith despite trials, expressing confidence in God's provision
and strength to endure temptation (*2 Timothy 4:7*).

Central to navigating trials and temptations is one's attitude. Job,
in the Old Testament, serves as a model of resilience and faithfulness in
the face of extreme adversity. Despite experiencing profound suffering
and loss, Job remains steadfast in his integrity, refusing to curse God
and recognizing that both good and trouble come from God's hand.

In emulating Job's example, believers are encouraged to maintain
their faith and integrity amidst trials, trusting in God's sovereignty
and provision. Rather than succumbing to despair or turning away
from God, they are urged to stand firm, seek refuge in Him alone, and
persevere under trial, knowing that their faithfulness will ultimately
be rewarded.

THE BEST OFFERING THAT THE LORD ACCEPTS

Does the Lord delight in burnt offerings and sacrifices as much as in obeying the voice of the Lord? To obey is better than sacrifice, and to heed is better than the fat of rams. 1 Samuel 15:22

This passage emphasizes the importance of obedience to God over the mere performance of religious rituals or sacrifices. It contrasts the value of obeying God's voice with the act of offering sacrifices, highlighting that obedience is far more significant and pleasing to the Lord.

In the context of King Saul's disobedience, the passage illustrates how he mistakenly believed that offering sacrifices could rectify his wrongdoing. However, the prophet Samuel makes it clear that God values obedience above ritualistic acts of worship.

King David acknowledges in Psalm 51 that God desires a broken and contrite heart rather than mere outward sacrifices. This sentiment is echoed in Proverbs and Micah, emphasizing that acting justly, showing mercy, and walking humbly with God are what truly matter to Him. Jeremiah further reinforces this message by stating that God's primary command to His people is obedience, rather than merely performing sacrifices.

Ultimately, the Scriptures presented suggest that genuine obedience, humility, and a contrite spirit are what God truly desires from His people, far surpassing the value of ritualistic sacrifices.

What does the Lord require of you? To act justly and to love mercy and to walk humbly with your God. Micah 6:8

In *Jeremiah 7:22, 23* God clarifies His commands about sacrifices: He says, *"When I brought your forefathers out of Egypt and spoke to them, I did not just give them commands about burnt offerings and sacrifices, but I gave them this command: Obey me, and I will be your God and you will be my people. Walk in all the ways I command you, that it may go well with you."*

FAITH AS SMALL AS THE MUSTARD SEED

Jesus said to His disciples, *"If you have faith as small as a mustard seed, you can say to this mulberry tree, 'Be uprooted and planted in the sea,' and it will obey you. Luke 17:5, 6*

> *"For truly I say to you, if you have faith the size of a mustard seed, you will say to this mountain, 'Move from here to there,' and it will move; and nothing will be impossible to you." Matthew 17:19, 20*

Jesus in these Scriptures emphasized the potency of even a small amount of faith, likening it to a mustard seed—a tiny yet vibrant symbol of faith in action. Hebrews 11:6 underscores the indispensability of faith in pleasing God, highlighting that faith devoid of action holds no value.

Yet, faith devoid of action isn't just too little; it is also too much i.e., excessive or redundant, as it lacks the vitality necessary for transformative power. Conversely, the faith embodied by the mustard seed epitomizes active trust in God's providence, willing to sacrifice and grow abundantly. Our faith should mirror this mustard seed—complete, wholehearted, and pulsating with life, firmly believing that God orchestrates all things for our ultimate good, as Romans 8:28 assures us.

Regarding moving mountains or uprooting trees, Jesus affirmed that such feats are attainable with mustard-seed faith, signifying unwavering trust in God's omnipotence. This faith, brimming with vitality, has the potential to manifest both figurative and literal miracles.

Therefore, our pursuit should prioritize the quality rather than the quantity of our faith. Understanding God's perfect will and actively exercising our faith must be our foremost endeavor—a commitment to vibrant, action-oriented trust in the One who can move mountains and shape destinies.

> *"Without faith, it is impossible to please God..." Hebrews 11:6*

HE WHO GATHERS CROPS IN SUMMER IS A WISE SON

He who gathers crops in summer is a wise son, but he who sleeps during harvest is a disgraceful son. Proverbs 10:5

Proverbs 10:5 emphasizes the importance of diligence and timely action, drawing parallels between agricultural work and spiritual responsibility. Just as a wise son gathers crops during the summer harvest, neglecting this duty brings disgrace. Farmers eagerly anticipate harvest time as the culmination of their efforts, but laziness during this crucial period leads to wasted yields, snatched away by birds or left for passersby.

Similarly, in our spiritual endeavors, merely sowing seeds of faith isn't sufficient; we must also engage in the crucial task of nurturing and reaping the harvest of souls. Beyond planting the Word of God, we're called to fervently pray for the salvation of others, ensuring they come to know Christ—a vital aspect of spiritual "harvesting" often overlooked.

Jesus Himself emphasized the abundant spiritual harvest awaiting, juxtaposed with the scarcity of laborers. He urged prayer for workers to engage in this plentiful harvest *(Matthew 9:37, 38)*. Moreover, biblical passages like Exodus 23:16 and *Proverbs 6:6-9* underscore God's design of harvest as a time for celebration and diligence, respectively. *Hosea 10:12* calls for righteousness in sowing and mercy in reaping, urging the breaking of fallow ground to seek the Lord's righteousness. Indeed, sowing demands labor, while harvesting evokes joy and festivity, as articulated in *Psalm 126:5, 6.*

Those who sow with tears will reap with songs of joy. Those who go out weeping, carrying seed to sow, will return with songs of joy, carrying sheaves with them. Psalm 126:5, 6

'Let us fear the Lord our God, who gives autumn and spring rains in season, who assures us of the regular weeks of harvest.' Jeremiah 5:24

New birth in Christ

He saved us, not because of the righteous things we had done, but because of his mercy. He washed away our sins, giving us a new birth and new life through the Holy Spirit. Titus 3:5

Titus 3:5 reminds us of the foundation of our salvation: not our own righteous deeds, but the boundless mercy of God. Through His mercy, we experience a profound transformation symbolized by a new birth and new life, facilitated by the Holy Spirit. This rebirth signifies a fresh start, a life infused with Christ's presence, nourished by His Word, and sustained by the Holy Spirit is guiding streams of living water.

The concept of being "born again" intrigued Nicodemus, prompting his inquiry to Jesus. Jesus clarified that this spiritual rebirth is essential for entering the kingdom of God. It transcends physical birth, signifying a spiritual awakening enabled by water and the Spirit. While physical birth begets fleshly existence, being born again through the Spirit signifies a spiritual regeneration, birthing us into God's family.

When we heed the Holy Spirit is prompting and accept Jesus as our Savior, we experience this spiritual rebirth, becoming children of God. Our assurance of being born again rests in our acknowledgment of Jesus's sacrificial death, resurrection, and eternal life. This faith, instilled by the Holy Spirit, marks us as new creations in Christ, with old patterns of life passing away and all things being made new *(2 Corinthians 5:17)*.

So, do you possess the assurance of being born again in the Holy Spirit? Do you affirm Jesus's atoning sacrifice, resurrection, and eternal reign? If so, rejoice, for you are a new creation in Christ, enveloped by His transformative grace and empowered by the Holy Spirit. May this faith continue to deepen in you, nurtured by the Spirit is presence and guidance.

If anyone is in Christ, he is a new creation; old things have passed away; behold, all things have become new. 2 Corinthians 5:17

New Life in Christ

Put off your old self, which is being corrupted by its deceitful desires; ......
put on the new self, created to be like God in true righteousness and holiness.
Ephesians 4:22, 24

If anyone is in Christ, the new creation has come: The old has gone, the
new is here! 2 Corinthians 5:17

These Scriptures underscore the profound transformation that occurs when individuals embrace Christ. It entails shedding their former selves, tainted by sinful desires, and adopting a new identity reflective of God's righteousness and holiness.

Ephesians 4:17-32 offers practical guidance for this metamorphosis, emphasizing a holistic renewal of mind and behavior. Believers are urged to reject worldly thinking, allowing the Holy Spirit to renovate their thought patterns and attitudes. This involves discarding old habits and embracing virtues aligned with Christ's character.

Truthfulness, integrity, and managing emotions constructively are encouraged, while guarding against temptation and cultivating a spirit of generosity and encouragement. The process includes honoring the Holy Spirit is presence within, avoiding actions that grieve Him, and fostering qualities like kindness, forgiveness, and compassion.

Through intentional effort and reliance on God's grace, believers embark on a journey of continual growth toward Christlikeness, embodying the transformative power of the Gospel.

GREAT LESSONS FROM LITTLE THINGS

There are four things which are little on the earth, but they are exceedingly wise: The ants are a people not strong, Yet they prepare their food in the summer; The rock badgers are a feeble folk, Yet they make their homes in the crags; The locusts have no king, Yet they all advance in ranks; The spider skillfully grasps with its hands, And it is in kings' palaces. Proverbs 30:24-28

The Book of Proverbs highlights the wisdom found in seemingly insignificant creatures on earth. Among these examples are the ants, which, despite their lack of strength, diligently prepare for the future by storing food in the summer. This behavior mirrors the importance of seeking the Lord and working diligently while it is still possible, preparing for the future (Isaiah 55:6; John 9:4).

Similarly, rock badgers, though small and feeble, display wisdom by swiftly retreating to the safety of rocky crags at the slightest hint of danger. They serve as a reminder for us to seek refuge in Christ, our Rock, especially in times of trouble (Psalm 61:2).

Locusts, despite lacking a leader, move in perfect harmony, functioning as a unified force. They inspire us to maintain unity and cooperation with fellow believers, acting together for the advancement of God's kingdom (Philippians 2:2).

Likewise, spiders fearlessly spin their webs even in the most regal settings, exemplifying diligence and purposefulness. They encourage us to use our talents diligently and without fear, working to fulfill God's purposes and bring others into His kingdom (Ephesians 2:10).

These humble creatures serve as teachers, imparting valuable lessons about preparation, seeking refuge in Christ, unity, and diligence. Despite their small stature, their wisdom surpasses that of many humans, reminding us to learn from all aspects of God's creation. Let us heed these lessons and apply them to our lives, seeking wisdom in the ways of the Lord.

THE DESIRES OF THE DILIGENT ARE FULLY SATISFIED

The sluggard craves and gets nothing, but the desires of the diligent are fully satisfied. Proverbs 13:4

Throughout the Book of Proverbs, the sluggard is consistently admonished for their lack of initiative and productivity. Conversely, diligent individuals are repeatedly praised for their hard work and dedication, which leads to fulfillment and blessings.

For instance, while the lazy neglect to utilize their resources effectively, the diligent take pride in their possessions *(Proverbs 12:27)*. Laziness results in poverty, whereas diligence brings prosperity *(Proverbs 10:4)*. Diligent hands are destined for leadership, while laziness leads to servitude *(Proverbs 12:24)*. Those diligent in their pursuits will find favor and success, even standing before kings *(Proverbs 22:29)*. The plans of the diligent invariably yield profit (Proverbs 21:5), ensuring their desires are fully satisfied.

But what does it truly mean to be diligent? Diligence entails striving for excellence in all endeavors, demonstrating perseverance and meticulous effort. However, true diligence transcends mere worldly pursuits; it encompasses a fervent commitment to God's kingdom, the propagation of the Gospel, holy living, and the salvation of souls.

By prioritizing godly endeavors, we invite divine blessings into our lives, effortlessly aligning our desires with God's will. As we seek first the kingdom of God and His righteousness, He promises to provide for all our needs and desires *(Matthew 6:33)*. Let us, therefore, pursue diligence in our pursuit of God's purposes, confident that He will abundantly satisfy our hearts' desires.

LOVE ONE ANOTHER

Love one another. As I have loved you. John 13:34

Be kind and compassionate to one another, forgiving each other Ephesians 4:32

Bear with each other and forgive whatever grievances you may have against one another. Colossians 3:13

Be devoted to one another in brotherly love. Romans 12:10

Encourage one another and build each other up. I Thessalonians 5:11

Submit to one another out of reverence for Christ. Ephesians 5:21

The Scriptures echo a resounding call for us to nurture healthy relationships with one another, rooted in love, kindness, and forgiveness. Yet, despite these exhortations, maintaining harmonious relationships can be challenging. As we grow older, we often find ourselves drifting apart from friends and family who may not align with our views or preferences. We may justify this distance, but it begs the question: Are our relationships with God unaffected by such detachment?

In truth, we may be deceiving ourselves if we claim perfect harmony in our relationship with God while neglecting our relationships with others. Let us humbly seek guidance from the Scriptures to illuminate the path of righteousness for us. May we earnestly endeavor to rebuild and nurture our connections with one another, anchored in Christ's love. Let us eagerly anticipate the transformative work of God in our relationships.

As we embark on this journey of reconciliation and renewal, let us extend grace, forgiveness, and love to those around us, reflecting the love of Christ in all our interactions.

BLESSINGS FOR THOSE WHO FEAR THE LORD

He will bless those who fear the Lord--small and great alike. Psalm 115:13

For as high as the heavens are above the earth, so great is His loving devotion for those who fear Him. Psalm 103:11

The blessings of those who fear the Lord are emphasized throughout the Psalms and other passages of Scripture. *Psalm 115:13* assures that the Lord will bless both small and great who hold Him in reverence. *Psalm 103:11* illustrates the vastness of His loving devotion for those who fear Him.

Psalm 128 further expounds on these blessings, detailing the prosperity and joy that come to those who walk in the ways of the Lord. Their labor bears fruit, their families flourish, and they are blessed with peace and prosperity. Scripture repeatedly calls for fearing the Lord, serving Him faithfully, and turning away from other gods. In *Joshua 24:14* and *1 Samuel 7:3*, the importance of serving the Lord wholeheartedly is emphasized, while *Psalm 135:20* encourages praise from those who fear Him.

As we reflect on these passages, let us renew our commitment to walk in His ways, serving Him faithfully with all our hearts. Let us turn away from any idols or distractions that vie for our devotion and instead wholeheartedly worship the Lord. May our lives be marked by reverence for God, leading to a rich outpouring of His blessings upon us and our families.

THE VALLEY OF WEEPING BECOMES A
PLACE OF REFRESHING SPRINGS

When they walk through the Valley of Weeping, it will become a place of refreshing springs. The autumn rains will clothe it with blessings. Psalm 84:6

Psalm 84 beautifully captures the joy of worshiping God at the Temple in Jerusalem. As believers journey toward this sacred place, they may encounter the Valley of Weeping—a metaphor for life's trials and hardships. Despite the challenges, we are reminded that we are merely passing through this valley, not dwelling in it permanently. Therefore, we should not lose heart but press on toward the ultimate goal of worshiping God in His sanctuary.

The Psalm beautifully outlines the qualities of those eagerly anticipating worshiping at the Temple. They are individuals who continually dwell in the presence of the Lord, offering songs of praise. Their strength is found solely in God, and they are wholly devoted to worshiping Him. Longing to be in His presence, they cry out for Him even amid the Valley of Weeping, where they transform adversity into a source of refreshing springs.

These worshipers remain undeterred by adversity, knowing that their sole focus is on encountering God. They understand that if they seek God's presence, He will provide for their needs and concerns, including their children's welfare. The imagery of sparrows finding a home near God's altar emphasizes the divine care and provision for all creatures, instilling confidence in God's faithfulness.

Even the sparrow finds a home, and the swallow builds her nest and raises her young at a place near your altar. Psalm 84:3

SEEING GOD FACE TO FACE

So, Jacob called the name of the place Peniel: "For I have seen God face to face, and my life is preserved." Genesis 32:30

Then she called the name of the Lord who spoke to her You-Are-The-God-Who-Sees; for she said, "Have I also here seen Him who sees me?" Genesis 16:13

Now Gideon perceived that He was the Angel of the Lord. So, Gideon said, "Alas, O Lord God! For I have seen the Angel of the Lord face to face." Judges 6:22

And Manoah said to his wife, "We shall surely die because we have seen God!" Judges 13:22

I speak with him face to face, Even plainly, and not in dark sayings; And he sees the form of the Lord. Why then were you not afraid To speak against My servant Moses?" Numbers 12:8

The encounters of individuals with God or His messengers face-to-face, as recorded in Scripture, evoke a sense of awe and wonder. To witness God's presence firsthand is indeed a profound blessing, worthy of praise and adoration. Personally, I have been blessed to encounter our Lord Jesus twice—once in a vision and another time in a dream. Both experiences were profoundly beautiful, leaving an indelible mark on my soul.

In our current state, our perception of God is limited, akin to seeing a reflection in a mirror dimly. However, a time will come when we shall know Him fully, even as we are fully known (1 Corinthians 13:12). The promise of His return is certain, foretold in Revelation 1:7, when every eye will behold Him, even those who crucified Him, ushering in a time of profound revelation and reckoning.

Are we prepared to meet Him face-to-face? The key lies in believing in Jesus and surrendering our lives to Him. Through His grace and transformative power, He prepares us for the sacred encounter of beholding God's glory. Let us, therefore, trust in Him and eagerly anticipate the day when we shall see Him face-to-face.

RETURN HOME

The Angel of the Lord said to her, "Return to your mistress, and submit yourself under her hand." Genesis 16:9

When he came to himself, he said, "I will arise and go to my father and will say to him, "Father, I have sinned against heaven and before you. Luke 15:17, 18

Perhaps you find yourself at a crossroads, uncertain of which path to take, akin to Hagar's plight, struggling amidst family turmoil. Maybe you have yearned for independence among friends, away from the confines of familial expectations, or endured ridicule for illness, poverty, or other trials, prompting departure from home.

In each scenario, the divine directive echoes: "Return home." Yet, this return demands humility—seeking forgiveness, submitting to authority—but it leads to restoration and acceptance, fostering familial love and respect. By obeying God and reconciling with family, we pave the way for deliverance and elevation. Just as Hagar birthed a nation and the repentant son became favored, and the healed man became a herald of Jesus' miracles, our return home becomes a testament to God's transformative power.

Therefore, let us heed the call to return home, sharing the story of God's intervention in our lives, for in doing so, we witness His faithfulness and grace.

"Return to your own house, and tell what great things God has done for you." And he went his way and proclaimed throughout the whole city what great things Jesus had done for him. Luke 8:39

CARRY YOUR CROSS AND FOLLOW JESUS

And whoever does not carry their cross and follow me cannot be my disciple.
Luke 14:27

This Scripture reminds us that carrying our cross and following Jesus is an essential aspect of discipleship. Regardless of our beliefs or circumstances, each of us faces challenges and burdens—our own cross to bear. Whether we perceive it as small or significant, these burdens are part of our human experience, stemming from the toils of life since Adam and Eve were expelled from Eden.

The crucial question is whether we are willing to follow the Lord despite the weight of our cross. Will we remain faithful and steadfast in our service to God, even amidst adversity? True discipleship means maintaining our devotion to the Lord through thick and thin, offering praise regardless of our circumstances, and unwaveringly trusting in God's provision, even when our resources dwindle.

Carrying our cross and following Jesus requires resilience and unwavering faith. Rather than turning away from God when faced with hardship, we are called to draw nearer to Him, finding solace and strength in His promises.

The hidden truth lies in the fact that as soon as we take a single step towards Him, He hastens to welcome us and shoulder our burdens for the remainder of the journey. As Jesus Himself affirms: *"Come to me, all you who are weary and burdened, and I will give you rest. Take my yoke upon you and learn from me, for I am gentle and humble in heart, and you will find rest for your souls. For my yoke is easy and my burden is light." Matthew 11:28-30*

GOD HAS CALLED US TO LIVE A HOLY LIFE

God did not call us to be impure but to live a holy life. 1 Thessalonians 4:7

Apostle Paul instructs us on living a holy life, outlining God's will for our sanctification: *For this is the will of God, your sanctification: that you should abstain from sexual immorality; that each of you should know how to possess his own vessel in sanctification and honor, not in passion of lust, like the Gentiles who do not know God; that no one should take advantage of and defraud his brother in this matter because the Lord is the avenger of all such. 1 Thessalonians 4:3-6*

The gravity of sexual immorality is a recurring theme in Paul's writings, addressed not only to the Thessalonians but also to the Corinthians, Ephesians, and Colossians, resonating with us today:

> *"Flee from sexual immorality. All other sins a man commits are outside his body, but he who sins sexually sins against his own body." (1 Corinthians 6:18)*

> *"Among you, there must not be even a hint of sexual immorality, or of any kind of impurity, or of greed, because these are improper for God's holy people." (Ephesians 5:3)*

> *"Put to death, therefore, whatever belongs to your earthly nature: sexual immorality, impurity, lust, evil desires." (Colossians 3:5)*

Despite societal perceptions of sexual immorality as mere instinct, we cannot trivialize it as such. Our God is holy, and as His children, we are called to reflect His holiness. His standard is unwaveringly high. Let us embrace our calling to lead lives of holiness. The Holy Spirit serves as our guide, convicting us of sin, righteousness, and judgment, leading us into truth (John 16:8, 13).

For those grappling with impurities, let us humbly approach the Lord, confessing our shortcomings and seeking cleansing through His redeeming blood. God beckons us to pursue lives marked by holiness.

FOLLOW THE WAYS OF YOUR HEART, BUT FEAR GOD'S JUDGMENT

Be happy, young man, while you are young, and let your heart give you joy in the days of your youth. Follow the ways of your heart and whatever your eyes see but know that for all these things God will bring you to judgment. Ecclesiastes 11:9

But if a man lives many years and rejoices in them all, let him remember the days of darkness; for they shall be many. Ecclesiastes 11:8

King Solomon, renowned for his wisdom, extensively researched all aspects of life under the sun. His conclusion? Childhood and youth are fleeting, characterized by vanity. Youthful desires often center around self-gratification, resisting rules and regulations. Solomon cautions the young that while they may indulge in whatever pleases them, they remain accountable to God's judgment. Their freedom is not absolute; enjoyment should be tempered with awareness of divine accountability.

As believers, we are bound by God's standards, not the indulgences of the world. Yet, this does not entail a joyless existence. God grants us numerous blessings to enjoy—family gatherings, church fellowships, outdoor activities—gifts meant for our happiness. Solomon urges the young to contemplate the inevitability of aging and its associated challenges. In the twilight years, pleasure wanes, replaced by ailments and difficulties. Therefore, he implores them to remember their Creator before the onset of adversity.

In conclusion, Solomon's wisdom resounds: Fear God and keep His commandments, as this is humanity's ultimate duty. Every deed, whether seen or hidden, will face divine scrutiny *(Ecclesiastes 12:13-14)*. Thus, young ones, heed not only your own understanding but also the wisdom of the elderly. Embrace the fear of the Lord and shun evil *(Proverbs 3:7)*.

Dishonest scales are an
abomination to the Lord

Dishonest scales are an abomination to the Lord, But an honest weight is His delight. Proverbs 11:1

Differing weights and differing measures, the Lord detests them both. Proverbs 20:10

These verses remind us of the importance of integrity in our standards of measurement. Reflecting on these scriptures prompts us to evaluate our own standards. Do we apply consistent benchmarks to all individuals, or do we show favoritism? As parents, do we distribute our wealth among our children with fairness and transparency? And how do we treat those under our authority? These questions challenge us to examine whether we uphold integrity or practice double standards.

God has established honest rules for us to follow, and all measurements are His own. Therefore, let us uphold His standards and judge others accordingly. Let us not employ double standards when treating others. Jesus's words in *Luke 6:42* remind us to address our own faults before pointing out others'. Likewise, Jesus's warning in *Matthew 7:2* emphasizes the reciprocity of judgment based on the measure we use.

In our business dealings, let us demonstrate utmost integrity, for God abhors deceitful practices. As *Proverbs 16:8* teaches, it is better to have a little with righteousness than to gain great wealth through dishonest means.

Furthermore, we are reminded that honest scales and balances belong to the Lord, and all the weights are of His making *(Proverbs 16:10)*. *Leviticus 19:35-36* instructs us not to use dishonest standards when measuring length, weight, or quantity, but instead to use honest scales, weights, and measures.

By aligning our standards with God's, we honor Him and ensure fairness and righteousness in all our dealings.

No matter how big our sea

In the journey of faith, certain stories stand as timeless pillars of inspiration. One such tale unfolds in Exodus 14, where the Israelites, liberated from bondage, confront the daunting expanse of the Red Sea with their pursuers hot on their heels. In the face of seemingly insurmountable odds, divine intervention reshapes their narrative, paving a miraculous path to freedom.

Drawing from this poignant narrative, I was moved to pen the poem below, encapsulating the essence of Exodus 14 in verse. As we delve into these lines, may we find echoes of hope and courage resonating across the ages, reminding us of the unwavering faithfulness of our God.

Merry and cheer they left,
Out of Egypt with their clan,
Gold and silver as gifts,
Slaves no more but free.

Away they travelled with dance,
Much singing and chatting as they fled.
A few days and a few nights into their trek,

Oh no! Red Sea in the front,
As they looked back to check,
Oh no! The army behind,
Their hearts all ached with fear,

With nowhere to flee from both.
They looked to their leader, and with prayer,
Be begged the Father in Heaven.
As they watched with so much fear,
An amazing event occurred.

The sea parted in half giving way,
They hurried on foot all the way.

All grannies, the young and the sick,
All mommies, babies, and kids
With daddies, the animals, and all
With fear and trembling and hope.

The sea stood as high walls you see,
On both sides, it was a great sight.
The wind was so harsh on the sea,
Yet so gentle to the folks as they walked.

Armies behind them to chase,
In chariots and fast-running horses.
While the army was still midway,
The sea came back with force to kill them all.

Not one of His people was lost in the sea,
And it is a constant reminder to us:
No matter how big our sea,
No matter how fast the foe,
God opens a way for us out,
For sure as He is true!

All glory be to God almighty!

POUR OUT TO OTHERS AS I POUR INTO YOU

I stumbled upon a beautiful poem that deeply resonated with me, and I felt compelled to share it with you. While the author of this poem remains unknown, its message carries profound significance, especially in the context of our daily reflections and spiritual journey.

The Master sought a vessel true,
On the shelf, where many grew.
"Choose me," cried the gold so bright,
"My value shines, a perfect light.
For someone like You, I'll stand tall,
With beauty that outshines them all."

But the Master passed with silence still,
To the silver, standing on the hill.
"I'll serve You well," the silver said,
"With grace and style, I'll share Your bread.
My lines are true, my form is grand,
A worthy vessel at Your command."

Yet the Master's gaze did not linger there,
Nor on the brass, so bright and fair.
"I'm ready!" cried the brass, so loud,
"To stand with pride among the crowd.
Place me on Your table, for all to see,
A vessel fit for royalty."

Then the crystal, clear and fine,
Called out, "Choose me, for I shine.
Though fragile, I'll serve You well,
With transparency, my story to tell.
In Your house, I'll proudly stay,
To reflect Your light each day."

But the Master's eyes fell upon the clay,

Empty, broken, in disarray.
No hope had the vessel, so plain and small,
To be chosen by the Master of all.
But the Master smiled, His heart so kind,
"This vessel is the one I'll find.

For I need not grandeur or shining gold,
Nor silver, polished, strong and bold.
Not crystal clear, nor wood so fine,
But a vessel humble, and truly mine.
With My power, I'll make it whole,
And fill it with My very soul."

So, the Master took the vessel of clay,
Mended and cleansed it without delay.
"I'll use you now," the Master said,
"To pour My love on hearts that bled.
Just pour out to others as I pour into you,
For in this simple vessel, My love shines true."

(Original source unknown)

"For God, who said, 'Let light shine out of darkness,' made his light shine in
our hearts to give us the light of the knowledge of God's glory displayed in
the face of Christ. But we have this treasure in jars of clay to show that this
all-surpassing power is from God and not from us." 2 Corinthians 4:6, 7

Let us reflect on the profound message of this anonymous poem.
May we remember that like the vessel of clay, we are chosen by God,
mended, and filled with His power. As we go about our days, may we
pour out His love, grace, and compassion to others, just as He pours
into us. Let this be our guiding principle as we strive to live out our
faith every day.

The Armor of God

The Armor of God

Finally, my brethren, be strong in the Lord and in the power of His might. Put on the whole armor of God, that you may be able to stand against the wiles of the devil. Ephesians 6:10, 11

The Apostle Paul reminds us that our struggle is not against flesh and blood but against the rulers, authorities, the powers of this dark world, and the spiritual forces of evil in the heavenly realms. To overcome this battle, we must don the full armor of God.

The armor of God consists of several components: the belt of truth, which is buckled around our waist; the breastplate of righteousness, guarding our hearts; the sandals of readiness, equipping us to spread the gospel of peace; the shield of faith, with which we can extinguish all the flaming arrows of the evil one; the helmet of salvation; and the sword of the Spirit, which is the word of God.

To attain this armor, Paul suggests that we pray in the Spirit on all occasions, with all kinds of prayers and requests. We should always be alert and keep on praying for all the Lord's people. Additionally, we are encouraged to pray for the ministers of God, that whenever they speak, words may be given to them so that they will fearlessly make known the mystery of the gospel *(Ephesians 6:12-19)*.

Let us, therefore, be vigilant and proactive in putting on the full armor of God at all times, ensuring that we are equipped to resist the schemes of the enemy and stand firm in our faith. Paul emphasizes the importance of being alert and praying in the Spirit on all occasions to receive the armor of God.

BELT OF TRUTH

In *Ephesians 6:13-17* we read about the armor of God consisting of the Belt of truth, the Breastplate of righteousness, the Sandals of readiness, the Shield of faith, the Helmet of salvation, and the Sword of the Spirit.

The Belt of Truth holds significant symbolism. Our adversary, the father of lies, stands in stark contrast to our Lord Jesus, who declares Himself as "the Way, **the Truth**, and the Life." King Solomon, in *Proverbs 6:16-19*, lists seven detestable things to the Lord, with "a lying tongue" at the forefront. *Revelation 21:8* warns of dire consequences for all who engage in falsehood.

Throughout Scripture, we are repeatedly urged to speak truthfully: *Zechariah 8:16* calls for truth, justice, and peace in our judgments. *Ephesians 4:25* emphasizes the importance of honesty among members of the body of Christ. *Psalm 15:1, 2* highlights truthfulness as a characteristic of those who dwell in God's presence.

Buckling the Belt of Truth entails a commitment to honesty, rejecting falsehoods in all forms. Let us renew our commitment to shun lies, both big and small, and instead strive to embody the truth exemplified by our Lord.

Each of you must put off falsehood and speak truthfully to your neighbor, for we are all members of one body. Ephesians 4:25

BREASTPLATE OF RIGHTEOUSNESS

Above all else, guard your heart, for everything you do flows from it. Proverbs 4:23

The Breastplate of righteousness, emphasized in *Ephesians 6:14*, takes precedence in the armor of God, akin to a metal vest shielding the soldier's chest and vital organs, particularly the heart. Guarding our hearts is paramount, as everything we do flows from it *(Proverbs 4:23)*.

But what exactly is this breastplate of righteousness? It symbolizes the righteousness we obtain through Jesus Christ, serving as a protective barrier for our hearts. Many of us grapple with various heart-related issues: burdens, past wounds, fear of the future, harboring records of wrongs, pride, guilt, and even hardening of hearts over time, becoming desensitized to sin.

To guard our hearts effectively, we must adhere to God's statutes, seeking Him wholeheartedly *(Psalm 119:2)*, remain faithful in relationships *(Malachi 2:16)*, and fill our hearts with goodness, particularly the Word of God and His Spirit *(Luke 6:45)*. Setting our hearts on the right path, receiving and retaining the Word, and praying for a renewed heart are also vital steps in safeguarding this crucial organ *(Proverbs 23:19; Luke 8:15; Ezekiel 36:26)*. Let us therefore don the breastplate of righteousness, guarding our hearts diligently and allowing God's righteousness to shield and guide us in all our endeavors.

I will give you a new heart and put a new spirit in you; I will remove from you your heart of stone and give you a heart of flesh. Ezekiel 36:26

Sandals of readiness to spread the gospel

Watch, therefore, for you know neither the day nor the hour in which the Son of Man is coming. Matthew 25:13

As we continue our discussion on the Armor of God, detailed in Ephesians 6:13-17, let us shift our focus to the Sandals of Readiness. Sandaled feet symbolize a constant state of preparedness—ready to pray, worship, embrace God's presence, extend a helping hand, go the extra mile, lead others to Christ, and share our faith testimony. Most importantly, they signify readiness to greet our Lord when He returns.

Consider the parable Jesus shared about ten virgins awaiting the bridegroom's arrival. Five were foolish, neglecting to bring oil for their lamps, while the other five wisely came prepared. As the night wore on, a cry announced the bridegroom's imminent arrival. While the foolish virgins scrambled to find oil, the bridegroom came, and those who were ready joined him at the wedding banquet. The door closed to those who were unprepared *(Matthew 25:1-12)*.

Jesus concluded this parable with a clear directive: Be ready to receive Him upon His return as the Bridegroom. Are we prepared to share the gospel and meet Jesus when He comes? To be prepared, Jesus instructed us to *"Take heed, watch, and pray; for you do not know when the time is" (Mark 13:33)*.

Let us heed this advice and remain ready, not forgetting to wear our sandals of readiness as we journey in faith.

SHIELD OF FAITH

Let us hold firmly to the faith we profess. Hebrews 4:14

Faith is the substance of things hoped for, the evidence of things not seen.
Hebrews 11:1

Much like a shield in a soldier's armor, faith intercepts attacks from the enemy, redirecting them or stopping them altogether. But how do we obtain such faith? *Romans 10:17* tells us that faith comes by hearing and believing the Word of God.

In moments of trial, Jesus questioned His disciples about their faith, highlighting its significance in overcoming challenges *(Luke 8:25)*. Recognizing the importance of faith, the disciples even pleaded with Jesus to increase their faith *(Luke 17:5)*. Jesus himself emphasized the power of even a small amount of faith, likening it to a mustard seed capable of remarkable feats *(Matthew 17:20, Luke 17:6)*.

Our faith serves as a shield against the devil's attacks, bolstered by the promises of God such as His unwavering presence and assistance *(Hebrews 13:5, 6)*. As we embrace and nurture our faith, we find ourselves protected and strengthened against the schemes of the enemy.

So let us, with unwavering faith, dress ourselves with the shield of faith, confident in the Lord's provision and protection. Anchored in the assurance of God's promise, *"I will never leave you nor forsake you"* *(Hebrews 13:5)*, we boldly declare, *"The Lord is my helper; I will not fear. What can man do to me?"* *(Hebrews 13:6)*.

HELMET OF SALVATION

'To be carnally minded is death, but to be spiritually minded is life and peace. Because the carnal mind is enmity against God; for it is not subject to the law of God, nor indeed can be.' Romans 8:6, 7

This Scripture highlights the contrast between being carnally minded and spiritually minded, emphasizing the importance of guarding our thoughts. Just as the head is vital for our physical well-being, Apostle Paul urges us to protect our minds with the helmet of salvation *(Ephesians 6:17)*, as it shields us from spiritual attacks that could be fatal.

The helmet of salvation symbolizes the blood of Jesus, which serves as a powerful defense against the devil's assaults on our thoughts. Holding onto the assurance of salvation through Christ's sacrifice grants us victory over negative thinking patterns.

King David's wisdom in *Psalm 141:5* reminds us to welcome correction from the righteous, likening their rebuke to the soothing effects of excellent oil on our heads. *Proverbs 4:8-9* underscores the value of wisdom, adorning us with grace and honor as a crown. Acting with kindness and generosity towards others, as suggested in *Proverbs 11:26*, results in blessings that serve as a protective crown upon our heads. Additionally, *Ecclesiastes 9:8* encourages us to seek the anointing of the Holy Spirit, ensuring continual protection and guidance. Ultimately, when we safeguard our minds with the helmet of salvation, we experience the joy and gladness promised by *Isaiah 35:10*, free from sorrow and despair.

The helmet of salvation serves as our spiritual protection, guarding our minds against the attacks of the enemy and ensuring our thoughts align with God's truth. As we clothe ourselves with this vital piece of armor, we find joy, gladness, and everlasting peace in the assurance of our salvation through Jesus Christ.

SWORD OF THE SPIRIT

Take the helmet of salvation and the sword of the Spirit, which is the word of God. Ephesians 6:17

This verse emphasizes that the Word of God is likened to a sword, specifically the sword of the Spirit. Regularly reading the Word of God is essential for our spiritual endurance during times of warfare. In today's world, the spoken Word of God is scarce, but thankfully, the Scriptures contain the spoken Word of God written down.

In Hebrews, Paul writes, *"For the word of God is alive and active. Sharper than any double-edged sword, it penetrates even to dividing soul and spirit, joints and marrow; it judges the thoughts and attitudes of the heart" (Hebrews 4:12).* The more we immerse ourselves in the Word of God and familiarize ourselves with His promises, the more equipped we are to face the daily struggles against our own flesh and the world. Without knowledge of the Word, our communion with God remains one-sided and incomplete, as we fail to hear His voice through His written Word.

The Word of God serves multiple purposes in our lives. It acts as our guide, illuminating the right path for us. As the Psalmist proclaims, *"Your word is a lamp to my feet and a light to my path" (Psalm 119:105).* It also sustains us spiritually, as emphasized by Jesus when he declared, *"Man shall not live on bread alone, but on every word that comes from the mouth of God" (Matthew 4:4).* Additionally, it serves as the Sword of the Spirit, a potent weapon enabling us to combat the temptations presented by the devil. Jesus himself employed the Word of God to rebuke the devil during times of temptation *(Matthew 4:1-11).*

Let us commit to filling our hearts and minds with the Word of God daily. Through it, we gain the strength to resist the devil's schemes and invite the transformative power of God into our lives.

CALL OF DUTY: BE ON GUARD

Be on your guard; stand firm in the faith; be men of courage; be strong. 1 Corinthians 16:13

This is our call of duty: to be on guard, to stand firm in our faith, to show courage, and to be strong. But what does it mean to be on guard, and why is it important?

Being on guard entails being alert and vigilant against the schemes of the devil, as well as being prepared for the imminent return of our Lord. As stated in *1 Peter 5:8, "Your enemy the devil prowls around like a roaring lion looking for someone to devour."* Thus, even a moment of carelessness can lead to spiritual harm. However, Scripture reassures us with the admonition to resist the devil, causing him to flee *(James 4:7)*. Additionally, the apostle Paul advises us in *Ephesians 4:27* not to give the devil a foothold, as he seeks any opportunity to establish control over our hearts and minds, robbing us of joy and influencing our thoughts and actions.

A little temptation, a slight stumble, or even a hint of pride or self-pity can divert us from our spiritual journey. Hence, it is crucial to be watchful against the devil's cunning schemes. Paul reinforces this in *Ephesians 6:11*, urging believers to put on the full armor of God to stand against the devil's strategies.

Furthermore, being on guard also involves readiness for the return of our Lord, as emphasized in *Matthew 24:42*. Our call of duty is to remain vigilant so that the devil does not gain entry into our lives. Let us, therefore, heed this call to be on guard, ever watchful and prepared to stand against the forces of darkness.

CALL OF DUTY: STAND FIRM IN THE FAITH

*Be on your guard; stand firm in the faith; be men of courage; be strong. 1
Corinthians 16:13*

This is our call of duty: to be on your guard, to stand firm in the faith, to be men of courage, and to be strong. But what does it truly mean to stand firm in faith? The apostle Paul provides clarity on this matter, urging believers to hold fast to the teachings they have received, whether through spoken word or written letter. This instruction, found in *2 Thessalonians 2:15*, emphasizes the importance of unwavering commitment to the principles and doctrines of the Christian faith.

Standing firm in faith entails adhering to the teachings passed down to us through the Scriptures. However, it is essential to exercise caution and discernment, ensuring that these teachings align with the Word of God. In *Galatians 5:1*, we're reminded not to be burdened by a yoke of slavery or sin but to stand firm in the freedom granted to us by the blood of Jesus.

We must avoid any habits or practices that may lead us back into bondage. Paul emphasizes in *2 Corinthians 1:21-22* that it is God who enables us to stand firm in Christ, sealing us with His Spirit as a guarantee of our future inheritance. Moreover, Jesus Himself proclaimed in *Matthew 24:13* that those who persevere and stand firm in faith until the end will be saved. This underscores the significance of unwavering commitment to our faith amidst life's challenges and trials.

Standing firm in our faith is not merely a suggestion but a vital aspect of our journey as believers. Let us embrace this call with determination and perseverance, knowing that God Himself strengthens us and empowers us to stand firm. Together, let us anchor ourselves in the truth of His Word, resisting any temptation to waver or compromise.

Will you join in this commitment to stand firm in faith, trusting in God's promises and relying on His unfailing grace?

CALL OF DUTY: BE MEN OF COURAGE

Be on your guard; stand firm in the faith; be men of courage; be strong. 1
Corinthians 16:13

This powerful exhortation from 1 Corinthians 16:13 highlights the importance of courage in the life of a believer. In Acts 4:13, we witness the remarkable courage of Peter and John, who, despite being recognized as unschooled men, boldly proclaimed the Gospel. Their fearless commitment astonished onlookers and testified to their close association with Jesus. Their example challenges us to reflect on our own actions—are we boldly proclaiming the Good News or succumbing to societal pressures?

For instance, if we were to share a faith-based video on social media that raises concerns among our non-believing friends, what should our response be? Should we refrain from sharing such content, distance ourselves from these friends, or even deactivate our accounts? Alternatively, should we courageously stand by our beliefs, even in the face of potential losses or criticism?

This dilemma underscores the pivotal role of courage in everyday decisions. As believers, do we possess the courage to confront challenges and potential losses, even if it means risking friendships, in order to stand firm in our faith in Jesus Christ? Will our commitment to Jesus be evident in our actions? This is the call to duty within this context.

In Acts, disciples faced threats from both Roman and Jewish authorities for preaching the gospel. Despite the risks, they persisted, boldly spreading the gospel and leading to daily additions to the Church. This courage remains crucial for the Church's growth in our time. Let us heed our call of duty to be courageous, just as the early disciples were (1 Corinthians 16:13).

CALL OF DUTY: BE STRONG

*Be on your guard; stand firm in the faith; be men of courage; be strong. 1
Corinthians 16:13*

Strength, in this context, extends beyond mere physical prowess to
encompass spiritual resilience. Just as we understand the importance of proper diet and exercise in building physical strength, the
same principle applies to spiritual strength. We must nourish ourselves
spiritually by consuming the Word of God, which is often likened to
bread, honey, and milk throughout the Bible.

In 1 Peter 2:2-3, believers are encouraged to crave pure spiritual milk
like newborns, recognizing its crucial role in their growth towards salvation, especially after experiencing the goodness of the Lord. Similarly,
John 6:51 portrays Jesus as the living bread from heaven, offering eternal
life to those who partake of Him. Psalm 119:103 beautifully illustrates
the sweetness of God's words, surpassing even honey in their delightful
and nourishing essence.

Just as our bodies require daily nourishment for physical health,
our spirits need regular feeding with the Word of God to maintain
spiritual strength. To live out the Word of God, it is crucial not only
to hear or read it but also to put it into practice in our daily lives. This
involves actively doing what the Word instructs us to do, whether
it is showing love, forgiveness, or kindness to others. Additionally,
we must accept and believe the Word with sincerity and conviction,
allowing it to shape our beliefs and attitudes. Moreover, proclaiming
our faith boldly and sharing the Word with others demonstrates our
commitment to living out its truths. Finally, living a life that aligns
with God's principles and values is essential for reflecting His character
and pleasing Him in all that we do.

Our call of duty is to be strong in our faith and in our knowledge
of the Word of God. We have heard the call of duty loud and clear.
Let us perform our duty!

BE ON YOUR GUARD AGAINST GREED

*Watch out! Be on your guard against all kinds of greed; a man's life does
not consist in the abundance of his possessions. Luke 12:15*

Greed, defined as an excessive desire for more material wealth
than necessary, often leads to envy and discontentment, causing
us to lose sight of what truly matters. While some may argue that
greed serves as motivation for improvement, its consequences are
far-reaching. It fosters selfishness, workaholism, reckless spending, and
indebtedness, ultimately distracting us from our spiritual priorities and
the pursuit of eternal glory. Jesus' warning against greed reminds us to
prioritize spiritual wealth over material possessions.

Here is another verse to set us on track. In *1 John 2:15*, we read, *Do
not love the world or anything in the world. If anyone loves the world, the
love of the Father is not in him.* King David shares similar lines in one
of his Psalms. In *Psalm 62:10* he writes ...though *your riches increase, do
not set your heart on them.*

God abundantly provides for our needs, often giving us more
than we require so we can share with those less fortunate. Everything
we receive is meant to be shared, as we are merely channels through
which God's blessings flow to others. Jesus instructs us not to hoard,
but to give generously, even if it means sharing what we have. While
this concept may seem challenging to adhere to, there are those who
faithfully practice it. We are reminded that what God blesses us with
is not for selfish accumulation but for sharing with those in need.

Let us be vigilant against all forms of greed.

BE ON YOUR GUARD AGAINST HYPOCRISY

Be on your guard against the yeast of the Pharisees, which is hypocrisy.
Luke 12:1

Hypocrisy involves professing to be more religious or virtuous than one truly is, opposing integrity by concealing our true nature from others. However, such duplicity does not escape the notice of God, who discerns the depths of our hearts.

Jesus compared hypocrisy to leaven or yeast, illustrating how even a small amount can cause significant inflation. Similarly, hypocrisy fills us with pride and vanity, fostering a 'holier than thou' attitude. Just as a small amount of yeast added to flour mixed with water causes it to rise, hypocrisy in our lives fosters haughtiness and snobbery, resulting in a judgmental attitude of superiority.

Jesus cautioned his followers to *"take heed and beware of the leaven of the Pharisees and of the Sadducees" (Matthew 16:6)*. These religious leaders, though well-versed in God's law, burdened people with additional man-made rules and rituals, earning Jesus's condemnation as "blind guides" who imposed heavy burdens but did not lift a finger to help *(Matthew 23:4)*. Outwardly righteous, they were inwardly full of hypocrisy and iniquity.

Jesus extended this warning to include the leaven of Herod, cautioning against the deceitful ways of political leaders who may outwardly appear righteous but act with duplicity *(Mark 8:15)*. Despite Herod's initial interest in Jesus, his true intentions were revealed, leading Jesus to label him "that fox." Herod's involvement in John the Baptist's imprisonment and execution, along with his attempt to manipulate Jesus's trial, exemplifies the danger of such hypocrisy.

Paul urged the Corinthian church to rid themselves of malice and wickedness, encouraging them to embrace sincerity and truth (1 Corinthians 5:6-8), a lesson we too must heed to.

PUT ON THE ARMOR OF LIGHT

The night is nearly over; the day is almost here. So let us put aside the deeds of darkness and put on the armor of light. Let us behave decently, as in the daytime, not in orgies and drunkenness, not in sexual immorality and debauchery, not in dissension and jealousy. Rather, clothe yourselves with the Lord Jesus Christ, and do not think about how to gratify the desires of the sinful nature. Romans 13:12-14

In 1 John 1:5, it is stated that God is light, and in Him, there is no darkness at all. John further elaborates on this in 1 John 1:7, explaining that if we walk in the light, as He is in the light, we have fellowship with one another.

Wearing the armor of light signifies cultivating genuine fellowship, setting aside our differences, denominations, and divisions. However, the prevalence of divisions within the Church indicates our failure to achieve the unity desired by our Lord Jesus Christ. This discrepancy suggests that we are not truly walking in the light as He does—a realization that is truly disheartening.

Let us henceforth cultivate fellowship among one another, embracing believers from different divisions of the Church instead of casting judgment upon them. How marvelous it would be if Brethren, Baptists, Lutherans, Methodists, Pentecostals, Protestants, Catholics, Orthodox, and believers from various other denominations could unite in worship of the Lord! Let us extend friendship to those outside our faith and showcase how we embody the teachings of our Lord through our actions. Let us diligently steer clear of deeds associated with darkness. If our aim is to walk in the light as He does, then darkness must find no foothold within us! Indeed, this is attainable! With God's guidance, we can achieve it! Amen!

Come, O house of Jacob, let us walk in the light of the Lord. Isaiah 2:5
That (Jesus) was the true Light that gives light to every man coming into the world. John 1:9

Jesus has said, *"I am the light of the world. He who follows Me shall not walk in darkness but have the light of life." John 8:12*

Conclusion

THE CONCLUSION OF THE WHOLE MATTER

Let us hear the conclusion of the whole matter: Fear God and keep His commandments, for this is man's all. For God will bring every work into judgment, including every secret thing, whether good or evil. Ecclesiastes 12:13, 14

I have seen all the works that are done under the sun; and indeed, all is vanity and grasping for the wind. Ecclesiastes 1:14

Let us heed the conclusion of King Solomon's wisdom. Solomon, known as the wisest person, to have lived on this earth, reflected deeply on life's meaning. Despite all his endeavors, he found everything to be vanity, like grasping for the wind (Ecclesiastes 1:14).

Yet, Solomon recognized that the essence of life lies in revering God and obeying His commandments. Recognizing that God will assess every deed, whether good or bad, fosters a reverent awe within us and motivates us to obey. Is it difficult to honor God? Not at all. With the Holy Spirit as our guide, it becomes instinctive, natural and effortless.

In *Deuteronomy 10:12*, we read of Moses's instructions for the Israelites: "*O Israel, what does the Lord your God ask of you but to fear the Lord your God by walking in all His ways, to love Him, to serve the Lord your God with all your heart and with all your soul?*"

Moses outlines the fundamental requirements the Lord has for the Israelites: to fear Him by walking in His ways, demonstrating love for Him, and dedicating themselves to His service with unwavering commitment from the depths of their hearts and souls. Fear God and obey His commandments. This is what is required of every man. This is the conclusion of the whole matter.

The fear of the Lord is the beginning of wisdom. Psalm 111:10

Is the Bible truly the Word of God?

There are moments when we confront the question, "Is the Bible truly the Word of God?" Our immediate response is a resounding 'yes!' Yet, how do we substantiate this claim? Our instinct may lead us to cite passages from the Bible. However, many may dismiss this approach as a circular reference. Contrary to this notion, the Bible is not a singular text penned by a lone author at a specific time. Rather, it is a compilation of 66 books composed by over 40 individuals over a span of 1500 years. The Spirit of God has divinely influenced the entirety of these writings. This is evidenced by the consistent message of salvation woven from the beginning to the end of the Bible: the creation of humanity, the fall of mankind, and the redemption offered through Jesus Christ. This, fundamentally, is the essence of the Bible.

The historical events documented in the Bible remain remarkably accurate even today. The scientific insights provided by Scripture regarding the earth, sun, moon, stars, galaxies, oceans, and depths only serve to affirm the Scriptures as reliable and truthful. While a minority of scientists may dissent, the majority recognize the Bible as the genuine Word of God.

How can it be those diverse individuals from various backgrounds, spanning numerous geographical regions and centuries, convey the same message? They speak of the same attributes of God, deliver the same message of salvation, and proclaim identical prophetic revelations. Such unity could only result from the divine intervention of Almighty God.

All Scripture is God-breathed and is useful for teaching, rebuking, correcting, and training in righteousness, so that the man of God may be thoroughly equipped for every good work. 2 Timothy 3:16, 17

For prophecy never came by the will of man, but holy men of God spoke as they were moved by the Holy Spirit. 2 Peter 1:21

THE WICKED WILL NOT INHERIT THE KINGDOM OF GOD

Do you not know that the unrighteous will not inherit the kingdom of God? Do not be deceived. Neither fornicators, nor idolaters, nor adulterers, nor homosexuals, nor sodomites, nor thieves, nor covetous, nor drunkards, nor revilers, nor extortioners will inherit the kingdom of God. 1 Corinthians 6:9, 10

Sexual immorality, idolatry, adultery, homosexuality, covetousness, drunkenness, verbal abuse, and swindling are all considered wicked. The aforementioned verse indicates that those who engage in such wicked behaviors will not inherit the kingdom of God. Sodom and Gomorrah, cities destroyed by fire from heaven, serve as a testament to God's detestation of homosexual sin (*Jude 1:7; Romans 1:26, 27*). Despite arguments to the contrary, the cited verses explicitly declare homosexuality as wicked, affirming that homosexuals cannot inherit the Kingdom of God.

Do not heed arguments that suggest homosexuals are naturally different from "normal" individuals. In the eyes of the Holy God, it is considered a sin, punishable by eternal hell. Those with same-sex attractions should not deceive themselves into believing it is natural or normal. Instead, recognize that God detests this unclean and wicked act. We must free ourselves from such unnatural and abnormal inclinations.

The wicked will not inherit the kingdom of God; they will be cast into the lake of fire. Therefore, we must reject wickedness and ungodly practices to enter the kingdom of heaven.

"It is not the healthy who need a doctor, but the sick. I (Jesus) have not come to call the righteous, but sinners to repentance." Luke 5:31-32

WHAT HAPPENS TO THE DEAD?

But now that he is dead, why should I go on fasting? Can I bring him back again? I will go to him, but he will not return to me. 2 Samuel 12:23

In this verse, King David expresses his hope of being reunited with his deceased son, acknowledging that the son cannot return to him. Many debate whether we will recognize our loved ones in heaven, but numerous Bible verses suggest that we will. For instance, Abraham in the Old Testament spoke of being gathered to his people, indicating his expectation of seeing them after death *(Genesis 25:8)*. Jesus, in his teachings about the rich man and Lazarus, implied that they recognized each other after death *(Luke 16:19-31)*. He also advised his disciples to use their wealth to make friends who would welcome them into eternal dwellings *(Luke 16:9)*.

Thus, we find comfort in the assurance from the Holy Spirit that we will be reunited with our departed loved ones when we pass away. We will not only see and recognize them but also rejoice in the absence of death, which can no longer separate us. Praise the Lord.

In our perception, earthly life may seem permanent, but in truth, it is fleeting, merely a preparation for our eternal life, which is everlasting. And in that eternal realm, our Lord Jesus Christ reigns supreme. It is akin to a fully paid, all-inclusive resort – this heaven.

Brothers and sisters, we do not want you to be uninformed about those who sleep in death, so that you do not grieve like the rest of mankind, who have no hope. For we believe that Jesus died and rose again, and so we believe that God will bring with Jesus those who have fallen asleep in Him. 1 Thessalonians 4:13-15

Take heart, dear ones. Let us eagerly anticipate meeting our Lord in the air when He comes, accompanied by our departed loved ones who have fallen asleep in Him.

THERE SHALL BE NO MORE DEATH

*Now I saw a new heaven and a new earth, for the first heaven and the first earth had passed away. Also, there was no more sea. Then I, John, saw the holy city, New Jerusalem, coming down out of heaven from God, prepared as a bride adorned for her husband. And I heard a loud voice from heaven saying, "Behold, the tabernacle of God is with men, and He will dwell with them, and they shall be His people. God Himself will be with them and be their God. And God will wipe away every tear from their eyes; there shall be no more death, nor sorrow, nor crying. There shall be no more pain, for the former things have passed away." Then He who sat on the throne said, "Behold, I make all things new." And He said to me, "Write, for these words are true and faithful." And He said to me, "It is done! I am the Alpha and the Omega, the Beginning and the End. I will give of the fountain of the water of life freely to him who thirsts. **He who overcomes shall inherit all things**, and I will be his God and he shall be My son. Revelation 21:1-7*

Behold, in accordance with *Isaiah 65:17*, God promises to create new heavens and a new earth, where the former will not be remembered or come to mind. This vision of renewal is echoed in *2 Peter 3:13*, where believers anticipate a new heaven and a new earth, characterized by righteousness. *Isaiah 11:9* further portrays a future where there will be no harm or destruction in God's holy mountain, as the earth will be filled with the knowledge of the Lord. The profound nature of this promise is expressed in *1 Corinthians 2:9*, where it is declared that the things God has prepared for those who love Him are beyond human comprehension, unseen by the eye, unheard by the ear, and unimaginable to the human heart.

These Scriptures convey the promise of God creating a new heaven and earth where righteousness reigns, with the assurance that those who overcome will inherit this eternal blessing. It underscores the ultimate fulfillment and conclusion of our lives. Therefore, let us overcome the challenges posed by the devil through the redeeming power of Jesus' blood and live in hopeful anticipation of receiving our divine inheritance.

THE LORD HIMSELF GOES BEFORE YOU

The Lord himself goes before you and will be with you; he will never leave you nor forsake you. Do not be afraid; do not be discouraged. Deuteronomy 31:8

Look, I am with you, and I will watch over you wherever you go, and I will bring you back to this land. For I will not leave you until I have done what I have promised you. Genesis 28:15

Keep your lives free from the love of money and be content with what you have, for God has said: "Never will I leave you, never will I forsake you." Hebrews 13:5

And the Lord answered, "My Presence will go with you, and I will give you rest." Exodus 33:14

The Lord turned to him and said, "Go in the strength you have and save Israel out of Midian's hand. Am I not sending you?" Judges 6:14

These scriptures collectively paint a portrait of God's faithful and unwavering commitment to His people, offering solace, strength, and guidance in every circumstance. With God Himself by our side, there is no need to fear anything. Let us rejoice in our great and greatly praiseworthy Lord. Amen.

Dear Readers,

Thank you for choosing to embark on this journey with *Table for Two: One-on-One with Jesus*. I hope that this book has enriched your spiritual life and deepened your relationship with Jesus.

Your feedback is invaluable to me and to others who are seeking to grow in faith. If you enjoyed the book, I would be grateful if you could take a moment to share your thoughts in a review. Your insights will not only help me improve but also assist potential readers in discovering this journey.

To make it easy, you can scan the QR code below to leave your review. Thank you for your support and for being a part of this journey.

Blessings,
Hephzibah

ABOUT THE AUTHOR

HEPHZIBAH QUEENSTAR ISRAEL is a passionate follower of Jesus Christ, committed to sharing her faith through her writing. Born and raised in southern India, Hephzibah accepted Christianity in her early teens, a decision that has profoundly shaped her life and work.

Hephzibah's academic journey began in Tirunelveli, Tamil Nadu, and continued with undergraduate studies in Bangalore. She holds a Master's degree in Computer Applications from Trichy and is currently pursuing a Doctorate in Business Analysis through an online program at Liberty University, Lynchburg, Virginia.

With a rich blend of technological expertise and spiritual insight, Hephzibah offers a unique perspective in her writing. Her journey as a writer began with the blog *Coffee with Jesus*, where she faithfully shared daily meditations on Bible verses for over a decade.

Now residing in New Jersey with her supportive husband and three grown children, Hephzibah and her family are active members of their local church, regularly attending Sunday worship and striving to live out their faith in everyday life.

Through her writing, Hephzibah seeks to inspire and uplift her readers, encouraging them to deepen their relationship with Jesus Christ. Her dedication to her faith and commitment to spreading its message are at the heart of all her work.